GARDENS OF THE WORLD
THE GREAT TRADITIONS

GARDENS OF THE WORLD
THE GREAT TRADITIONS

RORY STUART

FRANCES LINCOLN LIMITED
PUBLISHERS
www.franceslincoln.com

This book is for Benito, who won't read it, and for Joy, who might.

Frances Lincoln Limited
4 Torriano Mews
Torriano Avenue
London NW5 2RZ
www.franceslincoln.com

Gardens of the World
Copyright © Frances Lincoln Limited 2010
Text and illustrations copyright © Rory Stuart 2010
First Frances Lincoln edition 2010

A catalogue record for this book is available from the British Library.

ISBN 9780711231306

Printed and bound in China

9 8 7 6 5 4 3 2 1

HALF TITLE PAGE *Palazzo Farnese, Caprarola, Italy.*

TITLE PAGE *Knightshayes, Tiverton, Devon, England.*

CONTENTS

PREFACE 6

1. THE GENESIS OF THE PLEASURE GARDEN 10

2. THE ISLAMIC TRADITION 26

3. THE ORIENTAL TRADITION: CHINA 58

4. THE ORIENTAL TRADITION: JAPAN 90

5. THE ITALIAN TRADITION 118

6. THE ENGLISH LANDSCAPE PARK 162

7. THE ENGLISH FLOWER GARDEN 188

8. THE AMERICAN EXPERIMENT 218

BIBLIOGRAPHY 250

INDEX 252

ACKNOWLEDGMENTS 256

PREFACE

W HEN FACED WITH THIS VAST SUBJECT, the development of pleasure gardens in the major garden cultures of the world, it is impossible not to feel underprepared. Learned men and women have written in depth on the histories of all these gardening traditions, yet here is an attempt to cover the roots and development of the world's fundamental garden cultures in one book. How can the author not be aware of all he hasn't seen, hasn't read, doesn't know? Lytton Strachey, however, offers some comfort when he asserts in *Eminent Victorians*, provocatively but not entirely unseriously, that 'ignorance is the first requisite of a historian – ignorance, which simplifies and clarifies, which selects and omits, with a placed perfection unattainable by the highest art'. A little knowledge certainly allows one to see more clearly the outlines of a culture or a tradition.

This book is aimed at garden visitors and students of any age who are beginning to be interested in international garden history, in particular at the increasing number of visitors who are venturing farther afield, outside the confines of their own familiar garden culture. They may wish to know something of the social history of garden-making in an unfamiliar land, and thus to understand why those gardens are so different from the familiar gardens of their home territory. Gardens have meanings, in the way that other works of art have meanings, and by becoming, in a small way, students of gardens as items of cultural history we will understand them more fully, thus beginning to become garden critics. And this increased understanding of a garden's meaning should not detract from but rather enhance our enjoyment of the whole garden experience.

RIGHT *Branitz, Germany. This pyramid is the last resting place of one of garden history's most restless and extraordinary characters, and of his long-suffering wife. Prince Hermann von Puckler-Muskau was an obsessive park maker. He ran through his own and his wife's fortunes, had to sell his original park and then began all over again at Branitz.*

LEFT *The Japanese Gardens, the Curragh, Ireland. Created between 1906 and 1910 by Japanese garden maker Tassa Eida, they were some of Europe's finest Japanese gardens. Europe had only recently 'rediscovered' Japan, and all things Japanese were highly fashionable.*

As a universal rule gardeners are conservative beings, which is why it is not difficult to trace the history of certain national garden styles. At the same time garden-making, like the other arts, is always subject to the fashion of the moment; in England, for example, decking and indigo-blue flowerpots have gone the way of garden gnomes and 'currant bun' rockeries, which were the delights of a previous generation. But these are merely the bubbles on the surface of a deep-running river of national assumptions about what makes a good garden. Gardening programmes on television, urging us to be more daring with plastic and to recycle old oil drums, are really little more than entertainment: they may successfully teach the rudiments of planting, growing and pruning, but have little influence on fundamental, culture-specific assumptions about garden design.

It may be thought the scope of this book is too narrow: no French tradition? no German tradition? no Spanish? It is true that each of these, and many more, countries have a garden tradition that is typically and splendidly theirs, but it seems to me that all the world's pleasure gardens spring from one of the great traditions that are the subject of this book. Many European gardens, for example, are variations on an Italian theme, occasionally with a few English modifications getting the upper hand. The characteristically French *broderie* parterre can be seen as an elaborate variation on the box plantings that are found in Italian gardens as far back as the days of Pliny. And in Germany the great parks of the astonishing Prince Hermann Puckler Muskau at Branitz and Muskau are heavily influenced by the example of the English designer Humphry Repton, and indeed by the work of Repton's son, Adey.

In brief, the principal aim of this book is to examine why people from such very different cultures and in such different parts of the world made pleasure gardens, rather than utilitarian vegetable gardens, and then to examine why they made the kinds of gardens that they did.

RIGHT *Bomarzo, Viterbo, Italy. The Park of the Monsters, also known as the Sacred Grove, was created in the sixteenth century by Vicino Orsini, when other Roman noblemen were working on terraced, hillside gardens with abundant fountains. The grotesque sculptures may form part of a 'programme', but, if so, it remains teasingly obscure.*

BELOW *Biddulph Grange, Stoke-on-Trent, England. This remarkable nineteenth-century garden, restored since 1988, is a wonderful example of Victorian ambition. All the world was to be drawn on for inspiration, the more exotic the better. Hence this Egyptian Garden, and the astonishing Chinese Garden.*

1

THE GENESIS OF THE PLEASURE GARDEN

ABOVE *Villa Adriana, Tivoli, Italy.*
The statuary is not original but it gives a good
idea of how the Canopus must have looked
originally. The recollection of Egypt must have
been painful to Hadrian, since his young lover,
the beautiful Antinous, had died there.

LEFT *Villa Adriana, Tivoli, Italy. The*
Emperor Hadrian came to power in AD 117.
This was his retreat from Rome, but it was
also the seat of government when the Emperor
was in residence. Parts of the site were
landscaped to recall scenes from his empire –
the Vale of Tempe in Greece, for example, or,
here, the Canopus in Egypt.

PLEASURE GARDENS, in China or Italy, Tehran or Agra, have always been places of privilege, places set apart from the hurly-burly of daily life. They probably originated as sacred precincts, dedicated to the deities of the mountains, or of the water springs on which the whole community depended; only certain castes, the leaders and the priests, would have been allowed to enter these holy places. In later times, rulers lavished water, land, time and money on creating pleasure gardens in a display of their superiority to those who needed these resources just to produce the food they lived on. Entry into such places of delight was conceded only to the family and guests of the ruler. Thus gardens became political statements, miniature demonstrations of power, even examples of the order that successful rulers imposed on their kingdoms. Later still, less powerful people began to impose their own kind of order on nature, to demonstrate not their religious or political power but their skill in creating something beautiful: all artists aim to make aesthetically pleasing shapes and patterns – out of sounds, words, colours, stone – and gardeners out of plants. Creating a work of art on a small scale, a private garden, required no patron, no court, no church. Today, gardeners the globe over find pleasure in making beautiful gardens in which they find spiritual refreshment when alone, but which they can also enjoy with their friends, proudly displaying their skill as designers and plant collectors.

'A river went out of Eden to water the garden' (Genesis 2.10); the very earliest gardens are all associated with places made sacred by the presence of life-giving water. And it was not long before savvy rulers began to associate themselves with the mystical powers that emanated from these sacred sites. In Mesopotamia and Assyria the control of water was a vital element in survival, and if the ruler could present himself as the one who brought water to his people, so much the greater would be his fame and influence. In the second half of the third millennium BC the King of western Mesopotamia took the title 'gardener', which was also the epithet given to the region's most important deity, Marduk. The title signified the one who made the land fertile, guaranteeing and regulating the supply of water, and thus the growth of crops. It is for this reason also that the kings of Babylon and Assyria are often represented carrying bronze pruning sickles.

Letters from the royal archives at Mari, a city on the river Euphrates, show that the rulers were involved in planting gardens as far back as the second millennium BC. In one letter the King of Assyria, Ishme-Dagan, asks his brother to send him seeds of juniper to be planted at the temple in Arrapkha, where it was permissible to grow only this species of tree. Rulers were also involved in encouraging the planting of timber, an important building material in a land where most buildings were made of mud. Another Assyrian king, Assur-Uballit (who ruled from 1365 to 1330 BC), brought water to his city and its gardens, an achievement recorded in this inscription: 'My lord, the god Assur, allowed me to construct the Canal of Abundance, which brought fertility to all.' (All quotations here are from di Pasquale and Paolucci – see the bibliography on page 250.) And provincial governors were required to supply trees and seeds to the capital; sometimes demands were made for hundreds, even thousands, of plants, which suggests how extensive were the royal pleasure grounds. One governor of a mountain province writes to excuse himself for not having supplied the King with seedling almonds and plums, but the late snow and frost had made it impossible to dig them up.

And what exactly did they grow in these gardens and parks? Two centuries after Ishme-Dagan, the Assyrian king Tiglat-Pileser (1307–1275 BC) took such pride in his plantings that he recorded them in an inscription: 'I have taken cedars, box and oak trees from the countries I have conquered; none of my royal predecessors had planted these trees, but I planted them in the gardens of my country. From their orchards I have taken rare fruit trees, such as never existed in my country, and have filled the gardens of Assyria with them.' Not all these gardens were created as demonstrations of political power, nor even for commercial purposes, as Tiglat-Pileser makes clear: 'I planted [at Nineveh] a garden for my royal pleasure . . . and in this garden I had a palace built.' And as the empire spread so did the range of plants that could be used in irrigated areas of the kingdom. A later king of Assyria, Assur-Nasir-Pal, moved his capital from Assur to Nimrud, which made it necessary to excavate a new canal of which he was clearly very proud; he records, 'I excavated a canal which cut through a mountain pass. And I irrigated the plain of the Tigris and there I planted gardens with all kinds of fruit trees. I made wine and offered the first fruit to my lord, the god Assur.' He goes on to list the plants he had introduced into his garden following military expeditions against other countries: cypresses, junipers, almonds, date palms, olives, oaks, tamarind, ash, pears, figs and vines. And he includes a lyrical description of his pleasure garden: 'From a high point the canal descends in a waterfall into the garden. The walks are sweetly scented and streams, numerous as the stars of heaven, glint in the garden of pleasure.' We are already hearing the first hints of the Islamic paradise garden, but that religion was not to appear until 1,300 years later.

In the British Museum there is a delightful relief from Sennacherib's palace at Nineveh, which shows a line of servants, all with characteristically permed hair and beards, carrying plants in pots on their shoulders. Sennacherib, however, was interested in grander projects than pleasure gardens: he boasted that he had constructed an artificial marshland in his hunting park, 'and there I planted a bed of rushes where I made herons, wild boar and buffalo live. The reeds prospered and herons from far and wide made their nests, while the boar and the buffalo had many young.' In these parks the King demonstrated his power over all creation by hunting wild animals, particularly the lion, symbol of royalty.

But the royal gardens were not only for such violent pastimes, or political symbols of the king's semi-divine power to supply his people with water: they were also for gentler pleasures. The famous ivory carving from the north palace at Nineveh shows the king, Assur-Banipal, in a garden of palms, reclining on a couch with a cup of wine, while his queen is seated in a chair at his feet. Both are drinking in the shade created by a vine draped between two cypress trees. The servants in attendance seem to be carrying fans to cool the air, while one is playing some kind of harp. Such civilized garden pleasures! The date is between 668 and 631 BC.

Gardens have always been, and indeed always are, associated with fertility. So these Middle Eastern gardens were also used for other kinds of sensual pleasure, including love-making; most of

Pasargadae, Iran. Cyrus the Great established the capital of the first Persian empire here in about 540 BC. The garden, which he created immediately outside his palace, was divided into four equal sections. Water was brought along these stone channels, which are still in place.

the surviving textual evidence points to love and sex between gods and goddesses, but who is to say that humans did not enjoy gardens for the same purpose? The god and his spouse were often carried into a garden at the climax of the sacred ritual, and there they received offerings of fruit, a sophisticated kind of fertility ritual. Many of these texts recall the seductive garden in the Song of Songs, which is planted with nuts, vines and pomegranates; these last were celebrated for their aphrodisiac effects. Fruit was also used as a metaphor for the male and female genitalia, the woman often being praised as a beautiful garden. This strain of metaphor persists into Latin literature, where the female genitalia are sometimes referred to as *hortus*.

Most famous of all the gardens built for love were the Hanging Gardens of Babylon, created by Nebuchadnezzar II in the seventh century BC to satisfy, it is said, his wife, who was homesick for the green landscapes of her mountain birthplace. Diodorus Siculus records that the gardens covered an area 121 metres by 121 metres/400 feet by 400 feet and were 'built up in tiers so they resembled a theatre'. The gardens rose on brick vaults to a maximum height of 23 metres/75 feet, the height of the city walls, and the beds above the vaults were lined with lead so that the water for the plants would not leak through and weaken the structure of the arches. To the amazement of visitors, well-grown trees flourished in these elevated beds. And how was water raised from the Euphrates to keep the plants alive? Some think by chain and bucket, others think by the use of the Archimedes' screw. Such an amazing garden was not only a message of love: it was also a political statement to rival kings of neighbouring states – 'Look on my works, ye mighty, and despair.'

In Egypt, too, water was scarce, but here the annual flooding of the river Nile guaranteed the fertility of the land, so long as the gods were appeased with ritual sacrifices. The earliest gardens here were also associated with royal palaces and temples, though later we find evidence of private gardens belonging to noblemen. An early image of a garden, from about 3000 BC, shows a rectilinear layout, no doubt dictated by the utilitarian pattern of the irrigation channels. In a second-millennium private villa a similar formal pattern is apparent in the layout of the garden. Temples were often surrounded by sacred groves, whose shade must have been much valued; Queen Hatshepsut imported incense trees from the mysterious land of Punt to plant around her mortuary temple at Thebes, but the introduction proved a failure. Trees were revered, so much so that the capitals of stone columns in temples were often carved in the form of plants, and jewellery has been found which uses motifs from the lotus and papyrus.

Private gardens are found in Egypt as early as 2600 BC. The governor of the northern Delta during the reign of Sneferu recorded his garden in the memorial inscription on his tomb. This 1 hectare/2 acre garden contained a large lake, a vineyard, fine trees and a pool. In tombs of the New Kingdom period a conventional prayer expresses the importance of a garden in the lives of rich Egyptians: 'May I walk each day on the banks of my water, that my soul may repose on the branches of the trees that I have planted, and may I refresh myself under the shade of my sycomore.' This last tree was not the European sycamore but *Ficus sycomorus*. Later houses had courtyards frescoed with paintings of gardens, and funeral garlands have been found, making it possible to identify some of the flowers the Egyptians prized, such as cornflower, poppy and mallow. Here too the fertility of gardens proved a stimulus to love. In a papyrus of the second millennium BC a wife invites her lover to take advantage of her husband's absence by visiting her in the garden. Later, love poems became a conventional part of the literature, often spoken by a tree who promises to assist the lovers and keep their secrets, providing they water it well.

Assyria, Mesopotamia, Syria, Egypt and, later, Greece were constantly trading with each other, and almost as constantly at war, all of which led to cultural exchanges which must have influenced the gardens each of these nations made. For example, when the Persians conquered Egypt in 525 BC, they were perhaps influenced by the sophistication of the formal domestic gardens they found. The Greeks defeated the Persians at Marathon and Salamis, while later Alexander led his Macedonian/Greek army as far as India. Xenophon records how much the Greeks admired the emphasis the Persian king placed on garden-making (see Chapter 2), but of Greek gardens themselves little is known. From the earliest times there are reports of sacred groves, usually associated with springs; in Asia Minor some of the most celebrated temples were built near springs, at Miletos, Ephesos and at Didyma, where the spring inspired oracular pronouncements. Particularly famous was the grove surrounding an Arcadian cave, sacred to Demeter, goddess of fertility. Gradually these sites were adorned with altars, statues and sometimes even a temple, and cultivated trees were added to the wild groves, for example around the Demeter shrine at Dorion in Thessaly. Thus when the Greeks built temples in less isolated sites, in their cities for example, it remained the custom to surround them with groves of trees. And, borrowing a technology that came from Egypt via Mycenae, decorative plants were grown in pots watered by irrigation canals, such as those found in the foundations of the Temple of Hephaistus at Athens.

In the western suburbs of Athens the hero Academus was venerated at a sanctuary dedicated to him, described as 'a well-watered grove with trim avenues and shady walks', while at the Lyceum there was a temple to Apollo also surrounded by trees. Baths, gymnasiums and open spaces for athletic contests developed in these areas made agreeable by the trees' shade. In the fourth century the 'peripatetic' philosophers Socrates, Plato and Aristotle began to teach in these groves, giving the rest of Europe the words for two kinds of educational institution: 'academy' and 'liceo'. The upkeep of these public spaces and the nearby religious sites had to be funded, of course, and in the famous temple of Apollo on Delos records have been found detailing the sale of produce from the temple's lands for the benefit of the cult. Another kind of commercial horticulture was the growing of flowers for garlands; these were used to decorate statues, to adorn the brows of newly wedded couples and to crown successful warriors or eminent poets. Of domestic gardens we hear little, an exception being the miniature gardens of Adonis, the beautiful youth with whom Venus fell in love, and whose fertility cult was imported into Greece from the Levant. These pot gardens were planted with whatever grew quickly and then died, to symbolize the brevity of human life and youthful beauty.

From this brief survey of the earliest gardens in Europe and the Middle East, it is possible to draw some general conclusions about their social functions. Usually these gardens were found near a source of water, without which life and growth in these dry lands was impossible. In a human attempt to overcome the vagaries of nature and to guarantee a constant supply of this vital liquid, the gods of these springs were invoked and placated with offerings. Later and further north, in well-watered England, holy springs continued to be centres of worship; at Bath, for example, the cult of the goddess Sul was celebrated. In the Middle Ages these pagan cults were suppressed and the wells were rededicated to Christian saints. An early example of a non-utilitarian garden was the sacred grove, a garden inhabited (permanently or temporarily) by gods, like the Garden of Eden in the Biblical story and the gardens of paradise in Islam, both of which contain significant rivers. As society became more organized and hierarchical these sacred precincts became the province of the ruler, who was also often the high priest of the cult. In dry countries he (most early rulers were men; Cleopatra and Hatshepsut were exceptions) presented himself as the giver or controller of the water supply, in this way displaying his almost divine power. This was also demonstrated in his introduction of exotic species from the further parts of his empire and from foreign countries he had conquered. Once places of religious reverence, gardens became the province of the social elite, and sometimes they were economically significant, since they grew timber, medicinal herbs and flowers for garlands. Ultimately they also became places of escape from the demands of city life, even places of sensual delight, where the nobility could indulge their taste for wine, women and song.

In tracing the subsequent social history of pleasure gardens we shall again and again find echoes of the motivation of these earliest garden makers. In the Mughal gardens of Kashmir, for example, the ruler would sometimes present himself to his people enthroned above a stream, so that all could see how he gave water to his people, and be grateful. In many Mughal tomb gardens the produce was sold to finance the upkeep of the garden and the tomb structure. Royal collections of exotic plants were to become the botanical gardens of medieval Islamic Spain and Renaissance Italy. Many later gardens are also demonstrations of power, most obviously Louis XIV's Versailles in France, but also the gardens of Italian villas, whose proprietors used water with such profligacy and imposed their will on nature by ordering the hillside into terraces. Like the sacred groves of Athens, medieval royal gardens were used often as places of retirement, for private pleasure, sometimes

The Chehel Sotun, Isfahan, Iran. The name means forty columns, but there are only twenty in the portico. The other twenty are supplied by reflections in the pool in front of this royal reception hall. This intimate association of architecture and water became a typical feature of the Islamic garden.

for dalliance. And when the Medici built their villas near Florence, their *giardini segreti* were consciously imitating the Athenian philosophers' gardens and groves which provided a calm setting for thoughtful debate. Gardens were always places apart, privileged spaces where the ruler hunted or made love, discussed political ideas or feasted honoured guests; essentially they were not part of the quotidian world, and in this way they recall their origins in the sacred groves dedicated to the gods and goddesses of fertility.

In tracing the genesis of the Western pleasure garden it should never be forgotten that its creation requires not just a social or religious motive but a period of peace and ample surplus funds – a point clearly demonstrated in any Third World country to this day. For example in Lao (once known as Laos),the second poorest country in Asia (only Bangladesh is poorer) where 85 per cent of the population still live on the land the sparse, urban middle class sometimes makes a collection of pot-grown plants to decorate the front porch. In the old capital, Luang Prabang, French colonial influence and the demands of the tourist have led to the creation of small front gardens behind picket fences. But in most villages there is neither the spare cash nor the leisure for the creation of pleasure gardens. The village of Tha Nam on the mighty Mekong River, to the east of Vientiane, is an interesting exception. Here Thai tobacco barons from the other side of the river frontier employ some of the inhabitants to grow and dry tobacco, with the result that there is sometimes a little cash to spare. In the village there are vegetable gardens, but no one has yet created a garden just for pleasure. However, on a visit I saw one curious small area, not close

to a house but carefully fenced off with bamboo canes, where it seemed that only flowers had been planted. When asked who was making a flower garden, our guide told us that marigolds were being grown here to decorate the temple, to make garlands for the divine statues and to hang around the necks of those who were celebrating a wedding or a birthday. This is typical of the development of the pleasure garden: when surplus cash and peace make it possible, flowers are grown first for the temple and for sacred rituals; only later will the village leaders perhaps have their own flower gardens.

ABOVE Padua, Italy. This botanical garden was founded in 1545 as a teaching aid for students in the University Medical School. Here apprentice apothecaries could learn their plants, which were laid out in carefully ordered beds.

Such motives have impelled humans to make pleasure gardens whether in Europe, the Middle East, India, China, Japan or the Americas. As we have seen, they may make gardens as places of spiritual retreat from the political, commercial or personal pressures of day-to-day life – the monastic cloister, for example, often with a fountain and planted with healing herbs, or the Islamic garden with canals, fruit and shade, reminiscent of paradise perhaps, but sometimes used for the carnal pleasures of drinking and wooing, or the Japanese Zen garden, which puzzles the mind. In this more secular age the garden maker may be looking to create a space in which to escape from stress, although with its constant demands on our time and energies, it is hard to see a garden as restful, unless someone else is doing much of the work. However, some people find the activity of gardening calming, particularly repetitive jobs like weeding, because they occupy enough of our minds to absorb superficial stresses, but leave enough thinking space unoccupied for semi-conscious cogitation. Joseph Addison, one of the earliest promoters of the 'natural' style in landscape design that was to become particularly English, found gardening an uplifting activity which 'fills the mind with calmness and tranquillity', gives 'a great insight into the contrivances and wisdom of Providence' and thus encourages 'a virtuous habit in man' (*The Spectator*, number

477, 6/9/1712); after a period of civil war in England such calm virtues were particularly prized. Other writers have suggested more than an entymological connection between humus and humility, particularly since so much gardening is done on our knees.

The garden at Stourhead in England was intended to transport the visitor into a higher realm; its idealized landscape recalls to our minds the backgrounds in Claude Lorrain's classical paintings, and the virtues of ancient Rome, or, perhaps more accurately, Whig interpretations of the classical world. The walk around the lake parallels a reading of Virgil's *Aeneid*, quotations from which were inscribed on the entrance to the Grotto and the Temple of Flora. Horace Walpole chose his words carefully when he described the view from the Temple of Apollo as 'one of the most picturesque scenes in the world'. Pictures were what the banker Henry Hoare had in mind throughout the construction of this garden – pictures by Claude Lorrain, Gaspard Poussin and Salvator Rosa. Stourhead attempts to give us an impression of paradise; here the garden has nothing to do with the house, and the classical Roman buildings in the landscape are there for the sake of the composition. We are as removed from the hurly-burly of real life as in any cloister.

If one motive for making pleasure gardens is to retreat from the world, a second universal motive is to create spaces in which to socialize, intimately, as in the castle gardens of medieval Europe, or less intimately, as in the rational, public gardens of nineteenth-century France. Medieval European literature and painting is full of references to gardens as places of courtship. The *Roman de la Rose*, which Chaucer translated into English, describes a walled garden which itself becomes a symbol of the beloved. In Chaucer's own *Merchant's Tale* January builds a garden that will be his private space, since only he has the key; here he takes his pleasure with his wife May. And here the unnatural conjunction of withered January and burgeoning May is threatened by the arrival of the attractive and youthful Damian; gardens, after all, are also about natural growth and the promotion of fertility. In China we find plaques set into the walls of many Song period (960–1279) scholars' gardens which recall pleasant evenings spent drinking in congenial company; these gardens were the settings not only for drinking parties but also for poetry-writing contests and musical entertainments.

RIGHT *The Church of the Santissimi Quattro Coronati, Rome, Italy. There has been a church on this site from the fourth century, but this beautiful cloister dates from the twelfth century. Its atmosphere of calm tranquillity, conducive to study and prayer, has been preserved in the hubbub of modern Rome.*

The function of public gardens and parks is similarly social and recreational, as the great nineteenth-century designer Frederick Law Olmsted acknowledged in one of his reports to the Commissioners of Central Park in New York:, 'It is one great purpose of the Park to supply to the hundreds of thousands of tired workers, who have no opportunity to spend their summers in the country, a specimen of God's handiwork that shall be to them, inexpensively, what a month or two in the White Mountains or the Adirondacks is, at great cost, to those in easier circumstances.' Even today in Tokyo it is striking to see groups of office workers in impeccable business suits gathering to drink together under a cherry tree full of blossom, thus celebrating the return of spring and the beauty of nature.

A third universal motive for making a garden is far from spiritual or social: it is to impress others with one's wealth and power – power over others and power over nature. When the remarkable Babur, first of the Mughal rulers of India, set up his new capital at Agra in 1526, he created gardens

LEFT *Stourhead, Warminster, England. This famous example of an idyllic English landscape park was laid out in the middle of the eighteenth century by the banker Henry Hoare. The lakes were created by damming the river Stour. The planting of rhododendrons and azaleas dates from the late nineteenth century.*

RIGHT *The City Palace, Udaipur, India. The palace is an accumulation of buildings of different periods, but most are built around courtyards shaded by trees and surrounded by porticos. The ruler could control how close any subjects got to his person by limiting them to the outer courtyards.*

for his own pleasure in which to escape from the oppressive heat. These gardens make a decisive political statement; they demonstrate the arrival of a more formal, Islamic aesthetic perception in 'charmless and disorderly Hind [India]', as Babur wrote in his diary. The lucidly symmetrical lines of these Mughal gardens, their formal planting and their abundant water show how Babur was able to impose himself not only on the landscape but on the conquered people and their cultural traditions.

It is, of course, possible to go too far in your garden, drawing too much attention to your power and wealth. The unfortunate Nicholas Fouquet employed the finest artists of his day to build the palace and garden at Vaux le Vicomte in France; Louis Le Vau was his architect, Charles Le Brun painted the interior of the house and designed much of the sculpture, and André Le Nôtre laid out the garden. On 7 August 1661 Fouquet invited his guests to admire the finished work. In a letter the poet Jean de la Fontaine described the event as he saw it from the hill at the far end of the garden: 'all the walks [were] animated with ladies and courtiers so that it was impossible to imagine a more beautiful spectacle, and there was such an abundance of good things that there are not words to describe them'. Fouquet, however, had made a grave mistake: among the guests was the young king, Louis XIV, who not only admired the achievement but envied it, and wondered how Fouquet, his finance minister, had paid for it all. Enquiries were made, and ten days later Fouquet was arrested for peculation; he spent the rest of his life in jail. Louis immediately employed the artists whose work he had admired at Vaux on his new palace, Versailles, commandeering most of the sculptures and uprooting many of the trees from Fouquet's garden for his new park. Louis' Versailles is one of the most deliberate statements of power that it is possible to find in garden history; the straight lines cut through woodland and the central avenue that had no ending

BELOW *Vaux le Vicomte, Seine et Marne, France. Nicolas Fouquet created this garden between 1656 and 1661, giving André le Nôtre his first major commission. This is gardening as a swaggering demonstration of power and wealth. He would pay for his ambition with life imprisonment.*

ABOVE *Orti Farnesiani, Rome, Italy. Little is left of the gardens that Vignola laid out for Pope Paul III Farnese in the 1530s. These were important botanical gardens, but also places for papal pleasures. Today these gardens on the Palatine offer a welcome escape from the heat and crowds of the Forum.*

proclaimed to the assembled French nobility, and to the world, Louis' complete self-confidence and his enormous ambition.

Few gardeners have had the resources or the desire to make quite so clear a political statement as Louis, but many have wanted to outdo their neighbours in splendour and display. During the sixteenth century around Rome one cardinal after another wanted to escape the politically and environmentally fetid atmosphere of the great city, and at his country seat each was determined to show off the wealth and status of his family in extravagant garden-making. Today we can find something similar happening around New Delhi and Jaipur, where the recently wealthy, with the same motive of escaping the noise and pollution of the city, vie with each other in the splendour and extent of the gardens at what they call their 'farms', really their country houses.

A fourth universal motive for making a pleasure garden, rather than a garden in which to produce food to eat, is the human desire to create beautiful patterns, to order our environment, to create works of art that express something of the aesthetic taste and the personality of their creator. The earliest gardens in most civilizations were highly patterned to draw the sharpest possible distinction between what had been created by a human and untamed nature, between the disorderly landscape where man felt threatened and the peaceful, contained setting he had created for himself. The earliest representations we have of gardens in Egypt show a geometric layout within a walled enclosure. The remains of first-century urban gardens found at Pompei are balanced, often symmetrical, even when they are not enclosed in the courtyard of a house. The earliest Chinese garden makers, by contrast, wanted to bring an idealized version of the landscape into their gardens (a tradition that continues), because mountains were the homes of the sages and the gods;

the garden versions of mountains and lakes are miniaturized and ordered into subtle patterns, so that even in the 0.4 hectare/1 acre of the Wang Shi Yuan in Suzhou the owner could experience something of the natural wildness in his carefully chosen and assembled piles of rock. Even the smallest suburban garden gives the owner space to express his or her own taste – to cram it with gnomes or heathers, grow a monkey puzzle or build a fountain; we are all gods when it comes to making a garden. Thus we express our own personalities, and perhaps raise our self-esteem.

If gardens once were places where man demonstrated his control, in our day they are also places where man encourages nature to take its course, because nature is no longer seen as threatening but rather under threat. So a fifth motive for garden-making – and this is a contemporary phenomenon – is to help the preservation of endangered species; butterflies are an obvious example. But there is perhaps something deeper that drives people to create wildflower, marsh and meadow gardens: a reaction to the loss of wilderness in many parts of Europe. In England, of course, the countryside is by now so tamed and managed that the wild element is almost entirely absent, and thus the enthusiasm for wildflower and bog gardens is particularly strong. By contrast in America, where the wilderness dominates, such gardens are of less interest.

Which raises the question of when the wilderness stops being the wilderness and becomes a garden. Anyone who has seen an Alpine pasture in full bloom, or the meadows of Vermont in spring, or an English beech wood carpeted with bluebells, may wonder why anyone bothers to make a garden when unaided nature is so beautiful. But gardens are an attempt to improve on the natural environment, working with, and sometimes against, nature. As soon as a human intervenes in the way plants are arranged in order to satisfy some aesthetic urge, not merely a pang of hunger,

ABOVE *Reconstruction of a Roman courtyard garden, Florence, Italy. This scholarly reconstruction of a Roman garden of the Imperial era was made for an exhibition on the history of gardening staged in the Boboli Gardens. The Romans' skill in hydraulics is apparent in the plentiful fountains and pools.*

RIGHT *Wang Shi Yuan, Suzhou, China. Chinese courtyard gardens are certainly retreats from the world, but they can seem claustrophobic with their clustering buildings and piles of rock. However, the reflections in the water create a feeling of space, and here another technique is used: the back of the pavilion is lined with a mirror.*

the art of the pleasure garden begins. As Roberto Burle Marx so succinctly put it, 'A garden is nature organized by man for man.' And the desire to arrange and grow plants in a way that satisfies our sense of beauty appears to be almost universal. The only part of the world where there seems to be no tradition of garden-making for the sake of beauty is sub-Saharan Africa, and this may well be for lack of the leisure and surplus funds referred to above. The exception is South Africa, where gardening is an art imported by the immigrant populations, who were also the imperial powers; here again gardens can be read as political documents. In a similar way the history of plant introductions can also provide us with evidence of the spread of political and economic power.

So we find humans making gardens in most parts of the world, sharing similar motives and aiming at aesthetically satisfying results. But of course, what satisfies one nation does not please another. Most Europeans, for example, would not readily enjoy the piles of contorted rock that are a major feature of many classic Chinese gardens, even when they come to understand the function these stones serve in the garden's composition. And the oriental gardener may wonder at the time spent on caring for lawns in much of Europe and America; grass, one Chinese scholar is said to have pointed out, 'may be of interest to a cow, but it offers nothing to the intellect of a human being'. Similarly, few Europeans perhaps find the greatest aesthetic pleasure in the raked sand and carefully placed rocks of the Japanese Zen garden. However, when we understand why these gardens are as they are, when we appreciate something of their history and meaning, then we can begin to enjoy them more intelligently.

RIGHT *Sitio Santo Antonio da Bica, Rio de Janeiro, Brazil, the home of one of the great geniuses of gardening, Roberto Burle Marx. His garden is a jungle of exotic species, many of which he collected himself on expeditions to the Brazilian interior, and some of which are named after him.*

BELOW *Ninfa, Latina, Italy. This great garden was made by three generations of Caetani women, who began to plant up the ruins of this medieval town in the 1920s. Gardens in ruins have a huge appeal to the post-romantic European imagination.*

2
THE ISLAMIC TRADITION

ABOVE *The Alcazar, Seville, Spain. This twelfth-century stronghold was rebuilt in the fourteenth century. The gardens are some of the largest in Spain that show evidence of Moorish influence, although some of the Islamic details have been destroyed in later developments.*

LEFT *The Taj Mahal, Agra, India. Dawn over the tomb of Mumtaz Mahal (died 1631), the favourite wife of the Mughal Shah Jahan. This is one of the most perfect buildings in the world; the same cannot be said of the garden. Originally there would have been parterres of flowers and fruit trees, as well as the extant symmetrical fountains and water channels.*

T HE KIND OF GARDEN we usually think of as Islamic in fact predates Islam; its origins are to be found in Persia. The gardens of paradise described in the Koran were of a type already existing, known to the prophet Muhammad either from direct experience or from travellers' tales. When the Arabs invaded Persia between 638 and 640 there was a productive exchange of cultures: the Persians converted to Islam, while the Arabs learned the uses of the scimitar and the horse in battle; they also learned of Persian gardens, which already had a long history. The Arab invaders quickly became experts both in warfare and in garden-making.

It is not hard to recognize the typical Islamic garden: it is walled, rectangular, often divided into four sections by four canals, perhaps representing the four rivers of the universe; it has elaborate water features, fountains, canals and water chutes; and there are shading trees, planted in rigidly formal patterns. But why did it develop like this? And after a little international garden-crawling, the next question will be 'And why are these gardens so similar whether they're in Spain, Algeria, Iran, Egypt or India?' Why does religious identity take precedence over national and climatic differences?

The consistency of design is remarkable, as is the reluctance to experiment or develop, emphasizing the close relationship between the religion of the conquering power and its garden culture – which is why these gardens are given the label 'Islamic', rather than being ascribed to a particular nationality. Appreciating this consistency of design and planting, a bored Vita Sackville-West concluded: 'There is very little else to be said for the Persian garden, except to say the same thing over and over again.' But having analysed why these gardens are as they are, and wondered at their uniformity, we might then consider some of the differences to be found in the gardens of the Dar al-Islam (the Islamic world); Mughal gardens, for example, while clearly within the great tradition of Islamic garden-making, are in many ways different from the much earlier Moorish gardens of Andalucia.

It is as rare to find the name of a designer, architect or owner recorded in an Islamic garden as it is to find the signature of an artist on a Persian or Mughal miniature; it is the tradition and the individual's submission to that tradition that is emphasized. Occasionally we find a reference to the ruler, as at the Alhambra in Spain, but even here there is an ambiguity in the references; the inscriptions could refer either to Allah or to the ruler. In a similar way the emphasis on geometry and proportion in the layout of the gardens reminds us of the theoretical perfection of mathematics, a science in which the Islamic world was particularly skilled, and this superhuman, mathematical precision is a major component of the beauty of the gardens' composition. The mind of the viewer is inevitably led towards thoughts of a better, more rational, more orderly world than that which exists outside the confines of the garden.

But Islamic gardens do not only transcend the human: they were also places for all kinds of very earthly, sensual pleasure, in particular love making and drinking (despite Koranic commandments against the use of alcohol). If Boccaccio gives us an idea of the ideal medieval Italian garden in his *Decameron*, then the Islamic equivalent must be the description of Harun al-Rashid's fictional garden in *The Thousand and One Nights*:

Ali Nour had seen at Basra some huge and beautiful gardens, but had never dreamed of something as wonderful as this. The great entrance was covered in rampant vines, from which hung heavy bunches of enormous grapes, some red as ruby, some black as ebony. The avenue we entered was shaded by fruit trees, which bent under the weight of ripe fruit. On the branches birds twittered in their own languages . . . Every fruit was represented by its best specimen; there were apricots with sweet fruit and apricots with sour fruits,

LEFT *The Alcazar, Seville, Spain. The straight lines, geometrical shapes and regular placement of the fountains are typical of the mathematical precision of the Islamic garden at its best. Such gardens may seem lifeless without the play of water, but in many parts of the Islamic world today water is too precious a commodity to lavish on garden ornamentation.*

and apricots from Khurasan. There were plums the colour of beautiful lips, whose sweetness would enchant you, red figs, white figs, and green figs, all wonderful to behold. The flowers resembled pearl and coral; the roses were more beautiful than the most beautiful young girl's cheeks; the violets were dark as burnt sulphur; the myrtle flowers were white, and there were wallflowers, pansies, lavender and anemonies. All the flowers' faces were wet with tears that fell from the clouds; the camomile bared its teeth as it smiled at the narcissus, and the narcissus stared at the rose with its large, dark eyes. The cedars were like goblets and the lemons hung like golden drops. All the earth was carpeted with flowers of a thousand colours, because spring reigned throughout the woodland; the nourishing streams were swollen with water and the fountains tinkled, the birds warbled, while the breeze sang like a flute, and the air re-echoed with joy.

(Quoted in Attilio Petruccioli, *Il Giardino Islamico*, p. 7)

Consider the number of senses that are appealed to here – sight, sound, touch, taste and hearing: the sensuous, sometimes almost erotic, luxury of such a picture must have contrasted strongly with the severe life of the desert nomads. Ali Nour is initiated into adult life in this garden of sensual delights; here he first succumbs to the pleasures of wine and kisses, with disastrous results.

Sometimes Islamic gardens are called 'paradise' gardens, because in the Koran we read about the gardens of the blessed, which are full of all the things the desert lacked – a temperate climate, shade, water and fruit trees; there true believers 'shall drink of a cup tempered at the Camphor Fountain, a gushing spring at which the servants of Allah will refresh themselves . . . they shall feel neither the scorching heat nor the biting cold. Trees will spread their shade around them, and fruits

BELOW *Madinat al-Zahra, Cordoba. This large palace complex, complete with terrace and courtyard gardens, was begun in 936 by Abd al-Rahman I. It was scarcely finished when it was sacked in the civil war of 1010.*

will hang in clusters over them.' The word Xenophon uses to describe Cyrus the Great's garden is *paradeisos*, which derives from a Persian word, *paradaida*, meaning 'walled about'. Unlike the Chinese garden with its borrowed landscape, or the English landscape garden with its open vistas, most Islamic gardens are surrounded by an enclosure; the surrounding landscape is excluded. It is not hard to appreciate why this was necessary in the desert, or on the high, arid Iranian plateau, where an escape from the blinding light and the harsh, sand-laden winds must have seemed like paradise indeed. In Greek the word *paradeisos* came to mean a pleasure park, clearly from the Persian example, although in the Greek Septuagint bible it was also used for the place that the blessed would enter after death. From the Greek the word entered English via Latin, although by the time it was used by the English translators of the Bible, by Shakespeare and Thomas Campion, the word had lost most of its connection to an enclosed Persian pleasure park; paradise was, however, still a garden, though for Christians a garden lost, and for faithful Muslims a garden to come.

As early as 480 BC in Xenophon's dialogue 'Oeconomicos' Socrates repeats the story of Cyrus the Younger, aspirant ruler of the Persian empire, showing his garden at Sardis to Lysander, commander of the Peloponnesian fleet, which had come to Cyrus' aid in the civil war: 'Lysander admired the beauty of the trees in it, the accuracy of the spacing, the straightness of the rows, the regularity of the angles, and the multitude of sweet scents that clung around them as they walked.' Lysander praises the skill of the designer who had laid out the garden, and Cyrus is delighted to tell him that he did much of the planting with his own hands. Later in the same dialogue Socrates comments: 'In all the districts that the Great King visits he takes care that there are "paradises", as they call them, full of all the good and beautiful things that the soil will produce.' (Loeb Edition translation.)

In the areas where the Persian garden developed, present-day Iraq and the high plateau of Iran, there is no agriculture without irrigation, so it is no wonder that water is central to the Islamic garden, as a sensuous delight for eyes and ears, but also of practical value, since it is used for irrigation, and for the ritual ablutions required of the devout Muslim. The science of the *qanat*, an underground water channel, is clearly very old and was born of necessity in these arid regions. First, it is necessary to tap into a water source high in the mountains; the water is then brought by the force of gravity through underground channels lined with plaster or brick; these channels keep the water cool and eliminate the risk of evaporation. Every 10 metres/30 feet or so there are

LEFT *A qanat pit, Iran. This method of water delivery, by underground tunnel lined with brick, was recorded by the Babylonians as early as 2000 BC. The water table is tapped in the mountains and water runs down the channels by gravity.*

ABOVE *Bagh-e Naranjastan, Shiraz, Iran. The mirror work in the pavilion is nineteenth century, but this traditional layout with a water tank immediately outside the building is traditionally Islamic.*

sloping access tunnels which give light to the tunnellers and allow access to maintenance engineers. These holes were a constant danger to merchants' caravans, which often travelled across the desert by night to avoid the scorching sun. In the first Persian garden we know about, that constructed by Cyrus the Great at Pasargadae in about 546 BC, the carved water channels, many of which still exist, defined the garden's geometrical layout. And when Darius the Great built Persepolis in about 500 BC, he provided his private quarters with flowing water for washing and for irrigating his garden. By this period the representation of flowers and plants was already an established theme of Persian art; on many of the ceremonial stairways of Persepolis rows of stylized roses, lotus, cypress and palms are carved in delicate, low relief.

These early Persian gardens set a precedent – unsurprising given the climate – that was to be followed in most of the gardens of the Islamic world: they were places to sit and contemplate, not to walk, let alone to work, as poor Adam and Eve had to do in the Garden of Eden, even before the Fall. The Koran promises that the faithful will be found not strolling in the shade of the garden but 'reclining there upon soft couches'. Sir John Chardin, a Huguenot jeweller, who visited Persia in 1686, noted the same thing: 'Nor do the Persians take any manner of pleasure in walking in them [their gardens], any more than in the fields, but set themselves down in some alcove or summer house as soon as they come in them, totally negligent of that exquisite variety that every foreigner is charmed with.' In Persian houses there was often an intermediate space between the house and the garden, a kind of shaded portico, called an *ayvan* or *iwan*. This was usually raised and looked out over water to the garden beyond; this close association of architecture and water was to become a hallmark of the Islamic garden. Later we also find detached pavilions from whose shade the owner could appreciate the sound of water, the scent of flowers and the delights of music.

Sometimes a pavilion, a *charbutra*, was placed at the crossing of two canals, to act as a focal point in the garden's design, and to catch any available breezes, cooled by their passage over the water.

The Arabs were not the only conquerors of the Persian empire who were themselves conquered by the wonders of Persian culture; something similar happened when Timur (known to many Westerners as Tamburlaine) invaded the empire from the east. He too was enchanted by the gardens, and the Spanish ambassador who visited him in 1403 describes him sitting in one of the many gardens he had created in Samarkand, his capital: 'He was sitting not on the ground, but on a raised dais before which there was a fountain that threw up a column of water into the air, and in the basin of the fountain there were red apples floating. His Highness had taken his place on what appeared to be a small mattress, stuffed thick and covered with embroidered silk cloth, and he was leaning upon his elbow against some round cushions that were heaped up behind him.' (Quoted in *New RHS Dictionary of Gardening.*) Though the Emperor, aged seventy and almost completely blind, is here described as sitting on a dais, it was more usual to sit on cushions on the floor, with the result that the point of view was lower than if the viewer had been sitting on a chair. This low viewing point was to have a decisive influence on the design of some later Islamic gardens.

The Islamic garden is also sometimes known as the *char bagh* (or *chahar bagh*), meaning a garden divided into four compartments, usually by two canals running at right angles, although in truth this is a subset of the Islamic garden. The first written reference to the *char bagh* is found in Narshaki's history of Bukhara, but this kind of garden seems to have existed earlier. At Samarra the Bulkawara Palace, built between 849 and 859, had what J.D. Hoag describes as 'a quadripartite garden, flanked by pavilions, overlooking the water', and from the mosaic vines found on a nearby portal he deduces that this may have been a deliberate evocation of the Koranic paradise.

ABOVE *The Alhambra, Granada, Spain. The gardens around the remains of the Partal Palace were built in 1924 on the ruins of part of the Nasrid Palace, but they imitate the earlier Hispano-Islamic style.*

In Sura 55 of the Koran Muhammad writes of two pairs of gardens for the blessed: one pair is 'planted with shady trees', 'each of which is watered by a flowing spring, . . . and each bears every kind of fruit in pairs'; 'and beside these there shall be two other gardens of the darkest green . . . A gushing fountain shall flow in each . . . and each shall be planted with fruit trees, the palm and the pomegranate.' So four gardens, symmetrically arranged in two pairs, are promised and all the blessed have to do is 'recline on green cushions and rich carpets', or 'on couches lined with thick brocade, and within their reach shall hang the fruits of both gardens' (translation by N.J. Dawood).

Timur was a Mongol, a nomad and a warrior, so he didn't spend all his time in his gardens reclining upon his elbow against soft cushions; his gardens were also used for a more practical purpose. He had parts of them planted with clover lawns so that he could use them as encampments for his troops and as the setting for his own tented court. The Mongols (when they became respectable, settled dwellers in India they were known as the Mughals) at this stage felt more at home in tents than in permanent structures. The biographer of Shah Rukh, Timur's son and successor, describes a Timurid festival at Herat: 'In the royal garden were erected tents which had from 80 to 100 poles, scarlet pavilions and tents made of silk. In these tents were thrones of gold and silver, encircled by garlands of rubies and pearls. From the carpets issued vapours of amber, whilst the durbar tent was filled with the soothing odour of musk.'

Carpets picturing formalized gardens are another source of information about the design of Persian gardens. The most celebrated of these was that of the Sassanian Khusrau (sometimes known as Chosroes), who ruled from 531 to 579. The brick span of his great audience hall still stands, possibly the longest span of unreinforced brickwork in the world, and beneath it was laid the bejewelled carpet known as the Spring of Khusrau. Part of a contemporary description

BELOW *El Badi Palace, Marrakech, Morocco. The palace was built by Ahmed al Mansour ed-Dahbi between 1578 and 1593. It was famous for its luxury, but survived for less than a century before being thoroughly sacked. However, the layout of vast sunken gardens and water tanks has survived in this monumental ruin.*

runs thus: 'The borders of the streams were woven in stripes, and between these borders tiny stones, the size of pearls, gave the impression of water. The stems and branches of the trees and flowers were woven from gold and silver, the leaves from silk like the rest of the plants, and the fruits were brightly coloured stones.' (Quoted in Roni Jay.) This extraordinary creation struck wonder into many beholders, but was divided as booty by the invading Arabs, who were perhaps suspicious of such ostentatious luxury. Their puritanical repugnance, however, did not last for long. Ambassadors of the Byzantine emperor reported equally expensive and exotic works of art when they visited in 917 – a tree with silver and gold boughs from which hung fruit made of precious stones, and mechanical silver birds, perched on the boughs of golden trees, which sang when hydraulic pressure drove air through their tubes.

The Arabs, took the traditions of the Persian garden to the West, along the north coast of Africa, as they set out on their remarkable period of conquest in the eighth century, and later the Asiatic peoples took the traditions of the Persian garden to the East, to Samarkand, Bokhara and Herat, from where Babur, the first of the Mughals, carried them into India. And the common thread in these gardens was the Persian design influence, in particular its insistence on the intimate connection between water and architecture, and the religion of the garden makers. Sadly, the heart of the Dar al-Islam has been fought over for so long (the warfare continues as I write) that few of the earliest gardens remain intact. For existing Islamic gardens we must look to Iran and to the fringes of the Islamic world – to Mughal India, to Andalucia in southern Spain, and to North Africa.

The astonishing conquests of the Arabs in the seventh and eighth centuries carried their faith, and the design of the gardens they had adopted, from Egypt, which was taken in 640, to the Atlantic seaboard in sixty years. In 711 the first Muslim army crossed the Straits of Gibraltar, defeated the Visigoth opposition and established itself in Andalucia. Fifty years later the Umayyad dynasty of caliphs that had ruled from Damascus was overthrown by the Abbasids, and the sole surviving Umayyad escaped to Spain, where he set himself up as the independent caliph of Al-Andalus. The Arabs and North African Berbers who established this caliphate found in the Iberian peninsula a country already developed by the Romans; there were Roman aqueducts, Roman agricultural practices, Roman roads and the vestiges of Roman law. It was a land of rich soil, and densely forested, so that it was said a squirrel could swing its way from the Straits of Gibraltar to the English Channel

BELOW *The Alcazar, Seville, Spain. After the collapse of the Cordoba caliphate, Seville became one of the most influential successor states. Water was brought to the town using the qanat system borrowed from Iran, and by Roman aqueducts where they were still usable.*

ABOVE *The Alcazar, Cordoba, Spain. Cordoba became the seat of the caliphate after the Islamic invasion of Spain, but there had been buildings on this site much earlier. Water was gathered in these great tanks, and was then distributed along lead pipes to fountains, pools and water chutes.*

without touching the ground. The Arabs brought with them their own skills in agriculture and hydraulics, skills they had learned from the Persians, and the tolerance their religion taught them. Their first capital, Cordoba, which had previously been the capital of a Roman province, became not only a flourishing commercial centre but also an intellectual powerhouse, where many Greek texts, often preserved in Arabic, were translated and made available to the rest of Europe.

Central to any Islamic society is the mosque, and the size of the mosque at Cordoba testifies to the importance of this city as the seat of a caliphate. Beside the mosque, which also contains what is now the cathedral, lies the Patio de los Naranjos; dating from *c.*990, it is the oldest surviving Islamic garden in the West. This courtyard was the place where worshippers would have performed their ritual ablutions before entering the mosque. The formal, regular planting must remind us of Lysander's amazement at the garden of Cyrus the Younger. In a space 120 by 60 metres/ 390 by 196 feet, divided into three equal rectangles, there is no decoration beyond the stonework of the arches, but the patio is now planted with orange trees, although earlier laurels, palms and olives had been used. Originally the arches of the mosque were left open and the trees were planted to continue the lines of the columns inside the building, creating a kind of shady porch, reminiscent of the Persian *ayvan*; these openings were walled up after the Christian reconquest of Cordoba in 1256, with the result that it is now much harder to appreciate the relationship between building and garden. The lines of trees are irrigated by narrow canals, which carry water from the overflowing fountains to the roots. Here are all the elements of the Islamic garden at their simplest: shade, scent, formal planting of fruit trees, regularly spaced, and flowing water, all contained in a rectangular frame. But, since this was a public space, it was not walled.

The Alcazar at Cordoba was adopted by the Muslim invaders as their seat of government; they adapted and extended the buildings erected by the Visigoths, who had themselves built on the foundations of an existing Roman building, so that what we see today is a palimpsest of different periods and styles. It is possible to see the Islamic influence in the great water tanks, fed by a Roman aqueduct, and in the water chutes beside the steps that lead down into the sunken garden. The garden of the Morisco patio is fourteenth century but based on a tenth-century design. It is enclosed, severely rectangular, with raised walkways above sunken beds; two large cisterns feed the irrigation canals that border the rectangular sections of the patio. There is also a first-floor balcony from which to appreciate the whole symmetrical layout of the garden.

As Cordoba grew in size, successful merchants began to build country houses around the city, making use of the agricultural land that was the source of their wealth. As in imperial Rome, three conditions made it possible to develop these estates: surplus cash, abundance of leisure and peace. These *munyats* or country estates were where the aristocracy relaxed, listening to poetry and music, admiring paintings, discussing ideas and entertaining their friends – just as the Medici were to do 600 years later at the Villa Medici outside Florence. The *munyats* were often described by visitors to Cordoba, and it was usually the gardens, not the architecture of the buildings, that were praised.

When Abd al-Rahman became the ruler in 756 he decided to build a palace from scratch 3 kilometres/1.86 miles from the city. His model was his grandfather's estate at Rusafa in Syria, where he had lived as a child, and it was from this palace that the Munyat al-Rusafa took its name. Recent excavations in Syria have revealed the remains of an eighth-century palace ascribed to the Umayyad Caliph Hisham. Among the ruins archaeologists found an enclosed, irrigated, four-part garden, which may be the earliest example of the *char bagh* layout in the Islamic world.

ABOVE *Patio de los Naranjos, Cordoba, Spain. One of the earliest gardened sites in Islamic Europe. The mosque, begun in 1171, was originally open on one side, and the lines of trees continued the lines of columns inside the building.*

Sadly, nothing remains of the Andalucian Rusafa, so we cannot tell if it was here that the four-part garden made its first appearance in Spain. It seems that Abd al-Rahman was sometimes homesick for Syria; he is said to have composed this nostalgic poem in his garden at Rusafa:

A palm tree stands in the middle of Rusafa, born in the West, far from the land of palms.
I said to it, 'How like me you are, far away and in exile, far from family and friends.
You have grown in a soil where you are a stranger; and, like you, I am far from home.'
(Quoted D. Fairchild Ruggles, *Gardens, Landscape and Vision*)

BELOW *Patio de los Naranjos, Cordoba, Spain. The courtyard has always been planted with trees, which were watered by rectilinear water channels.*

This poem also recalls how Abd al-Rahman encouraged the introduction of new plants, such as a finer strain of pomegranate, from the East. Within the Dar al-Islam there was a constant interchange of ideas on architecture and garden design; plant material was also disseminated by visiting merchants, and by artists called to Andalucia from Syria or Byzantium. One of the most celebrated was the musician Ziryab, a refugee from Abbasid Baghdad, who became an arbiter of taste in early ninth-century Cordoba, where among other points of refinement, he insisted on the use of toothpaste. This interchange of plants and ideas was also stimulated by the meetings in Mecca of hajj pilgrims, who came from all parts of the Islamic world. The dissemination of plants is often an achievement of empires; the Roman empire and the British empire both saw a radical extension of the range of plant material available in the mother country.

Some of the plants introduced into the gardens of twelfth-century Andalucia were the banana, the carob, whose seeds were used to weigh gold, the lemon, the medlar and for shade the oriental plane (*Platanus orientalis*). Cotton and sugar cane were of commercial value, but many plants, such as new varieties of jasmine, were introduced purely for the pleasure they gave the senses; at this period nowhere else in Europe was there such an emphasis on the aesthetic delights that gardens could offer. Plants were also systematically studied in royal gardens 500 years before the foundation of the botanical gardens at Pisa and Padua, often thought to be the earliest in Europe. In late eleventh-century Toledo Ibn Wafid laid out a botanical garden in an area of the city still known as Huerta del Rey, the King's Garden. His successor, Ibn Bassal, published an important treatise on gardening, which dealt with the choice of trees for particular situations, the preparation of the ground, pruning and grafting. Plants were also grown and studied for their medicinal properties; in the early thirteenth century Ibn al-Baitar of Malaga collected his enormous *Pharmacopoeia*, the most complete study of herbal remedies then available in Europe.

Ibn Luyun, writing a rhymed treatise on gardens in mid-twelfth-century Andalucia, describes the ideal setting for a country house:

With regard to houses set amid gardens, an elevated site is to be recommended, both for
    reasons of vigilance and of design;
And let them have a southern aspect, with the entrance at one side, and on an upper level
    the cistern and well,
Or in place of the well have a watercourse, where the water runs underneath the shade . . .
In the centre of the garden let there be a pavilion in which to sit, with vistas on all sides,
But so designed that no one approaching can overhear the conversation within, and no one
    can approach undetected.
(Ibid.)

Alberti, writing 100 years later, echoes much of this advice on the siting of Italian country houses, though he is less concerned to protect the ruler from the attention of spies and assassins. Like Alberti, Ibn Luyun derived his advice from existing examples of noble buildings, the most celebrated of which must have been Madinat al-Zahra, the extraordinary palace/city created by Abd-al-Rahman III in 936 about 10 kilometres/6.2 miles west of Cordoba; the building of an entirely new seat of government was a gesture of enormous confidence in the increasing power and influence of the Umayyad caliphate. This is the only one of the country estates that has survived, and, although excavations have only touched the surface of the remains, it is still possible to get an idea of its splendour. Unlike earlier *munyats* Madinat al-Zahra is sited on the southern slopes of a hill, on three distinct levels. The caliph and his family lived on the highest level; on the middle level he would receive visitors, confer with advisers and dispense justice; and on the lowest level lived the soldiers and servants who ran the palace. Here is urban design with a very precise political significance. Moreover, the siting of the city/palace had its own significance; from a mirador (a viewing point) in the walls of the middle level it is possible to enjoy the view of the garden below and then let the eye travel beyond the garden to the rich, flat, agricultural lands beyond, all of them part of the caliph's possessions. Just as the caliph could look down at his subjects serving him on the two lower levels of Madinat al-Zahra, so here the viewer was in the powerful position of being able to survey the lands below while remaining unseen. Arab poets and travellers were not interested in landscape or views; they rarely show any interest in nature untamed by man and instead they write of lands made fertile by irrigation and of gardens. The miradors we find in many Islamic gardens from this date on were there for a precise purpose, and it was not to enjoy the view but rather to emphasize the extent of the viewer's gaze and to flatter his ego by underlining the power implicit in seeing far without being seen.

Many poets and travellers celebrated the astonishing beauty of Madinat al-Zahra, although few were allowed into the inner sanctums of the caliph's residence, which in its turn contributed to the palace's almost mythical reputation for extravagance and luxury. In the main meeting hall stood a large tank of mercury, and when the caliph wanted to impress a visitor he would signal to a servant to agitate the tank so that the light reflected from the mercury's surface 'flashed like lightning bolts'. Water ran through the palace, brought from the mountains behind on a Roman aqueduct, providing bathing facilities; it also ran in channels through the gardens, where it collected in pools, like that in front of the great meeting hall, now called the Salon Rico. Here there is the traditional pavilion, protected from spies and assassins by a pool on each side, and the garden is divided into four unequal parts by canals. The pavilion was originally to have had a gold ceiling, but when the *qadi*, the judge appointed by the caliph, criticized Abd al-Rahman's extravagance, it was replaced by one made of wood. In the wall that enclosed this garden there were miradors from which to enjoy views over the lower garden and the surrounding country.

On the highest level there was also a much smaller, more private garden, the remains of which have been excavated; surrounded by buildings and almost square, this garden contains the traditional pool immediately outside the residential hall, while paved walkways with narrow water channels create the usual four compartments. This garden (it is tempting to call it a *giardino segreto*) is described in none of the literature that celebrates the beauties of Medinat al-Zahra, perhaps because none of the writers had been privileged to penetrate thus far into the private areas of the palace.

Adding to the legend of Madinat al-Zahra was the brevity of its existence: it came and went like a vision, so no one could be sure they had truly seen such opulent splendour – was it all really a dream? Civil war broke out in Cordoba in the early eleventh century, the walled city/palace was turned into a prison for Abd al-Rahman's grandson and on 4 November 1010 it was destroyed by fire. Cordoba ceased to be the seat of government for the whole of Al-Andalus; in its place individual cities became independent centres of power, the most celebrated being Seville, Granada and Toledo.

But these independent states were too weak to stand up against the Christian onslaught that began in earnest in the late eleventh century. With the help of forces from Morocco the Christians were held at bay for a time, but by the mid-thirteenth century the only Islamic state in the Iberian peninsula was the Nasrid kingdom of Granada, which survived until the Muslims and the Jews were finally expelled from Spain in 1492. However, it survived not as an independent state but as a tributary of the kingdom of Castile; thus its continued existence depended on its generating sufficient economic prosperity to pay the annual tribute. We hear of Granada in the early fourteenth century described as 'a mother surrounded by children, with luxuriant greenery adorning her sides as if she had worn a necklace'. This comparison of the gardens surrounding a city to a necklace worn by a beautiful girl was by this time something of a cliché; it had been used to describe Cordoba surrounded by its *munyats*, and the same comparison was used of tenth-century Palermo, when that city too was under Islamic control.

Like the Alcazar at Cordoba, but unlike Madinat al-Zahra, the Alhambra in Granada was not planned as a unit but grew in stages and was adapted to the uses of different rulers in different periods. However, in the Alhambra the visitor can at last experience the elegant impact of the Islamic garden style, not recreated in the imagination, as at Madinat al-Zahra, or from the documents of poets and historians, but first hand, because two of the palaces in the complex, the Comares and the Lions Palaces, remain almost unaltered from the late fourteenth century, and each is built around a garden courtyard, though these have been significantly modified. As at Madinat al-Zahra, the visitor approaches the inner parts of the palace through a confusing series of corridors and courtyards. From the Mexuar, the court where public business was conducted, you enter the Golden Court and from here a series of narrow, dark corridors leads to the Court of the Myrtles

The Alhambra, Granada, Spain. The Alhambra was a fort, and thus built on the top of a hill. The Arab builders showed immense expertise in hydraulics in order not only to bring water to this height but also to give it the pressure necessary to power a fountain.

and the so-called Hall of the Ambassadors. Through a narrow doorway, and quite unprepared for the splendour to come, you enter a space flooded with light, which is reflected off the enormous, rectangular central pool that occupies most of the courtyard. And it is a huge space, perhaps ten times as large as the Golden Court. The surrounding buildings crowd in, but the slender columns of the arcades that close each end of the space and the fretted marble work lighten the effect.

Ambassadors coming to do business with the sultan must have been left breathless by the exquisite elegance of this courtyard. They would have sat in the hall at the end of the Court of the Myrtles, looking down the length of the calm pool; over their heads hung a coffered wooden ceiling inset with mother-of-pearl stars and on the walls they would have read the words of the 67th Sura of the Koran, entitled 'Sovereignty'. This sura begins: 'Blessed be He to whom all sovereignty belongs: He has power over all things', and continues, 'He created seven heavens, one above the other. His work is faultless. Turn up your eyes; can you detect a single flaw?' Here the references to Allah can also be interpreted as referring to the sultan who had created the beautiful chamber with its ceiling of stars in which the ambassadors were received. And later the same sura seems almost to refer directly to the powerful position of one who looks, unseen, from the miradors in the same chamber: 'Those that fear the Lord, although they cannot see Him, shall be forgiven and richly rewarded.' Locked between two greater military powers, the Christians to the north and the Moroccan kingdom to the south, Granada could survive only by skilful diplomacy, and the impression made on visiting ambassadors by this hall and courtyard must have played a significant part in creating an image of a state under the firm and calm control of its ruler. Here is an example of a garden with a political message as clear as that of Versailles, though on a much smaller scale.

The courtyard is now planted only with two hedges of myrtle, which run parallel to the pool and are carefully pruned into a rigidly rectangular profile, although an early sixteenth-century traveller recalls seeing orange trees here. The scene is monumentally still and silent, except for the two bubbling fountains, at each end of the pool, which throw up a small finger of water; these make only a small impact, as they are set at ground level and the water runs back into the central pool with no kind of drama. But they do enough to give some animation and lightness to the scene. They also draw the eye down to the circular basins into which the water falls, and this circular shape makes an interesting contrast with the insistent right angles of the pool, the buildings and the hedges. The central pool, filled to the brim so that its reflections are as complete as possible, is scarcely disturbed by the two small runnels that feed it. The only colour here, apart from the dull green of the myrtle hedges, is supplied by a dado of *azulejos*, blue glazed tiles, that runs across the farther end of the rectangular space.

This mass of water in the Court of the Myrtles and the freedom with which it is used in the next courtyard, the Court of the Lions, must have been striking to any visitor, ambassador or humble servant. The fortress of the Alhambra is, as one would expect, on the summit of a hill, and it is impossible not to be struck by the engineering skill that can provide water so profusely at such an altitude, and under such a pressure that it can drive a fountain.

The Court of the Lions is reached from the Court of the Myrtles, again through an entrance that does nothing to prepare us for the splendours to come. Both courtyards are oblong in shape, but the Court of the Lions is divided into the familiar four segments by walkways and narrow canals, while at the centre stands the celebrated fountain supported on the backs of twelve lions. Here the water not only flows from the fountain but, miraculously, bubbles up inside two of the surrounding buildings and within the arcade that runs round the court, and flows thence to meet the water from the fountain. The arcade surrounding this courtyard makes the space feel more confined and more domestic than the elegant emptiness of the Court of the Myrtles. The visitor glimpses the central fountain through a forest of the slenderest possible columns, grouped in twos and threes, or standing alone. And the arcade itself invites you to take a leisurely stroll in the shade around the perimeter of the courtyard. There seems no evidence in either court of lights placed behind waterfalls or fountains, such as we find in the fort at Agra, even though in early eleventh-century Granada we read of a fountain shaped like a dome inside which lights were placed to gleam through the cascading water.

The Alhambra, Granada, Spain. The calm confidence of the Court of the Myrtles must have impressed visiting ambassadors from the more powerful Christian kingdoms to the north, and the more powerful Berber regimes to the south. Granada survived as an independent, Islamic, client state until 1492.

On either side of the Court of the Lions stand two halls, their floors about 15 centimetres/6 inches above the level of the courtyard, richly decorated with the honeycombed ceilings called *muqarnas*. From here those sitting on cushions (the low point of view is important) would have looked across the sunlit garden and seen the tops of the flowers planted in the four sunken segments of the garden, which must have appeared like a carpet, an effect which it is difficult for the strolling visitor to appreciate. We know from archaeological excavation that the level of these sunken beds in the fourteenth century was about 80 centimetres/31 inches lower than it is today. But we also know that there were orange trees growing here, as a French visitor who saw the Court of the Lions in 1502, only ten years after the Reconquista, remembers them as tall enough to stand beneath. Islamic garden designers gave little emphasis to the form and shape of a plant, although the painters and mosaic workers gave these details the most careful attention; they were interested in colour and patterns of colour in a single plane. In the Alcazar at Seville there is a courtyard called the Patio del Crucero where the raised walkway is 5 metres/16 feet above the surrounding beds and a seventeenth-century traveller remembers seeing orange trees that scarcely reached the height of the paths. An advantage of the sunken planting is that the clean lines of the architecture are not blurred or even hidden by foliage, except that of the orange trees, which may have been planted here, as in the Patio de Los Naranjos, to echo the architecture. And sunken gardens are also, of course, easier to irrigate.

The Lion Fountain itself has been the subject of much debate; the basin is certainly fourteenth century, but some believe that the lions themselves are from the eleventh century, and certainly their rather primitive carving, which makes them look more like lap dogs than ferocious wild beasts, would support that theory. The lion had long been a symbol of authority and power, and perhaps here they symbolize the sultan's gift of water to his people. The last verse of the sura on sovereignty which is reproduced in the Court of the Myrtles reads: 'Think, if all the water that you have were to sink down into the earth, who would give you running water in its place?' There is also a long tradition of fountains in the shape of lions. For example, there was a tenth-century example at the Munyat al-Naura near Cordoba: at the edge of a pool stood 'a lion, enormous in size, unique in design and fearful in appearance . . . It was plated with gold and its eyes were two brilliantly sparkling jewels. Water entered through the rear of the lion and was spewed into the pool. It was dazzling to behold in its splendour and magnificence.' (Ruggles, p. 50.) Here the fountain emphatically symbolizes the power of the caliph to make the land fertile, and perhaps his power to defend the most important source of life – water.

From the Lions Palace it is possible to direct the eye not only inward to the beauties of the courtyard but also outward over what used to be a garden, the Lindaraja Garden, and beyond that to the town in the valley and the hills beyond. From a mirador behind the Hall of the Two Sisters the eye is drawn to the outer view. It is certain that these narrow windows were not built for defence, since the Lions Palace does not lie on the outer extremity of the fortress. It may have

ABOVE *The Alhambra, Granada, Spain. In the Court of the Lions the water flows from the halls into the courtyard to meet the water from the fountain. The planting beds would have been some 80 centimetres/28 inches below the current level of the gravel; they would have contained fruit trees and other plants, some scented.*

been a place for the ladies of the court to enjoy the cooling breezes, while remaining unseen, but the inscription in the mirador suggests something more than that. Like some of the other inscriptions at the Alhambra this personifies the architectural feature it adorns; the mirador itself speaks: 'In this garden I am an eye filled with delight, and the pupil of this eye is truly, our Lord/Mohamed . . . He is the full moon of the empire's horizons . . . In me he looks from his califal throne toward the capital of his entire kingdom.' Here the role of the mirador is made clear; it is not a place from which to enjoy the wide view but rather a place to reflect on the power that the unseen viewer has over what is seen.

RIGHT *The Generalife, Granada, Spain. This was the garden of a pleasure palace built in the early fourteenth century on the hillside opposite the Alhambra. The jets of water that line the central pool of the Acequia Court are not original, but the site of the pool is.*

The gardens of the Generalife, on the opposite hillside, are earlier than the gardens of the Alhambra courtyards, and these are clearly pleasure gardens, although even here the inscriptions don't let the reader forget their political significance; at the entrance we read: 'Over this perfect palace of singular beauty shines the greatness of the Sultan . . .' They were built among orchards and farm land in long, wide terraces across the slope of Santa Elena Hill in the early fourteenth century; there were no formal reception halls, as this was not a palace where public business was carried out. The Acequia Court at the heart of the complex is named after the canal that stretches along the enclosed space, linking the three-storey harem building to the south with the north pavilion, which has a mirador looking down and out over the Albaicin area of the city. The two rows of fountains that throw their water in elegant arcs into the canal are modern, but there was always a central fountain, marking the mid-point of the four sections into which the oblong garden is divided. Along the west side another mirador allows superb views over the Alhambra. One of the charms of the Generalife gardens is the water staircase, which links the Garden of the Sultana (entirely modern) to the highest point of the enclosure. The water not only descends the steps, controlled by a series of small terraces where it pops up as a sequence of miniature fountains, but also runs along the handrail of the stairs, a detail found also at the Villa d'Este in Tivoli in Italy, a garden created 200 years later but perhaps influenced by this Islamic example. The presence of trees, the openness of the site, the playful use of water and the lace-like decoration above the arches make these gardens some of the most joyful it is possible to visit anywhere in the world.

As the Arab forces swept through North Africa in the eighth century, they brought the Islamic faith and its culture to each conquered country; so it is no surprise that we find Islamic gardens along

BELOW *Dar el Mokri, Fez, Morocco. In all parts of the Islamic world, courtyard gardens with trees and fountains such as this are common. This house takes its name from the grand vizir who held office under French imperial rule.*

ABOVE *San Giovanni degli Eremiti, Palermo, Sicily. The Muslims also ruled Sicily for a time, and, even after their overthrow, Moorish craftsmen were at work in this twelfth-century church, as the red domes make clear.*

the southern coast of the Mediterranean from Egypt to Morocco. Important cities like Cairo, Tunis and Algiers were all surrounded by pleasure palaces with famous gardens, irrigated by water drawn from a river or wells, often by the waterwheels that the Muslims introduced into Spain. These suburban gardens did not survive the stresses of the climate and the unrest caused by constant wars and invasions. But some of the courtyard gardens are still intact, particularly in Morocco: the great fourteenth-century *madrasa* gardens of Fez, for example, and the gardens of Aquedal and Mansounia. The impetus of the Arab advance carried the Muslims across the sea to Sicily, where they were the dominant power during the ninth and tenth centuries. Even in the time of Frederick II his Muslim subjects in western Sicily were sufficiently numerous that their constant revolts caused him severe problems. Little is left of the buildings, let alone the gardens, of Islamic Sicily, but the Arabs left their mark in the architecture, in the advanced irrigation techniques they taught the Sicilian farmers and in the plants they introduced, notably sugar cane.

Recently Arab water tanks and irrigation channels have been reconstructed at Kolymbetra, a beautiful garden of orange and lemon trees in the Valley of the Temples at Agrigento. Here it is possible to see Arab irrigation techniques in action, but where do we see evidence of their garden building? After their conquest of Sicily the Normans established a regime that was remarkably tolerant and sophisticated. Architectural evidence of the blending of the Islamic tradition with that of northern Europe is found in many parts of historic Palermo, perhaps most wonderfully for the garden visitor in the ruined cloister and deconsecrated church of San Giovanni degli Eremiti, with its tomato-coloured, hemispherical domes. On the edge of the city the Norman kings built their hunting lodges, in parks already established by the earlier Arab rulers; of these the most impressive is La Zisa (from the Arabic *el aziz*, 'the splendid one'). The first impression is of a typically sturdy

Norman tower, four square, heavy and severe. But in the great hall on the ground floor the atmosphere changes to playful lightness; here we find typically Arabic stucco work, mosaic wall decoration and a water chute feeding a series of pools. The water rises inside the building, as in the Court of the Lions at the Alhambra, and then runs through a set of internal pools out into a great collecting tank immediately in front of the main façade. There was a utilitarian as well as an aesthetic reason for the use of water here: it cools the air, which then rises through a series of ducts in the massive walls to the upper rooms of the building, a technology familiar in the wind towers of Persia and the Middle East. La Zisa was built in the twelfth century, 100 years after the Norman conquest, but this marrying of water to architecture can only be Arabic in inspiration and, most likely, in execution.

When Constantinople was taken in 1453, that city became part of the Dar al-Islam, but here the Islamic garden traditions are modified; there is no evidence of the quadripartite garden and the more ample rainfall made it less important to create irrigation canals. The new regime built its administrative centre on the old acropolis at Topkapi. The Topkapi Saray is a series of courtyards, increasingly private as one moves from the public gate to the interior, while a separate group of courtyards served the harem. There is little to remind us of the formal geometry of the Islamic garden here, although the fourth courtyard is enclosed and contains a series of gardens on several levels. There are fine fountains and pavilions known as Ottoman kiosks; these are a development of the *chabutra*, but free standing and seldom built near water. These kiosks were often elaborately decorated; when that intrepid traveller Lady Mary Wortley Montagu was received at Topkapi, she noted that the kiosk in which she met the sultan was lined with 'mother of pearl fastened with emerald nails'. Elaborate tulip festivals were held in the fourth courtyard in the eighteenth century,

BELOW *Topkapi Palace, Istanbul, Turkey. The palace was the seat of government for the Ottoman Empire for 400 years. But the gardens of Topkapi are surprisingly unlike other Islamic gardens, since the rainfall here is abundant.*

when prizes were given for the most perfect blooms; nightingales sang in cages, while tortoises wandered through the flower beds with lighted candles fixed to their backs. Tulips, which caused such hysteria in Holland in the 1630s, were first introduced to western Europe from Turkey in the late sixteenth century by the gloriously named Flemish diplomat Ogier Ghiselin de Busbecq, Ferdinand I's ambassador to the court of Suleyman the Magnificent. Legend has it that their name derived from a misunderstanding: Busbecq asked what they were called and his guide, thinking he was admiring the beauty of their shape, replied 'Tuliband', meaning shaped like a turban. In fact the Turks called these flowers *lale*, a name derived from Persian.

Eighty years after the capture of Constantinople by the forces of Islam, on the plain of Panipat in northern India the first of the great Mughal emperors, Babur, led his 8,000 troops into battle against the 100,000 men and 1,000 war elephants of the Sultan of Delhi. Babur was genetically well suited to being a successful fighter, since he was descended from both Ghengis Khan and Timur (Tamburlaine). But Babur was more than a fighter: even on campaigns he would keep notes of the flowers and trees he found along the way. When, at the age of fourteen, he captured Samarkand, he was impressed by the architecture and the gardens created by Tamburlaine, who had brought artists and craftsmen from Persia to carry out the work. These had impressed the Spaniard Ruy Gonzales de Clavijo, who visited the city in 1404 and recorded: 'So numerous are these gardens and vineyards surrounding Samarkand that the traveller who approaches the city sees only a great mountainous height of trees, and the houses embowered among them remain invisible.' Babur was a man of the mountains who was driven into the plains of India by his inability to establish a stable empire in central Asia, so it is no surprise that in his memoir, the *Baburnama*, he wrote: 'Three things oppressed us in Hindustan [his name for India], its heat, its violent winds and its dust.' The answer to all these problems was the creation of well-watered gardens in his new capital, Agra.

Babur has left us an account of the difficulties he had in making his first garden.

We crossed the Jumna [the river] to look at the garden area, a few days after entering Agra. The place was so unpromising that we viewed it with a thousand disgusts and repulsions. So ugly and displeasing was the site that I abandoned the idea of making a garden there. But there was no other suitable land near Agra, so a few days later the work began.

A start was made with the large well whence the water comes for the hot bath, and the piece of land where the tamarind trees and the octagonal pool now stand . . . Then in charmless and disorderly Hind plots of garden were seen, laid out with order and symmetry, with appropriate borders and parterres in every corner, and in every border roses and narcissi perfectly arranged.

This emphasis on order, in particular the symmetrical layout, was typically Islamic, and showed that in garden art Babur had learned the lessons of his Persian masters. Although the regime he replaced was also Muslim (the sultanate of Delhi had been founded in 1206), Babur clearly felt he had much to do to civilize the 'charmless and disorderly' land he had conquered. Any garden had to be built near the river, as that was the only plentiful source of water in the plains of northern India, and an

Islamic garden without water was unthinkable. The basic layout was always geometrically rigid, with raised platforms from which to appreciate the pattern of the beds. However, it is interesting that the Mughals, for all their determination to impose order on nature, never showed any interest in topiary. The garden of the Ram Bagh on the banks of the Jumna in Agra was originally thought to be of Babur's making, though now it is considered to be the work of Jahangir's wife, Nur Jahan. Here the aqueduct and well to the south are original, and it is interesting to note how narrow

LEFT *Abhaneri, Rajasthan, India. Raising water to the surface has always been a problem for the inhabitants of Rajasthan. The step well, of which this is a remarkable example, was one method of doing so, though carrying the buckets to the top must have been hard work.*

ABOVE *Amber, Rajasthan, India. The Hindu rulers of Amber found it convenient to intermarry with the powerful Mughals, and both their architecture and their gardens show an interesting mixture of Hindu and Islamic features.*

are the watercourses; they were purely functional, to take water to the roots of the trees. In later Mughal gardens the irrigation channels widened into canals and became an important feature of the design. Babur made many gardens in his short reign (he died in 1530), and in them he would live and conduct his business in the tents to which he was used. His daughter recalls how he planned to fill the fountain of a garden at Dohlpur with wine, but then took an oath of sobriety and filled it with lemonade instead. Babur was buried in a garden tomb, open to the sky, which he had designed himself, and, significantly, not in 'charmless and disorderly Hind' but in Kabul, among the mountains of Afghanistan.

This tradition of the garden tomb is not typically Muslim, nor is it Persian; it is derived from Turkic traditions of commemorative architecture in Central Asia. Humayun, Babur's son, was not an effective ruler and in ten years lost most of the empire his father had conquered. He fled to Persia and begged the Shah for assistance; the latter agreed, but only on condition Humayun and his court abandoned their Sunni beliefs and became Shiites – something that was to prove a grave problem in the years to come. His flight was so precipitate that he left behind his infant son, who was to become the great Emperor Akbar. The fact that he fled to Persia shows how close the ties between the empires remained; indeed the language used at the Mughal court was almost always Persian. Humayun died as unfortunately as he had lived: he had scarcely retaken Delhi when he tripped and fell to his death while descending the steps from his library.

The tomb his wife had built for him is one of the great monuments of Mughal art. It was begun in 1564, eight years after Humayun's death, and designed by a Persian, Mirak Mirza Ghiyas. In many ways the garden that surrounds the tomb is typically Islamic, but it is centred on the gigantic, central tomb, which now contains more than a hundred Mughal family graves. The garden too

is enormous, 13 hectares/30 acres, and sited near the river Jumna, although the water for irrigation was drawn from wells. It is, of course, walled, and entered through two imposing gateways. The garden plan is an elaboration of the *char bagh* pattern; here each of the four quarters into which the garden is divided by wide paths is itself divided into four further parts. Down the centre of each of the four main paths runs a water channel, 35 centimetres/14 inches wide but only a few inches deep, so that the four rivers of the Islamic paradise seem to meet at the tomb. Rectangular or flower-shaped pools mark the intersections of the paths, with four fountains in the square pools along the major axes. Along the outer walls are planted giant neem trees (*Azadirachta indica*), and in the body of the garden lemon and orange trees (which Humayun himself particularly liked), and flowering shrubs such as hibiscus, which Humayun's son, Akbar, recorded seeing in the garden. The superb restoration that has recently been carried out, generously funded by the Aga Khan Trust, has revealed that the water for the 3.5 kilometres/2 miles of canals was originally lifted from wells, and after its decorative and irrigation work was done it drained into the river. This is the earliest of the great Mughal tomb gardens and, particularly after its scholarly restoration, the one that gives us the clearest idea of what such a garden would originally have looked like. In 1857 the last Mughal emperor, Bahadur Shah II, took refuge in Humayun's tomb during the First War of Independence (more usually known in Britain as the Indian Mutiny), and here he was captured; Bahadur Shah was condemned to exile in Burma, where he died.

Akbar the Great, the son whom Humayun had abandoned in his flight to Persia, ruled for nearly fifty years. He was not only a great warrior but also a great thinker and a great diplomat. At his death the Mughal empire stretched from Kabul and Kashmir in the north to the Deccan plateau in the south and to the Bay of Bengal in the east. He was more a builder than a garden maker; the two great building projects that he instituted were the fort at Agra and the city of Fatehpur Sikri. However, his capture of Kashmir in 1586 gave a huge impetus to Mughal garden-making, as we shall see later. Like his predecessors he did not neglect the gardens of his empire; among other

ABOVE *I'timad-ud-Daulah's tomb, Agra, India. This is the tomb of the Persian vizir Mirza Ghiyas Beg, who had been given the title I'timad-ud-Daulah, meaning 'pillar of the state'. It was built (1622–8) by his daughter Nur Jahan, the wife of the Emperor Jahangir. Some of the decorative techniques used on the Taj Mahal, many borrowed from Persia, were tried out here.*

plants he imported apple trees from Samarkand. Peter Mundy, an early seventeenth-century English traveller, recalls Akbar's gardens at Agra full of 'pretty flowers, all watered by hand in tyme of drought, which is nine moneths in the year'. Akbar is buried at Sikandra, just north of Agra, in a tomb garden that was begun in his lifetime and finished by his son, Jahangir. Akbar had married a Hindu wife and encouraged Hindus at his court, so it is no surprise to find that his tomb (surely the work of Hindu builders?) is a maze of stairways and turrets – a 'disorderly' building, as his grandfather might have said – but it stands at the centre of a rational Islamic garden. The walled enclosure is square, with a gateway in each wall, although only one is used. Over the south gate the

RIGHT *The gardens of the Amber Fort, Jaipur, Rajasthan, India, with their heavily outlined, geometrical compartments are typical of the blend of Islamic and Hindu taste.*

inscription reads, 'These are the gardens of Eden; enter them to live for ever.' The garden is divided into the usual four segments, which are planted with trees – cypress, pine, plane and palm. Water flows from tanks in the central platform down the four causeways that divide the garden.

Akbar may not have been a great garden maker, but his tax laws gave a huge incentive to his subjects to create gardens; death duties exacted on noble families were often 100 per cent, the whole estate going to the emperor, who then made a grant to support the dead man's family. This provided a great incentive to spend money before death, often on gardens that could be enjoyed during one's life and then become the site of a memorable tomb. One of the most beautiful tombs is that of I'timad-ud Daulah, which was built beside the river in Agra in 1622. I'timad-ud-Daulah had served as prime minister to Jahangir, Akbar's successor, but more importantly he was the father of Jahangir's wife Nur Jahan, a title meaning 'light of the world' that was conferred on her by her husband. She was a talented lady and may have designed the tomb and garden herself. The marble is inlaid with semi-precious stones picturing flowers and trees – one of the first times this technique had been used in India, though it was an art well established in Persia. The gardens are typically Islamic, rectilinear, with paths and canals; the gatehouse to the tomb is approached through orchards that are planted in regular patterns. The harvest from these orchards was used to pay for the upkeep of the tomb after the owner's death, a common practice which may explain why tomb gardens are better preserved than pleasure gardens.

The most famous Mughal tomb is, of course, the glorious Taj Mahal, built by Shah Jehan, Jahangir's son, between 1632 and 1654 for his favourite wife, Mumtaz Mahal. She had died giving birth to their fourteenth child and it is said that she selected the site of her tomb herself, after seeing

BELOW *Taj Mahal, Agra, India. The gardens show more sign of British than Mughal influence. The Mughals would have had green ground cover, but it would have been clover, not grass. The produce of the garden's fruit trees would have been sold to pay for the upkeep of the tomb.*

ABOVE *Agra Fort, Agra, India. The fort was begun by the Emperor Akbar in 1565. It contains two important gardens; this is the Anguri Bagh, the Grape Garden. The elaborate pattern of stonework outlining the planting beds has been recently restored.*

it in a dream. The innovation here is that the tomb is placed not at the centre of the garden but at one end, on a high plinth, a site usually occupied by a pleasure pavilion in other Islamic gardens. At the Taj the garden is walled on three sides but open towards the sacred river Jumna. The layout is the traditional *char bagh* with raised walkways carrying the irrigation canals; the centre of the garden is occupied by a raised tank in which the dome is reflected, and from which water flows to the four planting areas. The formal layout of the Mughal garden has subsequently been blurred by the use of specimen trees, perhaps to satisfy European taste; originally there would have been fruit trees and maybe cypresses to provide shaded walks. The fountains rise from carved lotus buds, an interesting Hindu detail, and are carefully controlled so that they reach the same height; under each fountain a brass pot has to be filled and not until all the pots are filled do the fountains begin to play. Shah Jehan slaughtered his way to the throne, disposing of two brothers and three of their children, thus breaking the code of honour of his family, which required that each family member care for the others. So it is hard to feel sympathetic towards him when he was deposed by his son and imprisoned in the Agra fort, from where he could watch the building work on the Taj Mahal.

Many Agra guides still claim that Shah Jehan intended to build himself a tomb of black marble on the opposite bank of the Jumna River, although archaeological excavations have found no sign of foundations for such a structure. But instead they have revealed the remains of a Mughal pleasure garden, the Mahtab Bagh or Moonlight Garden. Gardens to be enjoyed in the cool of the night were a Hindu rather than an Islamic tradition, but then we should remember that Shah Jehan was at least half Hindu; his mother and his grandmother were Rajput princesses. The remains have been found of a large octagonal terrace, at the centre of which lies an octagonal pool in which the Taj Mahal would have been perfectly mirrored; behind this pool the foundations of a pavilion have

been discovered, and the remains of a fountain system, and of paths surfaced in white plaster, which would have shown up well at night. Archaeobotanists have found traces of the so-called red cedar (*Toona sinensis*) and the champa (*Michelia* spp.), both of which have flowers that give off an alluring scent at night. The Mahtab Bagh is aligned along the same axis as the garden of the Taj, and it has been suggested that the two sites are linked in meaning: that the Moonlight Garden was a place to reflect on the death of the loved one, but also in which to enjoy the pleasures of this world, while not forgetting what was to come.

One delightful detail which can still be found at the Mahtab Bagh is a small waterfall with niches behind it, in which flowers or lighted candles were placed. These niches are called *chinikhanas* (the word means literally 'house for china'; it was a Persian custom to display prized items of china in such small niches inside the house), and they are found in other Mughal pleasure gardens, for example at the Agra fort. It was here that Shah Jehan was imprisoned by his son Aurangzeb, the last of the Great Mughals and the only one who seems to have had almost no interest in gardens; his time was taken up with warfare and the imposition of strict Shariah law. The walls of the Agra fort date from the time of Akbar, but much of the interior was remodelled in the time of Shah Jehan. There are the remains of two interesting gardens, the Machi Bhawan and the Anghuri Bagh or Grape Garden. The former was laid out in geometrical patterns of flower beds, water channels and tanks containing sacred fish. This garden was badly damaged in the eighteenth century, when the Jats pillaged most of the furnishings to adorn their extraordinary garden at Deeg. The Anghuri Bagh was the garden of the *zenana* quarter of the palace, the women's section. It was probably named the Grape Garden not because grapes grew there but because of the decoration

Humayun's Tomb, Delhi, India. Both tomb and garden have been magnificently, and accurately, restored, through the generosity of the Aga Khan. The wide walks, with water channels down their centre, are typical of Mughal tomb and palace gardens.

on the walls. Tavernier (who started the rumour of the black Taj Mahal in his book of travels of 1684) describes 'a kind of latticework of emeralds and rubies that represented to the life grapes when they are green and when they begin to grow red. But this design . . . required more riches than all the world could afford to perfect it, so it remains incomplete.' Just as in the Mahtab Bagh, here there is a reservoir reflecting an important building (the Khas Mahal) and a waterfall with *chinikhanas* behind.

Shah Jehan was also responsible for building the Red Fort at Delhi, originally called Shahjehanabad. As at the Taj Mahal three sides are walled and the fourth is left open to the river; on the narrow strip of sand between the fort and the river elephant fights and parades were staged. A seventeenth-century traveller describes the marvels of the Red Fort thus: 'There is almost no chamber but it hath at its door a storehouse of running water. 'Tis full of parterres, pleasant walks, shady places, rivulets, fountains, jets of water, grottoes, great caves against the heat of the day, and great terraces raised high, and very airy, to sleep upon in the cool. In a word you know not there what 'tis to be hot.' His awestruck wonder finds an echo in a carved inscription found in the Hall of Private Audience: 'If there is paradise on earth/It is here, it is here, it is here.' There was once a moonlight garden here too, planted with flowers that yielded their scent at night. And the garden of the Hayat Baksh (or Life-giving Garden) still exists, a typical *char bagh* with a central pavilion. This garden was once planted with cypresses, trees introduced into India by the Mughals and much used in their gardens; often cypresses and fruit trees were planted alternately in formal rows, the evergreen representing what is eternal, the deciduous what is transient. And there are records that the beds were planted with saffron, crimson and purple flowers, a combination of colours apparently much favoured by the Mughals. At the Red Fort it is hard to miss the importance of water; the Nahar-e-Bihisht or Canal of Paradise flows through several of the most important buildings.

Women were much involved in the creation and design of Mughal gardens, as we have seen in Nur Jahan's creation of the tomb garden for her father. Mumtaz Mahal herself designed a garden in Agra south of the Ram Bagh, which was inherited by her daughter, Jahanara, who renovated it and made it one of the most beautiful gardens along the riverfront. Sadly almost nothing remains. Another of Shah Jehan's wives laid out the Shalimar Bagh in Delhi, in imitation of the garden of the same name in Kashmir. A canal 5.4 metres/18 feet wide ran the length of this garden and fell in a series of waterfalls. Again nothing is left. And during the rule of Aurangzeb (1658–97) his sister, Roshanara Begum, made the Roshanara garden, also in Delhi, where the heat was less punishing than in Agra, but all that remains is one pavilion.

In 1586 Akbar captured Kashmir and built the garden palace of Nasim Bagh. Kashmir was an idyllic place for garden-making with its plentiful supply of water and definite seasons. Jehangir fell in love with the beautiful Srinagar valley, saying he would rather lose all his empire than that one state. In a memoir of his reign he describes his pleasure in 'mead after mead of flowers . . . the flowers of Kashmir are beyond counting and calculation' (*Memoirs of Jehangir*, translated by A. Rogers). He built several gardens in Kashmir and his courtiers followed suit, so that, when a count was made, it was discovered there were at least 700 gardens around the Dal Lake near Srinagar.

Many of these hillside gardens were laid out around a central, straight watercourse with canals branching off at right angles, and platforms in the centre of the canals. At Vernag little was done to modify nature; an octagonal pavilion was built around the spring and the water was made to run in a straight canal through the garden, before emptying itself into a stream. Perhaps the most celebrated Kashmir garden is the Shalimar, the lower part of which was designed in about 1630 by Prince Khurram, who was later to become Shah Jehan. As emperor he added a second part to this garden, again in the form of a *char bagh*, with a pavilion standing in the centre of a pool from which fountains sprang. The pavilion in which the Emperor would sit is placed, just inside the entrance of the older garden, in the middle of the central canal, above a waterfall, behind which we find niches for flowers or lamps. The word used for this pavilion is *talar*, a Persian word for the hall that usually lay behind the *ayvan*. Here the Emperor would receive the public, and be seen not only as the commander of his people but as the giver of water, the source of life.

The Emperor's nobles created magnificent gardens also; among the most celebrated is the Nishat Bagh (Garden of Gladness), which descends the hillside in twelve terraces (the number of signs of the Zodiac). Here the garden, far from being enclosed, 'borrows' the landscape; the views in one direction of the lake and in the other of the mountains are not excluded but form part of the composition. The Peri Mahal (Fairies' Palace) may have been designed by Shah Jehan's son Dara Shukoh. In a sense the Mughals had discovered in Kashmir the promised land from which they had been driven in the early sixteenth century; here were the steep hillsides, the cool air and the ample water of the mountains from which their family came, and here was the opportunity to create the gardens Babur had so much admired in and around Samarkand.

It is hard for a twenty-first-century visitor, especially if a non-Muslim, to appreciate fully the meaning of many Islamic gardens; for most people it is even harder to 'read' these gardens than to 'read' the programmes of the great Renaissance gardens in Italy. Their meaning is more abstract, purer (more mathematical, one might say), less human than that of other gardens, however worldly and sensual their use may from time to time have been. As at Madinat al-Zahra, there was often a political significance in the use of the different levels: for example, in the Kashmir Shalimar Garden the lowest level, the Divan-i Am, was the area for public audiences; the next, the Divan-i Khas, was reserved for the members of the court; higher still were the areas that were *haram*, forbidden, because they were totally private, and these included the *zenana*, the women's quarters. There were, of course, religious implications in all Islamic gardens; the octagon which we find in many Mughal gardens was a blend of the circle, eternity, with the square, ephemeral human kind. And the explicit references to the gardens of the Koranic paradise in the inscriptions over the entrances of not only

Jodhpur, Rajasthan, India. The Balsamand palace was built as a summer palace for the Maharajahs of Marwar. This marble cascade connects the lake to the garden that lies below.

Sikandra but the Taj and La Zisa in Palermo would have conditioned the response of any Muslim subject who was fortunate enough both to be able to read and to be given a glimpse of these great gardens. Religious symbols were themselves also a means of reinforcing the power and authority of the emperor; the gardens not only resembled the paradise of the Koran but also provided a frame for the public ceremonials that were so dear to the Mughal emperors.

It would be unwise, however, to deduce from the example of the well-preserved and more recent Mughal tomb gardens that all Islamic gardens were paradise gardens in the sense that they deliberately evoked the Koranic paradise promised to the faithful. Professor D. Fairchild Ruggles writes: 'In Cordoba through the tenth century, I have found no explicit conceptual link between the gardens of the "munyas" of Cordoba and the Qur'anic concept of paradise as a garden of shade-giving trees and flowing rivers. Rather, palace gardens were sensual places of worldly pleasure and arenas for political ceremony.' This surely was also true of the Mughal gardens in Kashmir. Ruggles quotes an interesting example of an eleventh-century Al-Andalus garden whose iconography changed after the death of its creator. The garden, which contains the tombs of al-Zajjali and his friend Ibn Shuhayd, seems first to have been used entirely for worldly pleasures. An inscription tells us Ibn Shuhayd 'enjoyed therein spells of well-being and rest both in the morning and afternoon. Fate gave him at that time whatsoever he desired, and the pleasures of sobriety and inebriation alternated with each other in his experience. He and the proprietor of the garden, who is buried alongside him, were companions in the youthful pursuit of the gratification of the senses and allies in joy.' Ibn Shuhayd himself composed the epitaph in which the Koranic gardens of paradise are referred to, but this inscription was written for a time when the owner and his friend could no longer enjoy earthly pleasures, and when the garden had become the centre of a mausoleum complex.

It is said that all Islamic gardens, like the garden that Ibn Shuhayd and his friend inhabited in life and death, have both a sensuous and a spiritual appeal – like most gardens, we may add! Many of us may be capable of responding only to the aesthetic merits of an Islamic garden, but even then their purity of line, their uncluttered planting (so different from the Anglo-Saxon tradition) and the harmony of their proportions make them supremely satisfying. The worldwide conservatism of the garden maker is even more marked in the gardens that are called Islamic. The obedient following of the traditional design, which has its origins in Persia, is perhaps symptomatic of the great strength and perhaps the great weakness of the Islamic world; the strength is the power of a faith which refuses to make any compromises with the conditions of the modern world, and the weakness is the same – the refusal to adapt, together with the suspicion of reform and innovation.

3

THE ORIENTAL TRADITION: CHINA

ABOVE *Shanghai Botanical Garden. These miniaturized plants are more familiar in the West as bonsai, the Japanese term for them; they are known in China as 'pengjing'. The dwarfed trees are often set off by rocks and water, to create miniature landscapes.*

LEFT *Beihai Park, Beijing. The Chinese characters for the word 'landscape' are 'san' (mountain), and 'shui' (water). In this popular Beijing park, partly created by Kubilai Khan, rocks and water are the principal components of the scene.*

CHINESE GARDENS ARE the most challenging gardens for someone who comes from another gardening tradition; they are so different from what we Westerners expect a garden to be, and the result is that the visitor may be at first repelled, but then, perhaps, fascinated. Repelled by the huge, disorderly piles of pitted rock hanging over the still pools, but fascinated by the way the garden is conceived dramatically, to lead us by winding paths from one space to another, never giving everything away. Among the great garden styles of the world the Chinese is the most demanding, both intellectually and emotionally, and the most difficult for the foreigner to appreciate. The first demand a Chinese garden makes is that the visitor take the experience slowly.

So let us begin by examining, slowly, the first reactions of a group of Western visitors to a Chinese scholar's garden in Suzhou. As we make our way down the narrow lanes, we will have seen little sign of any garden, perhaps a tree top waving its branches above the 4–5 metre/13–16 foot high white walls, which contain no windows, nor wrought-iron gates, through which a preliminary glance would have given an idea of what is to come. These walls surround the compound, which contains both dwellings and garden. The entrance is modest, perhaps a pair of trees, an unassuming gateway with a carved stone lintel and some chrysanthemums in a pot; thence visitors make their way along an unremarkable corridor, or through the forecourt of a house, from which they may at last be allowed a glimpse of the garden. And when finally we arrive, what do we find? A puzzling, intense mass of detail which baffles the mind; we don't know what to look at first, and there is an absolute absence of symmetry which would help to guide the eye. The higgledy-piggledy piles of rocks, some with narrow paths through or over them; the sparse planting; the zig-zag, flat bridges over narrow streams; a pool, seeming too large for the space it occupies, whose dark, unruffled surface throws back perfect reflections of its rocky shore, and of the white walls of single-storey buildings and corridors that run along its side; the pavilions perched on the tops of some of the rock piles, and other buildings distributed around the garden according to no very comprehensible plan; the paths with pebble pictures of fish or birds – everything is clearly thought out in such careful detail, but where to look first? We feel lost, puzzled, disorientated. No question but we must move slowly; there is so much to take in.

After the first stunned pause, we begin to move, and at once there will be a choice of paths; perhaps one leads up some rough steps that climb a rock pile, and the other along the flat, beside the informally shaped pool. Which should we take? Which is the right way to go? We move through a series of spaces that are unpredictably large or small, open or closed, dark or light, guided by bridges, pathways, corridors, all of which may be straight, curved or zig-zag. The variety adds to our bewilderment. We begin to take in the vivid contrasts of texture – the flat, dark, silky surface of the water against the pock-marked rock pile behind – and of light and shade – the darkness of a small cave in the rock pile sharply contrasting with the brilliant whiteness of the wall which encloses the garden. And against this wall no plant is trained, as would be the case in so many European gardens; instead it is allowed to be an uninterrupted white surface, a screen on which patterns of moving leaves throw their shadows, or which highlights the silhouette of a contorted tree.

Trying to take in all these new impressions, we move slowly towards a one-storey building; this, at least, is reassuringly symmetrical and rectilinear, although its swept-up corners have a startling, almost comic effect. It is a post-and-beam, wooden construction, painted a wonderful colour somewhere between deep plum and rust; at the front, pairs of doors open at right angles to the house front, so that, when thrown wide open, there is no barrier between interior and exterior. But what was this building used for? It contains some uncomfortable-looking wooden chairs, a scroll picture of a landscape, a dwarf tree in a simple container, some tables, on one of which a collection of incomprehensible instruments is carefully laid out, and little else. Its windows also are odd: the central pane is of clear glass, framing a perfectly formed composition of rocks, plants and paving, but around this central pane the glass is set in a crazy-paving pattern, allowing in the light but giving no view. Was this a sitting room, a bedroom, a study, a dining room – indeed did people live here, or just picnic? More puzzles.

We set out again, towards a distant pavilion atop a pile of rocks, and find ourselves walking along a kind of outdoor corridor, a roofed passage which must mean that the garden can be visited equally comfortably in wet weather and on a midsummer's day when the sun beats down. But this corridor, strangely, doesn't lead directly to the pavilion: it zig-zags, constantly changing direction. By now we're getting the idea; this is to slow us down if we are inclined to hurry, and to make us look at the different views of the garden offered with each abrupt turning. Sometimes the corridor has no walls, at other times it has walls with unglazed windows, and every window is a different shape – some round, some like a jar, some like a leaf, some fan-shaped and some abstractly indefinable. The windows are lovely both to look at and to look through. My, there's a lot to take in! We seem to be moving further away from the pavilion that was our first objective, but no matter.

BELOW Beijing Botanical Garden. Openings in walls take many unexpected forms in Chinese gardens. Notice also the tree growing in front of the cream-coloured wall, so that its form is readily apparent.

ABOVE *The Mansion of Prince Gong, Beijing. Gong was the youngest brother of the Xianfeng Emperor, who ruled 1851–61, and was father of the last emperor. This house and garden may have been the models used by Cao Xueqin in* The Story of the Stone, *the eighteenth-century novel sometimes known as* The Dream of the Red Chamber.

Suddenly, we get a glimpse through a moongate into another courtyard, of whose existence there had previously been no clue. And just beyond the gate, standing alone on a plinth, is a massive piece of pitted stone, 3 metres/9.8 feet high, curving in several directions, wider at the top than at the base, like a narrow, petrified wave. Should we go to explore that courtyard or go on to the pavilion? As we look along the corridor we have taken, the way back also seems to offer views and delights temptingly unlike those seen already. However, we proceed along a paved path that leads to a set of narrow steps, winding up a rock pile to the pavilion. As we have now come to expect, the ascent is not direct; we twist and turn, glimpsing new views of the garden and pool we have already visited, and, as we gain height, also of the other courtyard with the standing stone.

From the pavilion, which is shaped like a fan and has a fan-shaped window in two of its walls, we can see beyond the walled boundaries of the garden to a distant multi-storeyed pagoda. As we look down at the dark pool below, we notice that the benches along one side have curved backs, so that as you rest against them you can turn and look straight down into the water, which (we now observe) is teeming with golden fish. In one wall of the pavilion a plaque of black slate is elegantly inscribed with white Chinese characters; this is as incomprehensible as the rest of our experience. Now we look around for plants – after all, this is supposed to be a garden! Two huge, venerable pines have small planting beds around their base, in which some bulbs are pushing up through the earth. No lawn, just tufts of coarse, floppy grass (*Ophiopogon japonicus*, the botanist says) growing through the rocky edges of the paths and beds. In the courtyard we have yet to explore we can see the tops of some bamboo waving in the breeze; it seems to be planted as a thin ribbon in front of the wall. There are some smaller trees, prunus most likely, which have been pruned to reveal a beautifully patterned network of branches. And tucked away in a corner by itself is a bed full of tree peonies, looking rather ungainly, as it is too early in the year for them to have leaves, let alone flowers. Certain we are missing something, we sigh and wonder what it's all about, why this garden is so different from any other we have visited.

The occidental visitor is indeed missing something – 2,000 years of Chinese culture. This garden has almost certainly been restored, probably several times, but that is no problem, since, as we have observed elsewhere, garden makers are conservative people, and nowhere more so than in China. The garden just visited is as it is partly because that is the way private Chinese gardens have been for 1,500 years. And in their accumulated history there is buried not only a consciousness of other, older gardens but a whole tradition of poetry and landscape painting, for in China the garden makers constantly refer to the poets and the painters who have preceded them. The earliest Chinese book on garden-making to have survived, Ji Cheng's *The Craft of Gardens* (1631), typically demands that in a garden 'Shadowy temples should appear through round windows, like a painting by the younger Li' and there should be 'rocks cut to look as if they were painted with slash strokes, uneven like the half cliffs of Dachi'. Here the author is referring to one painter of the thirteenth century and another of the eighth, whose work should be imitated, or, if not exactly imitated, at least borne in mind by the garden maker, so that the cultivated visitor to the garden may feel the influence of the great painters of the past. Ji Cheng also constantly refers to the poets, whose reflections on the beauties and consolations of nature should also be present in the minds of the garden maker, and of the garden visitor. For example, his work is full of references to the fifth-century poet

Tao Yuanming, also known as Tao Qian, who abandoned his civil service career to live the simple life of a farmer. One of his best-known poems runs:

I built my house near where others dwell,
And yet there is no clamour of carriages and horses.
You ask of me, 'How can this be so?'
When the heart is far, the place of itself is distant.

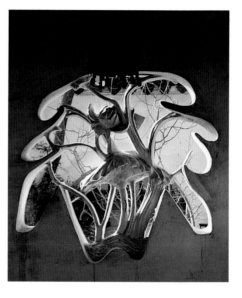

Cang Lang T'ing, Suzhou. Windows in Chinese gardens are often beautiful to look at, as well as to look through. In the low winter sun the cream walls act as screens for shadows; those of the sparse leaves of bamboo resemble Chinese characters.

Cang Lang T'ing, Suzhou. The history of this, perhaps Suzhou's oldest garden, can be traced back to the tenth century, but it was substantially modified in 1697.

And it was surely his garden that helped his heart to distance itself from his immediate surroundings; certainly we shall find that in China, as in many other parts of the world, this was one of the garden's most important functions. One of the oldest gardens in Suzhou (and one we can still visit) even takes its name from a work of literature. The garden of the Cang Lang T'ing (Surging Wave Pavilion) was built in 1044, and its name refers to a story in which a fisherman (always a symbolic figure of perfect Taoist adaptation of the self to circumstances) gives a pernickety, over-conscientious public official a lesson in how to be more relaxed: 'When the surging wave is clean, I can wash my hat ribbons in it; but when it is not clean, then I can wash my feet.'

And why did these poets retire from public service to spend more time 'fishing' – a word that came to imply a simple life of contemplation, of quiet, disciplined searching for truth? Confucius, who himself spent much time out of office and thus had time to develop his philosophy and write, taught the importance of the individual's serving the public good, but in China there were countervailing forces working against this emphasis on duty to the state. Taoism emphasized the submission of the individual to the processes of nature, while Buddhism preached turning your back on this world of illusion and suffering, perhaps retreating to a monastery to meditate and study.

What has all this to do with garden-making in China? The answer is: everything. To take one example, we have already noticed the contrast between the symmetry of the buildings and the apparently random form of the garden, with its twisting paths and zig-zag bridges; the former can be seen as rational, balanced and Confucian, while the latter is more mysteriously Taoist. Taoists taught that all living things, humans included, were infused with *ch'i*, the energy that gives life to all creation. This *ch'i* flows best in smooth curves; it hates to be trapped, but equally if it flows in straight lines, it might run too fast and thus get out of control, with dangerous results.

One explanation for why the roofs of Chinese buildings turn up so dramatically at the corners is that these upward sweeps prevented the *ch'i* from catapulting down off the roof in an uncontrolled way. For the Taoist the supreme gift was adapting oneself to the exigencies of life, not battling against them. Listen to Lao Tzu, the great philosopher of the sixth century BC, describing the Path:

> This is the Simple Path: to return to the simplicity and naturalness we once had. The path of the breeze that gently whispers through the trees, of the bird that climbs into the open, clear blue sky. The way of the simple flowers that bloom without effort and catch the warmth and blessing of the sun. The way of the waters that run through the veins of the earth, overcoming obstacles without effort, and pass at last into the wide ocean.
> (Quoted in Roni Jay)

There is no striving here, rather passive adaptation of the self to circumstances, and this quiescent attitude was fostered by a garden.

Few Westerners can begin to understand all these implications and references, which are implicit in a Chinese garden; it is not so much a question of meanings but of half-hidden references or allusions, which are sometimes found in the names given to parts of the garden. But if a point is made too plainly or a reference is too literal, the visitor's imagination and intelligence is circumscribed, whereas a successful garden should stimulate him or her to react in an individual way. Thus many Chinese feel uneasy with the literalness of the wall surrounding the Yu Yuan garden in Shanghai; the tiles that cap the wall are laid like a dragon's scales, but in this garden the implied presence of the benign dragon is made too plain, too obvious by the five, ferocious heads that the animal has been given. If we know something of the history, religion and philosophy of the country, we will begin to appreciate some of the layered suggestions that are present in a Chinese garden. But then there is more.

Chinese culture is full of symbols, so a good garden will appeal not only to the eye but to the mind; we must look beyond the surface appearance. To go back to the dragon, which was among other things an imperial symbol: he was a benign force not only as guardian of the garden but also as a symbol of male energy and creativity. He spent the winter under the earth, returning to heaven on the second day of the second month and thus causing the first rains of spring. In pictures we sometimes find two dragons playing with a ball; their vigorous games were the cause of thunder.

Flowers, too, have their symbolic meanings. The chrysanthemum, for example, is represented by the character *ju*, which is similar to the character for 'to remain', so the flower of autumn represents persistence and longevity. Traditionally chrysanthemums were picked on the ninth day of the ninth month for luck and long life, and often a tea was made with their petals. The peach was a tree freighted with suggestions; according to legend the peaches of immortality blossomed

BELOW *Yu Yuan, Shanghai. This sixteenth-century private garden has been much altered, not least by Western troops filling in the ponds to create more space for their tents. The dragon heads are thought by some Chinese scholars to be too literal; for them it would be more satisfactory to allow the walls, capped in scale-like slates, merely to suggest a dragon.*

once every thousand years. And peach wood was used for carving statues of gods who would protect the house, while bows made of peach wood could shoot down malign demons. Poets wrote of the peach and its flowers; the great eighth-century poet Li Bai described how 'Peach blossoms float their streams/away in secret/To other skies and earths/than those of mortals.' Here the reference to peach flowers recalls in its turn the fifth-century short story 'The Peach Blossom Spring', in which a simple fisherman follows a stream through a cave and emerges in an ideal land of perfect happiness. The tree peony, the famous Mu-dan, was the symbol of wealth and success, and also of an alluring girl, as a folk saying has it: 'When the peony begins to bloom, it is picked by the young man.' One last example is bamboo, commonly found in Chinese gardens; its empty core suggests modesty, a lack of 'ego', as does the way it bends with the wind, accommodating itself to its circumstances in the perfect Taoist way.

But what about all those rocks? At one level they represent the yang, the male, assertive element, contrasting with the yin of the water, the yielding, female element. But this is too simple a distinction between this permanent pair of opposite forces on which the world turns; water is also powerful, as these rocks demonstrate. Those most celebrated for their unusual shapes came from Tai Hu Lake, not far from Suzhou, and it was the waters of this lake that had pitted and carved the rocks. As Lao Tzu, the great Taoist teacher, wrote: 'There is nothing softer or weaker than water, and yet there is nothing better for attacking hard and strong things.' The rock piles in Chinese gardens are also mountains in miniature, so that the narrow, winding path to the summit of a rock pile, for the imaginative and learned visitor, can represent a walk in the mountains, or even a pilgrimage to one of the Buddhist monasteries, which were often built in remote and beautiful places.

BELOW *The Forbidden City, Beijing. This is a detail from the Complex of Peaceful Longevity, created by the eighteenth-century Qianlong Emperor for his retirement. The twisting channel contained moving water for the wine cup game, in which contestants had to compose verses before the cup reached them, or else drain its content.*

ABOVE *Liu Garden, Suzhou. This is a different style of 'pengjing' (miniature landscape), displayed on a plinth. Sometimes groups of miniature trees were displayed in the huge rock piles to give a false sense of perspective.*

Mountains have long been revered in China – so much so that the cult of the Five Mountains still has a great hold on the imagination of the country. These mountains, to south, north, east and west and in the centre, seemed to guarantee the stability of the world, and they were sources of wisdom as the places where the sages lived. In a small compound in Suzhou it was not possible to have a real mountain, but you could have an impression of rocky peaks and sheer slopes, perhaps with a cave, which in the garden would not only remind you of the dwelling of a hermit but could, more practically, act as a refuge from sun and rain. And the winding path up the rock pile could be a way of turning your back on the world and dedicating your life to simpler things, while searching for enlightenment. The Li Bai poem referred to above is called 'In the Mountains: A Reply to the Vulgar', and here it is in its entirety:

> They ask me where's the sense
> on jasper mountains?
> I laugh and don't reply,
> in heart's own quiet.
>
> Peach blossoms float their streams
> away in secret
> To other skies and earths
> than those of mortals.
> (Translated by Arthur Cooper)

And the individual standing stones? These are easier to appreciate, as natural sculpture, for the strange shapes into which the force of nature has twisted them. However, it should be remembered

that they are not all entirely the product of unaided nature; stonemasons were known to carve indentations in promising rocks and then sink them in Lake Tai Hu so that they would seem to have been formed naturally. The fissures and holes in the rock also represent a form of yin and yang, the solid playing against the void. And as the sun lights them from different directions during the course of the day, the shadows moving across their surface may suggest different pictures to the visitor's imagination. The Taoist might also find in their twisted shapes an expression of the *ch'i*, the energy that informs all creation, while the more literary might recall the beginning of *Monkey*, the delightful sixteenth-century tale by Wu Ch'eng-En. Here is Arthur Waley's translation:

> There was a rock which since the creation of the world had been worked upon by the pure essences of Heaven and the fine savours of Earth, the vigour of the sunshine and the grace of moonlight, till at last it became magically pregnant, and one day split open, giving birth to a stone egg, about as big as a playing ball. Fructified by the wind, it developed into a stone monkey, complete with every organ and limb.

By now the Western visitor is probably beginning to be overwhelmed by the multiplicity of inferences that can be drawn from the components of the Chinese garden scene; it all seems so cerebral, so full of allusions, so demanding. But when visitors come across a pavilion with a very explicit name – it may be 'The Hall for Listening to the Wind in the Pines', or 'The Pavilion for Enjoying the Scent that Comes from Afar' – they are reminded that these gardens also celebrate sensuous pleasures in a perfectly simple, universal way. Chinese gardens have always been places for meditating, for practising calligraphy, for painting or writing poems, for self-improvement,

Liu Garden, Suzhou. The initial impression in many Chinese gardens is of chaos, but out of this different compositions appear as the visitor moves and changes the point of view. And the angle of the sun at different times of the day, and of the year, changes everything yet again, so that what seems static is in reality constantly mutating.

but they have equally been important for flirting and drinking; some of the beautifully penned inscriptions we find hanging in the gardens recall particularly delightful evenings spent getting drunk or writing poems, or both, in the company of a small group of friends. This poem from the fourteenth century should remind us that Chinese gardens were not just for spiritual self-improvement but also places for having a good time:

When peach blossoms open in the court
Oh, happy, joyous drunk
When lotus blossoms perfume the pool
Oh, mornings, evenings, drunk
When golden asters cluster by the hedgerow path
Oh, falling, tumbling, drunk
And when the wax-plum on the mountainside
First blooms to herald the spring
Oh, coming, going, drunk
Getting drunker, getting drunker
Drunk and sober; sober, drunk
(Translated by Jerome P. Seaton)

To get an idea of what a Chinese garden maker was aiming at, here is the late eighteenth-century scholar, public servant and painter Sheng Fu giving advice on how to make a successful garden:

In laying out gardens pavilions, wandering paths, small mountains of stone, and flower plantings, try to give the feeling of the small in the large and the large in the small, of the real in the illusion, and of the illusion in the reality. Some things should be hidden and some obvious, some prominent, some vague.

This is the way of showing the small in the large: in an unused corner plant some bamboo, which will grow quickly, then plant some luxuriant plum trees in front to screen it.

This is the way to show the large in the small: the wall of a small garden should be winding and covered with green vines, and large stones decorated with inscriptions can be set into it. Then one is able to open a window, and, while looking at a stone wall feel as if one were gazing out across endless precipices.

Here is the way to show the real amidst an illusion: arrange the garden so that when a guest feels he has seen everything, he can suddenly take a turn in the path and have a broad, new vista open up before him, or open a door in a pavilion only to find it leads to an entirely new garden.

The visitor to a Chinese garden has to be receptive, imaginative and thoughtful, not only looking at the surface of things but also considering what they suggest, what lies behind them both physically and metaphysically.

Visiting a Chinese garden has many similarities to viewing a Chinese painting, and both offer challenges to the Westerner. First, the multiplicity of points of view challenges our conventional way of looking at a painting and confuses us in the garden; then the marks on the paper, like the components of the garden composition, may be interpreted in so many ways – they suggest rather than define a meaning. Thus the garden visitor and the viewer of a Chinese painting have work to do; they must enter into the work of art with an alert imagination, so that in a sense they themselves become the creators. According to the Japanese critic Okakura Kakuzo, writing of Taoism and its influence, the viewer of garden or painting must be given 'the chance to complete the idea, so that a great masterpiece irresistibly rivets his attention until he seems to become actually part of it. A vacuum is there for him to fill up.' This vacuum is also present in Chinese poetry; the reader must fill the gaps between one character and another, must establish a pattern in his or her own mind which may not be the definitive meaning of the poem, but will be the essential experience it offers.

Maggie Keswick, who has written so well on Chinese gardens, sums up the problems we Westerners have:

> For the foreigner, however, the 'magic realism' of China's few remaining old gardens may still be elusive. They were, after all, meant to be savoured over a lifetime, and they often took a lifetime to make. For a woman with bound feet, the garden of her family home (if she was lucky enough to have one) might represent the sum total of her freedom. In traditional China a group of friends might have spent a whole afternoon in the corner of one courtyard watching the sun move round on a rock – revealing in the cracks and fissures lions perhaps, or cranes, or even the faces of the Immortals – or another, in autumn, 'appreciating the chrysanthemums', or, in the late spring, the peonies.

The subtle pleasures of Chinese gardens do not easily reveal themselves to the tourist group on a tight schedule.

The Chinese reverence for the past and for tradition means that the history of their gardens demonstrates no dialectical struggle between, for example, the formal and the informal, nor any restless search for novelty; rather than any linear development, it shows an accumulation of influences, so that no famous garden of the past, whether in painting or poetry or a real creation, is devoid of influence on the educated garden maker. It is for the same reason that the Chinese, to the surprise of so many Westerners, neglected the botanical richness of their own country, continually planting the same traditional trees and flowers; only these carried with them the layered suggestions of many hundred references in poems and paintings of the past.

The first Chinese gardens were the work of rulers intent on demonstrating their power and the security of their dynasty. Like the rulers of Mesopotamia, they enclosed huge areas as hunting parks and filled them with exotic trees and animals from the far corners of the lands they had conquered. These parks were used not only for hunting but also for military training; some good rulers, like Wen of the Zhou dynasty (1027–256 BC), opened them to the public, and used them for religious or magical rituals. Boys, armed with bows made of peach wood, fired arrows into the sky to break the bridges that allowed evil spirits to invade the earth. However, the making of parks was a temptation and evil emperors notoriously squandered their own fortunes and the resources of the country on their parks, as did the tyrant Zhou, last ruler of the Shang dynasty, which fell in 1122 BC, and, worse, Jie Gui, whose park became the scene of orgies, its lakes filled with wine while pieces of meat dangled from the trees. Both these semi-legendary rulers were severely censured for their profligate spending by Mencius, the fourth-century-BC philosopher and follower of Confucius, who protested: 'They pulled down houses in order to make ponds, and the people had nowhere to rest. They turned fields into parks, depriving people of their livelihood.' In 221 BC China was finally unified under Ch'in Shih Huang, a ruthless conqueror and a resolute park maker. He walled in the huge Shanglin park to the south and west of his capital city, Xi'an; its contents came to represent the extent of his empire, containing:

> Unicorns from Chiu Chen
> Horses from Ferghana
> Rhinoceros from Hang Chih
> And birds from T'iao Chih.
> (Quoted by Maggie Keswick)

So much was this park a symbol of the empire that when the Qin dynasty fell in 207 BC, it was not destroyed; indeed the great Emperor Wudi (140–87 BC), of the subsequent Han dynasty, enlarged it, so that it stretched 160 kilometres/100 miles west and south.

However, for Wu Di the park was not only a place where the range of animals and plants could demonstrate the extent of his power: it was also a means to discover the secrets of longevity.

The Immortals were beings who had escaped death but were not gods; they had two homes, one in the Himalayas to the far west, and another on the floating Islands of the Blessed off the eastern coast of China. These islands had been seen by humans but, as sailors approached them, they dissolved into the mist. Wu Di's plan was to build a garden so beautiful that the Immortals would mistake it for their island home and come to live there. The Emperor would then be able to learn the secret of how to defeat the one enemy that had so far evaded him, death. The garden he created, the Jian Gong, was begun in 104 BC and carved out of the imperial hunting park; it contained huge lakes and islands but also pavilions and terraces to make it as beautiful and tempting as possible. This model of a garden, with its lakes, islands and miniature mountains, was to have an enormous influence on subsequent gardens in both China and Japan. The pines and chrysanthemums of present-day Chinese gardens, as we have already noted, still point to a search for longevity, though no longer for immortality.

During the Han period (206 BC to AD 220) private individuals began to imitate their rulers' passion for garden and park making, not always with happy results. The rich merchant Yuan Guanhan created an impressive garden with a rockery said to be 30 metres/32 yards high; he built pavilions, covered walkways and lakes; he collected rare animals – yaks, white parrots and purple mandarin ducks. But the competition with the gardens of the Emperor was a little too challenging and, like the unfortunate Fouquet at Vaux le Vicomte, he suffered for his presumption.

After the fall of the Han, China was plunged into a period of turmoil for three centuries, 221–581, as the northern states were overrun by barbarian hordes. The capital was moved first to Loyang and then to Jian Kang (Nanjing), but some gardens continued to be made, though none of them have survived. Most notable were the botanical collections of trees and aquatic plants in the gardens of the Southern Song. To escape the uncertainties of the cities during this period scholars took refuge in the hills, some pursuing the path of Buddhist or Taoist enlightenment, and many wrote about the consolation offered by their gardens, which were necessarily much smaller than the great imperial parks. Buddhist monastery gardens also became centres of innovation; for example, the first water clock was installed in the garden of the Ji Ming temple in Nanjing. These monasteries were not only remote but sited amidst scenes of great natural beauty, and they made ideal refuges from the turmoil of the times. The Buddhist monastery on the holy mountain Lu Shan provided a refuge for many, who never forgot its beautiful scenery and, when they left, tried to reproduce these inspiring scenes in so called Lu Shan parks. Among those who found peace there was the remarkable Hsieh Ling-yun (385–433), poet, politician, herbalist and garden maker. In his poems he celebrated the refreshment he found in his intricately planned but secluded garden:

Hemmed in by mountains, there seems no way out.
The track gets lost among the thick bamboos.
My visitors can never find the way,
And when they leave, forget the path they took.

This removal from the world in a landscape so complex that it puzzles the mind was to be an influence on many later garden makers. And the beauties of Lu Shan continued to inspire poets, including Li Bai, who wrote this delightful quatrain, 'The Waterfall at Lu Shan', 400 years later:

In sunshine, Censer peak breathes purple mist.
A jutting stream, the cataract hangs in spray
Far off, then plunges down three thousand feet –
As if the sky had dropped the Milky Way.
(Translated by Vikram Seth)

With the Sui (589–618) and Tang (618–906) dynasties some peace returned to the empire. The first Sui emperor, Yang Guang, restored the old eastern garden in Xi'an, and built a new garden, the

Xi Yuan (Western Garden), in Loyang. This garden was designed by Hung Shen, who made it a labyrinth that would confuse and constantly surprise the visitor with cunningly contrived new views, through windows, doorways and arches. The Xi Yuan, too, was to have a huge influence on the later development of private gardens, where the elements of surprise in the layout and the skill in creating a wide variety of sensuous experiences, however small the site, became highly prized.

The most influential gardener of the Tang period was undoubtedly Wang Wei (699–759), who was celebrated not only as a gardener but as a painter, poet and a calligrapher; as Maggie Keswick writes, 'He was the ultimate gentleman – brilliant, cultivated, unworldly, and a model of filial piety.' He was prodigiously talented in many of the arts; at the age of seventeen he wrote *The Ballad of the Peach Tree Spring*, and in many of his poems he celebrated the pleasures of rustic isolation, as in 'In Answer to Vice Magistrate Zhang':

> Late in my life I only care for quiet.
> A million pressing tasks, I let them go.
> I look at myself; I have no long-range plans.
> To go back to the forest is all I know.
> Pine breeze: I ease my belt. Hill moon: I strum
> My lute. You ask – but I can say no more
> About success or failure than the song
> The fisherman sings, which comes to the deep shore.
> (Translated by Vikram Seth)

In and out of office as a civil servant, Wang Wei would retreat to his country estate when unemployed and during periods of political unrest. He left a scroll painting of the estate around his Wang Ch'uan villa, which was copied many times – fortunately, since the original does not survive. The site of the garden was a valley among rolling hills that contained streams and a lake, around which Wang Wei devised a set of twenty views; each of these could be enjoyed from a hut or pavilion, some of which were simple, rustic buildings, others more elaborate, two-storey halls. The halls and pavilions were joined by paths, bridges and the covered, outdoor corridors (*lang*) that were to become an essential part of the Chinese garden. The scroll painting gave the viewer something of the experience of exploring the garden, since it too could not all be seen at once but required slow appreciation as one moved from one scene to the next. From a distance the pavilions and halls in the garden seemed to have been placed at random; only when visitors entered them would they have understood their purpose: each building provided a place from which to view a carefully organized landscape composition, a pleasure which could be enjoyed whether it was raining or the sun was blazing. Many subsequent garden makers followed this example; pavilions in Chinese gardens came to serve the purpose of drawing the visitor's attention to a garden composition, so that, far from being placed randomly, they are sited with the greatest care.

Continued invasions from the north forced the Song (960–1279) to move their capital to Lin An (now known as Hangzhou), a place already famous for the beauty of its 'ten scenic spots'. And garden-making continued in the softer southern climate. The last Northern Song emperor, Hui Zong (ruled 1101–26), became notorious for his addiction to strangely shaped rocks. He sent surveyors all over his empire to search out rocks of the most bizarre form, and the barges bringing his booty home blocked the Grand Canal, so that vital convoys of rice could not pass. One of these barges sank in the mouth of the Huangpu River, where Shanghai stands today, but the rock (known as the Exquisite Jade Stone) was eventually dredged up and is now one of the glories of the Yu Yuan garden in that city. Marco Polo, who visited Hangzhou when the city was already in decline, records seeing a large park beside the lake full of deer, hares and rabbits, which were hunted by the courtiers and the imperial concubines. In 1210 the dreaded Ghenghis Khan invaded northern China, saying he would flatten the whole country and use it as a pasture to feed his horses. By 1279 the Mongols were masters of all China, but Kublai Khan, far from flattening the country as his grandfather had threatened, established a new capital around a hill created from the spoil thrown up when excavating a lake; this is the Bei Hei (Northern Sea) of present-day Beijing. By the end of the Song dynasty the key features of the Chinese garden were well established – lakes or pools are dug, rocks piled up, groves of bamboo planted, pavilions sited as viewing points and joined by covered walkways (*lang*), and fruit trees, prized for their blossom, collected; only in the imperial parks are animals still hunted.

The Ming dynasty (1368–1644), which succeeded the Mongol Yuan regime, seemed more interested in running an efficient civil service than in building gardens, but during this period some

Yu Yuan, Shanghai. The 'lang', or covered walkway, allows the garden to be enjoyed on even the wettest and the hottest days. Notice also the seat with its back curving out over the water, so that the sitter can look straight down into the dark depths.

classic private gardens were built (the Chinese always write and speak of 'building' a garden, while Westerners more often 'plant' a garden); and some of these wonderful gardens we can still visit – the Yu Yuan in Shanghai and several scholar gardens in Suzhou. The Yu Yuan, like a number of historic gardens, has survived many vicissitudes of fortune; it has been a private garden, a temple garden and even, in the nineteenth century, a barracks for foreign troops engaged in putting down the T'aiping rebellion. These barbarians filled in some of the ponds with stones from the rock piles to make more flat space for their tents. But each time the Yu Yuan was damaged, the local population repaired it, so though the garden we see today is not exactly the garden made by Pan En in the mid sixteenth century, it gives us a good idea of what a wealthy, retired bureaucrat's garden of the period must have looked like.

Pan En left a document in which he relates how the garden came into being:

> For twenty years I continued to build the garden. I sat a sit, and thought a thought, and rested a rest, but it was still not very good. [In 1577] when I returned from Szechuan where I had held the office of Provincial Treasurer, I gave my entire heart to the affair. I thought only of the garden . . . I increased the size of the ground, adding fifteen plots of land. I made seventeen pools.

BELOW *Yu Yuan, Shanghai. The doorways in the shape of vases are a kind of visual pun. The character for a vase, 'p'ing', is also the character for peace. Notice how the shape is emphasized by the dark lining to the opening.*

He goes on to explain that he did all this to give his mother pleasure (another model of filial piety!), and to provide a place where he could entertain his friends to banquets, at which they composed poems together; poetry writing was a compulsory part of the examination for entry to the civil service. It seems that the garden grew without any overall plan, and that originally there was not even a wall. The present undulating dragon wall, white plaster with a dark grey tile coping, makes a huge impression; the purist may shudder at the unsubtle literalness of the representation, but most visitors enjoy the five snarling dragons' heads with teeth bared, nostrils flaring, eyeballs bulging. Pan En took great pains to point out the significance of various elements in the garden by giving them carefully chosen names; just inside the entrance was a gate with the inscription 'Chien Chia', meaning 'Beauty Penetrates Gradually' – that is, don't hurry through my garden. And above another arch he had inscribed 'Jeng Ching Hu T'ien' (Man's Place in the Immortals' Heaven), a title that takes us back to the origins of Chinese gardens. He ends his description of the Yu Yuan by comparing it to the estate of Wang Wei, who was by then well established as the ancient master of all garden makers.

Pan En wrote of his intention to 'cut off the noise and bustle of the city', which is especially important today when Shanghai has grown to be one of the most populous cities on earth. We now enter the garden by a zig-zag causeway across a lake, and then through a narrow door; at once we are confronted by a building, so that nothing is revealed of the garden; after all, we are entering the realm of the immortals and are reminded that beauty penetrates gradually. The visitor's experience of the garden is controlled with great subtlety; sometimes we are allowed long views down a corridor, or through vase-shaped doorways, and here we are tempted to move swiftly; at other times we find ourselves in spaces so small they seem almost claustrophobic, the exit from which is often concealed, or we slowly ascend the rockery by a narrow path that twists and turns. (The doorways in the shape of vases are themselves a kind of visual pun: the character for vase, *p'ing*, is also the character for peace, the effect of the garden.) Views are allowed at certain carefully selected points, and sometimes our attention is drawn to a particularly beautiful composition by a pavilion;

ABOVE *Shanghai Botanical Garden. Another shape of opening. The plants in pots are used for seasonal displays.*

for example, the Jade Bright Hall stands in front of the garden's great T'ai Hu rock, the Exquisite Jade Stone. One two-storey building even allows a view over the Hangpu River beyond the garden wall, a characteristically Chinese use of landscape 'borrowed' from outside the garden.

Other parts of the Yu Yuan have suggestive names – Old Gentleman's Court, Moon-gaining Storey, Quietly-looking Hall; the Looking Mountains Hall stands opposite the 15 metre/16 yard high rockery, for which 2,000 tons of yellow rock were brought from Zhejiang province and glued together with rice glue. The upper part of this building is named the Chamber for Gathering the Rain – perhaps a Taoist reference to catching the pure rain before it is sullied by contact with the earth, or perhaps a reference to a seventh-century poem which contains the line 'Pearl curtains gather the rain from the western mountains in the dusk.' Typically the name suggests a reference, but doesn't insist upon it.

The Chinese expression for 'landscape' is *shan shui*, literally mountain and water. Mountains were places of magic and spiritual wisdom, while water suggested the Taoist ideal of adapting oneself to one's setting and circumstances without complaint. All good gardens must contain at least these two elements, but they must be handled carefully. In the Yu Yuan there is a strange place where the stream flows under a wall; human visitors are enclosed by the wall and can go no further, but the moving water must be allowed to express its ch'i and flow on unimpeded. Interrupting this life energy, or trapping it, can have disastrous results. The contorted rocks also express the force of the ch'i, and the mountains, miniaturized to fit into a garden, do not lose their energy by being represented in little; rather their ch'i is concentrated. The miniature plants and landscapes, known in the West more often by the Japanese name *bonsai*, but in Chinese called *pengjing*, similarly represent the force of nature concentrated into miniature form. In the Yu Yuan a few dishes containing miniaturized trees were placed among the stones of the rockery, perhaps to heighten the illusion that the visitor is seeing the mountains from so far away that the trees and even the mountains themselves are dwarfed. Gardens cannot, indeed should not, aspire to the awe-inspiring and spiritually uplifting qualities of nature; but their winding paths and unpredictable developments, so much more natural according to the Chinese than the formality of Western gardens, should rather inspire in the visitor the quintessence of the uplifting effect that nature has upon us.

'Heaven above; Hangzhou and Suzhou below', goes the ancient Chinese saying. Both of these cities, famous for their gardens, are sited close to water: Hangzhou on Lake Xi Hu and Suzhou near both Lake T'ai and the canal system of southern China. Carved on stone, a 1229 plan of Suzhou (it was then known as Pingjiang) shows ten gardens, five of them in private hands. The only garden recorded on this plan that still exists is the Cang Lang T'ing (Surging Wave Pavilion). Though records of this garden go back to 907, when it was used to grow flowers for the imperial court, its development as a pleasure garden dates from 1044, when the place was bought by Su Shunqin, who retired from his post as a judge to spend more time writing. This pattern of retiring from the service of the government (which showed a Confucian sense of duty) to devote oneself to writing, painting and spiritual refinement became typical among the makers of Suzhou gardens.

The retiring civil servant would often claim he wanted to spend more time 'fishing', and from this euphemism comes the name of one of the best gardens in Suzhou, the Wang Shi Yuan or

BELOW *Wang Shi Yuan, Suzhou. This is one of the world's great gardens, so much is achieved in about 0.4 hectare/1 acre. Two visitors are enjoying the benches with backs curved out over the water, allowing them to gaze directly down at the fish*

the Master of the Fishing Nets' Garden. This was first laid out in 1140 and its purpose is made clear in its original name, the Hall of Ten Thousand Books; it was to be a place of study for the retired official Shi Zhenglong. The Wang Shi Yuan is just 0.4 hectares/1 acre, but so complex is the layout of interlocking courtyards that it seems much larger. The illusion of size is helped by the irregularly shaped lake in the main courtyard, which is much too big for its space but offers perfect reflections of the sky, surrounding trees and buildings, and by the rock piles, which require slow, even laborious exploration. Some of the walls of this garden are painted not white but soft grey, so that in the humid air of low-lying southern China the garden seems not so much shut in by its walls as wreathed in a boundless mist. This illusion is heightened by half rocks, which are butted up against the wall, so that we imagine them fading into the distance and the wall itself becomes an illusion. And there is a final detail that adds to the sense of space in this small garden: in the raised pavilion that looks down on the pool of the main courtyard, the Pavilion of the Clouds and Moon, one wall is a mirror, so looking from below and from a distance we seem to be looking into vacancy.

There is, of course, a rock pile, here concealing a staircase, and a fine collection of characterful rocks from nearby Lake T'ai; one fine, curling monster stands against the wall, under a roof, and has a pair of seats on each side for those who would pause and wonder at its magnificent, poised energy. And the planting? The soft floppiness of mondo grass contrasts with the sharp angles of the rocks among which it is planted; bamboo waves its wands against wall and rockery, and in the study courtyard (known as the Courtyard of the Late Spring), perhaps the heart of the garden, a fine sophora adds height and movement to the composition on which the scholar/owner would gaze out as he sought inspiration. One ancient, twisted shrub is provided with a stone prop, so that it can continue to express its reverent character and all the coiled *ch'i* it contains. Pruning in a Chinese

garden seeks not to impose itself on the plant, as when shrubs are sculpted into some topiary shape, but rather to reveal the essential character and growth pattern of the individual plant.

A pavilion with no view of the central pool, because it lies behind the main rockery, has the function of drawing attention to the plants near by; this is the Hall of Small Mountains and Osmanthus Spring. Another building is the Hall for One who Looks at the Pines. Pines had played an important part in the history of Suzhou. The great Confucian administrator Fan Chung-yen (989–1052) contributed enormously to the prosperity of the town by initiating drainage works; when confronted by a difficult problem, he would climb into the branches of an old pine tree in his garden in search of enlightenment. The windows throughout the Wang Shi Yuan are as diverse in shape as we have come now to expect, and their tracery is equally varied. The pebble paving is beautifully executed: sometimes it is laid in intricate patterns, in other places pictures are made out of pebbles – a fish shows its scales and the stork, on whose back the Immortals fly, spreads its wings so that each feather is visible. This magical garden exerts its own kind of yin and yang: the urge to move forward and explore round each corner, through each archway, working against the urge to stand still and examine the detail of what lies around.

The two largest historic gardens in Suzhou are the Liu Garden and the Humble Administrator's Garden. The former was built in 1522 by Xu Shitai, another retired civil servant, but the name derives from subsequent owners called Liu. When they sold the garden, their successors kept the name but changed the character to another with the same pronunciation, so that the word *liu* now means 'to linger'. Even in these large gardens the spaces are inventively varied, so that intimate courtyards where the whole composition may be three bamboos and a rock contrast with broad,

LEFT *Wang Shi Yuan, Suzhou. Sometimes the paving pebbles are used to create pictures – the crane, symbol of longevity, or, as here, the fish. The Chinese character for fish, 'yu', is phonetically almost identical with the character for abundance or affluence.*

open spaces of the water down which the eye is led by the distant 'borrowed' landscape of the Beiji pagoda roof. In these classic Suzhou gardens there are the pavilions (*ting*) and the walkways (*lang*) we have come to expect, but they are never dully predictable in use or construction. In the Cang Lang T'ing (Surging Wave Pavilion), for example, the walkway is doubled, so that under the same roof there are two corridors separated by a wall, which is occasionally pierced by a window so that the visitor can see through to a landscape which, at that moment, it is impossible to enter. And in the Liu garden the *lang* changes direction twelve times in 40 metres/43 yards, each time drawing the visitor's attention to a new view. The pavilions, too, are varied, with roofs more or less extravagantly swept up at the corners, while some are fan-shaped with windows also in the form of fans. Bridges show the same variety: some are flat pieces of stone exactly parallel to the water; some zig-zag, because it is said evil spirits can move only in straight lines; some are hump-backed, so their reflections in the water make a complete circle.

But while the layout may be complex, many of the pavilions continually remind the visitor how simple garden pleasures can be. In the Humble Administrator's Garden, for example, we find the Wind in the Pines Pavilion, the Pavilion of the Perfumed Snow, reminding us of the scented beauty of *Prunus mume* blossom, the Listening to the Rain Terrace, and the Pavilion for the Scent that Comes from Afar; this is the scented flower of the lotus, which emerges pure and beautiful from the muddy bed of a pond, thus representing the pure soul living in the world but untainted by it.

RIGHT *Liu Garden, Suzhou. Single stones are used like pieces of natural sculpture. Often they are more pitted than this example, so that there is more play of light against shade, and of solid against void.*

LEFT *The Humble Administrator's Garden, Suzhou. This garden is as much water as it is land. Most Chinese gardens are crowded with parties taking photos of each other; the ice on the pool explains why on this occasion the garden is empty. Note the pagoda in the distance used as a focal point, a typical example of landscape 'borrowed' from outside the garden.*

BELOW *The Humble Administrator's Garden, Suzhou. Moon gates serve to frame views of the garden, and to create compositions, all of which are carefully calculated.*

Certainly some earlier visitors had enjoyed this garden and not only for the sensuous variety that it offered; there is a plaque in immaculate calligraphy, dated 1747, with this inscription: 'The lord of the garden prepared wine and bade his guests drink; they chanted songs, chatted and rejoiced. Their pleasures were very refined, not in the least coarse . . . Although one had scarcely left the market place, one seemed to have reached the hills and forests.' This was the ultimate test of a successful Chinese garden: could it mentally transport the visitor from its urban setting into the inspiring scenes of the natural countryside?

The example of these classic Suzhou gardens lies behind the first surviving Chinese book on the art of garden-making, Ji Cheng's *The Craft of Gardens*, written in 1631. While conceding that towns are not ideal places for gardens, Ji says that if a secluded spot can be found, the owner may find 'that the hermit's life in a city far surpasses a distant mountain retreat. If you can find seclusion in a noisy place, there is no need to yearn for places far from where you live. Whenever you have some leisure, you are already at your goal, and whenever the mood takes you, you can set off with your friends for a walk.' And a classic garden usually offers the owner, at the very least, the choice of a mountain walk, up and down the twisting paths of a rockery, or a flat walk beside a pool.

But Ji was not writing a book of instructions; as Zheng Yuanxun writes in his original introduction, 'He goes by the concept, not by a fixed set of rules.' This is necessary as Ji stresses the importance of fitting the garden into the site, and every site is different. Here is Ji telling his readers how to begin: 'Excavate a pool and dig out a moat, arrange rocks and build up a mountain, construct a gate to welcome arriving visitors, and keep a path open to connect it to the

nearest building. With bamboo growing elegantly and trees flourishing, with shady willows and bright flowers, an area of 5 mu [roughly 0.3 hectare/0.8 acre] is not a restriction. In fact you can rival Lord Wen's Garden of Solitary Delight.' Three-tenths of the area, he says, should be water, and the shape of the pool should be irregular 'so that it is interesting'; this determination that gardens should engage the mind is particularly Chinese. Views over water are very important: 'a curving bay of willows in the moonlight cleanses the soul' and he quotes from a Wang Wei poem: 'The river flows beyond the edge of the world/The prospect of the mountains lies between being and non-being.' He is very critical of many people's attempts at creating mountains; too small and they look 'like the decorations in a goldfish bowl', too large and they look like 'the scenery in the haunted town of Fengdu'. 'Instead,' he writes, 'the depths of your imagination should be full of pictures, and your feelings should overflow into hills and valleys.'

Garden buildings should have 'order in variety' and always a 'pleasing unpredictability' – though these are the most stable, predictable and formal parts of the garden. Doorways, too, should arouse interesting thoughts of entry into another world, while paths up rock piles should twist and turn 'like playing cats'. And no garden is complete – he is firm on this point – unless it contains pavilions (*ting*) and covered walkways (*lang*). Here is the last paragraph of his book, cautioning designers not to begin before they have thought long and hard: 'Making use of the natural scenery is the most vital part of garden design . . . But the attraction of natural objects, both the form perceptible to the eye and the essence which touches the heart, must be fully imagined in your mind before you put pen to paper.' It is always necessary in a Chinese garden to look beyond the 'form perceptible to the eye', in an attempt to find the essence.

Ji Cheng stresses the importance of pavilions and we have already noted the way these are often carefully named to draw attention to a particular sensuous delight, which, if it cannot be experienced at that particular moment, may be remembered, or anticipated. And just as Chinese paintings are not complete without inscriptions, either by the artist or by other cognoscenti, so gardens need their literary references and suggestive names. An eighteenth-century novel, *The Story of the Stone*, sometimes known as *The Dream of the Red Chamber*, gives us a clear idea of the importance attached to naming parts of the garden (all quotations are from David Hawkes' translation). Early in the story Jia Zheng goes to inspect his new garden, which at this stage has no name, to see if it is ready for the formal visit of his daughter, Yuan-chun, who has been taken into the palace as an imperial concubine. (Between 1984 and 1988 this garden was recreated in Beijing under the name

LEFT *The Humble Administrator's Garden, Suzhou. Here we see the choice of paths: along the side of the water is the easy, flat path, but the young couple on the left have decided on a kind of country stroll among the piles of rock, which are miniaturized mountains.*

ABOVE *Daguanyuan Gongyuan, Beijing. This garden was built between 1984 and 1988. It is a replica of the garden described in the late eighteenth-century novel called* The Story of the Stone, *or* The Dream of the Red Chamber.

Daguanyuan Gongyuan, and it is now a popular place to visit in the capital.) Jia Zheng is pleased by the complex layout, and by the way the small space has been made to seem larger, in part by the use of a mirror, so that after a thorough exploration of several areas of the garden 'they were surprised to find that even now they had covered little more than half of the whole area'. He is accompanied by a group of elderly literati and his young son Bao-yu, who 'showed no aptitude for serious study' but is reported to have a gift for composing poetic couplets. Jia Zheng feels he should wait until his daughter's visit so that she can name the scenes in the garden; on the other hand 'all those prospects and pavilions – even the rocks and trees and flowers will seem somehow incomplete without that touch of poetry which only the written word can lend a scene'.

Climbing the winding path up one of the rock piles Jia Zheng comes across a stone that has been polished ready to receive an inscription, so he turns to the group and asks for their suggestions. After various uninspired attempts by the literary gentlemen, Jia turns to his son. Like the well-educated Chinese that he is, Bao-yu replies to this demand, 'I remember reading in some old book that "to recall old things is better than to invent new ones". We ought, then, to choose something old.' He points out that this rock pile is not the garden's chief mountain and that therefore they need a quotation that suggests 'a first step to more important things'. So he proposes calling the place 'Pathway to Mysteries', recalling a line of poetry by Chang Jian: 'A path winds upwards to mysterious places'. The literati receive this suggestion with applause, but Bao-yu's autocratic father pretends to be less satisfied.

So the group proceeds through the garden with the young man suggesting names for its various parts, and inventing couplets of poetry to hang on either side of the entrance to each new scene. Sometimes Jia Zheng rejects suggested names as 'too obvious', sometimes as 'too contrived'. When the great day of the Imperial Concubine's visit comes, the garden is decorated with 'hundreds of tiny lanterns, and flowers of gauze, rice paper and bast had been fastened to the tips of the branches'; all this is necessary since it is winter, so there are no leaves or flowers. Yuan-chun alters the names of some parts of the garden, gives names to other views and finally decides the garden should be called Prospect Garden.

The eighteenth century was a period in which the emperors too were again building great gardens. The Emperor Yongzheng ordered the extension of a private Ming garden on the north-western outskirts of Beijing into an imperial garden, and he himself wrote the inscriptions for the twenty-three scenes that were to be created. His successor was an obsessive garden maker; the Emperor Qianlong (ruled 1736–95) added another twelve scenes and incorporated two other gardens into what was called the Yuan Ming Yuan, the Garden of Perfect Brightness. The combined gardens covered about 350 hectares/864 acres and were hidden behind an enormous wall. The Qianlong Emperor justified the huge expenditure on his gardens by saying: 'Every Emperor and ruler, when he has retired from audience, and has finished his public duties, must have a garden in which he may stroll, look around and relax his heart.' So the good government of the empire depended on the construction of multiple gardens! By all accounts the Yuan Ming Yuan was the most stupendous Chinese garden ever created; some called it the garden of ten thousand gardens because it contained such a variety of different spaces within it. Water was brought from the Western Hills through meandering streams to fill the great central lake, the Fu Hai or Sea of Felicity.

From 1725 the Yuan Ming Yuan became the very heart of the Chinese empire, since imperial business was daily conducted there; a new stone road between the garden and Beijing made communication between capital and garden easier. The emperors' royal quarters were called the Nine Continents, a reference to an ancient Chinese way of describing the world; in fact they were a series of nine linked islets along the shore of the Hou Hu, the Rear Lake. But this was more than an administrative hub: it was also a scholar's garden on an enormous scale, with a library where the Qianlong Emperor gathered together an extensive collection of Confucian classics, history and literature, and fine collections of paintings and calligraphy. The emperor's favourite place for writing verses was the Peony Terrace, on which each spring the imperial household would gather to admire the flowering of the tree peonies. Another part of the garden was called Peach Blossom Cove, recalling the traditional story of the fisherman who loses his way and finds himself in an ideal world, in which everyone lives happily. He returns home but can never again find his way to Peach Blossom Cove, although he tells everyone about it. (This had been the subject of a famous ballad by seventeen-year-old Wang Wei.)

The Qianlong Emperor often visited the southern parts of his empire and brought back with him from Hangzhou and Suzhou ideas of gardens, which he would then incorporate into the Yuan Ming Yuan. He was also inspired by the illustrations of fountains he found in some books presented to him by Jesuits who were guests at his court. He found these so appealing that he ordered two of the Jesuits, Giuseppe Castiglione and Michel Benoist, to build him a baroque fountain in the Eternal Spring Garden. Working largely from sketches and illustrations in books, these amateur architects and engineers managed to construct a swaggering baroque palace, in front of which they sited a European-style fountain, remains of which can still be seen. They also designed a maze on instructions from the Qianlong Emperor. But the Yuan Ming Yuan was not merely a pleasure garden: it had become, like earlier imperial parks, a symbol of imperial power. In this lay the cause of its destruction.

After the First Opium War (1839–42) the British had extorted trading concessions from the Chinese empire, but twenty years later these were thought to be inadequate, so, after helping to suppress the Taiping rebellion, they made a new set of demands. France was also intent on expanding its influence in the area, citing as a pretext the execution of the French priest Auguste Chapdelaine. The result was that these long-term imperial rivals decided to act together, at first in defence of and then against the tottering Chinese empire. The Emperor Xianfeng, who had recently acceded to the throne, decided to resist the aggressors, but had little chance against the advanced military technology of the allies. At 7.00 p.m. on 6 October 1860 the French troops under Baron Montoubon arrived at the gates of the Yuan Ming Yuan. The Supreme Supervisor of the Garden,

Wenfeng, made a token attempt to keep the foreigners out of the imperial precinct, but when he saw that his efforts were useless drowned himself in the Sea of Felicity. The next day the British arrived under the command of Lord Elgin. Many of them were enchanted by the beauty of the garden; Robert Swinhoe, General Grant's interpreter, for example, wrote:

Here a solitary building would rise, fairy-like, from the centre of a lake, reflecting its image in the limpid, blue water, in which it seemed to float, and then a sloping path would carry you into the heart of a mysterious cavern artificially formed of rockery, and leading out on to a grotto in the bosom of another lake. The variety of the picturesque was endless, and charming in the extreme; indeed, all that is most lovely in Chinese scenery, where art contrives to cheat the rude attempts of nature, seemed all associated in these delightful grounds. The resources of the designer appear to have been unending, and no money spared to bring his work to perfection. All the tasteful landscapes so often viewed in the better class of Chinese paintings, and which we had hitherto looked upon as wrought out of the imagination, were here brought to life.

The Summer Palace, Beijing. Another doorway in the shape of a vase. The Summer Palace was a royal preserve, allowing the emperor and his family to escape the intolerable heat of the Forbidden City. These gardens were much enhanced in the eighteenth century by the Qianlong Emperor, an energetic garden maker.

All this beauty did not save this wonderful garden from being thoroughly looted. The British blamed the French for this shameful episode; the French blamed the British. Discipline had entirely broken down and officers were seen loading carts with booty. 'Everything of value that could be carried off, consisting of gold, silver, clocks, watches, enamels, porcelain, jade stones, silks and embroidery, with numerous articles of vertu were removed by the allies,' wrote Major General Allgood. What could not be carried off was smashed in an orgy of destruction. It wasn't long before the locals joined in the free-for-all, and later the allies tried to blame them for the sack of the garden.

But the worst was to come. Some Allied prisoners, who had been released by the Chinese, told stories of their mistreatment, and Elgin decided that in order to punish and humiliate the Emperor the Yuan Ming Yuan should be burned. The French did not agree, but Elgin argued that it was necessary to 'make the blow fall on the Emperor, who was clearly responsible for the crime committed'. On 18 October the order was given to burn down this masterpiece of garden art, and since all the buildings were wooden it was quickly destroyed. Captain Charles Gordon of the Royal Engineers wrote: 'You can scarcely imagine the beauty and magnificence of the places we burnt. It made one's heart sore to burn them; in fact, these palaces were so large, and we were so pressed for time, that we could not plunder them carefully. Quantities of gold ornaments were burnt, considered as brass. It was wretchedly demoralising work for an army. Everybody was wild for plunder.' Was it demoralizing, the reader may wonder, because the garden was so beautiful, or because the army had not been able to plunder the place thoroughly? The Chinese, who were negotiating a peace treaty, were shocked: 'The barbarians put all our royal garden under restraint and wilfully set fire to it. Their behaviour made our hair stand up in great anger. Having seen what happened, we conclude that we absolutely cannot continue peace talks with them.' But for the Chinese there was no option; a peace was signed, which conceded all the Allied demands.

The imperial house didn't stop building gardens after the destruction of the Yuan Ming Yuan. The terrifying Empress Dowager (1835–1908) rebuilt the garden around the Summer Palace in Beijing, one of the many gardens laid out by the Qianlong Emperor. As was appropriate for an imperial garden, the water and mountains of this garden are on a huge scale: the shore line of the Kunming lake was developed in a series of islets which run along under Longevity Hill. Beside the water runs an immensely long gallery with 273 rooms from which

LEFT *The Summer Palace, Beijing. The Long Corridor, the 'chang lang', 730 metres/2,550 feet long, runs along the north shore of Kunming Lake, which occupies 75 per cent of this royal park. Pictures of birds and flowers decorate the 'lang', and the views across the lake are so beautiful that courting couples are said to find it impossible to emerge from a visit unbetrothed.*

different views across the lake can be enjoyed. Some of these scenes and indeed the shape of the Kunming Lake itself echo those of the West Lake in Hangzhou. When the Empress came to rebuild these gardens, she raised money by appealing for funds to re-equip and modernize the navy, which was imperative to defend China against the Japanese. However, the money was spent on the gardens and not one naval vessel was built; indeed, as wits of the time pointed out (very quietly, no doubt), the only ship the nation got was a marble boat, in reality a tea house in the gardens of the Summer Palace. This ungainly creation, perhaps inspired by the marble boat in Suzhou's Lion Grove garden, takes the form of a particularly graceless, top-heavy Mississippi paddle steamer. But by this time the empire was on its last legs and funds for garden building and everything else were running very low.

The memory of the extraordinary Yuan Ming Yuan lived on in the paintings, commissioned by the Qianlong Emperor, of the forty most beautiful views in the garden, for each of which he had himself written a couplet. And these gardens exerted an influence far beyond the boundaries of the Middle Kingdom, for the first European eyes to see and admire this garden were not those of the Allied soldiers who destroyed it. Among the painters the Qianlong Emperor employed were the European Jesuits, whom we've already met as amateur architects, engineers and designers of fountains. One of these, Père Jean-Denis Attiret, was allowed a studio inside the walls of the Yuan Ming Yuan, and in 1749 he sent home a description of the garden. He was struck by the inventive irregularity of the layout; how the water 'serpentizes, and then spreads away, as if it was really pushed off by the hills and the rocks. The banks are sprinkled with flowers; which rise up even through the hollows of the rockwork, as if they had been produced there naturally.' He was particularly taken with the *lang*, the covered walkways, and by the fact that 'they never go in a straight line. They make a hundred detours, sometimes behind a clump of bushes, sometimes behind a rock, or sometimes round a lake; there is nothing so agreeable. In all this there is an enchanting, elevating impression of the countryside.' He was perceptive enough to see that all the elaborate artifice aimed at producing the 'impression' of the countryside. 'But what is the most charming thing of all is an island or rock in the middle of this sea [the Sea of Felicity] raised in a natural and rustic manner, about six feet above the surface of the water. On this rock there is a little palace, which however contains a hundred different apartments. It has four fronts and is built with inexpressible beauty and taste; the sight of it strikes one with admiration.' This fairytale element, appealing so strongly to the imagination, was what also struck the soldiers who were ordered to destroy the garden. Attiret admitted, 'I had never seen anything that bore any manner of resemblance to them [the Yuan Ming Yuan gardens] in any part of the world.'

His letter was translated into English by Joseph Spence, using the pseudonym 'Sir Harry Beaumont', and published in 1752 under the title *A Particular Account of the Emperor of China's Garden near Pekin*. Nothing could have been more timely. English park makers were beginning to throw off the shackles of formality in their designs, and here was the example of a garden tradition that valued irregularity and made of it something beautiful. No surprise, then, that in France the new style of park was known as 'Anglo-Chinois', or that in Kew Gardens to this day there stands a ten-storey Chinese pagoda, designed in 1761 by Sir William Chambers. He had visited China twice and his books, *Designs of Chinese Buildings* (1757) and *A Dissertation on Oriental Gardening* (1772), were to be enormously influential. In this way the secretive beauty of Chinese gardens, usually hidden away behind tall walls, became influential in Europe. Deeply embedded as these gardens are in the culture of the country, when plucked out of their context, as are the beautiful Chinese gardens in contemporary Vancouver and Sydney for example, they lose many of their remarkable qualities, but these complete gardens are infinitely preferable to the chinoiserie fragments that became so popular in later eighteenth- and nineteenth-century European gardens.

BELOW *The Summer Palace, Beijing. This is the so-called Marble Boat. In fact it is neither: it is a tea house and it is made of stone. It was built by order of the terrifying Dowager Empress, who held effective power in China for forty years in the late nineteenth century, enforcing her rule by bribery and murder.*

ABOVE *The Dr Sun Yat Sen Garden, Vancouver, Canada. This was the first full-scale classical garden, imitating the gardens of Suzhou, to be constructed (1985–6) in the West. Most of the materials were brought from China, including the pebbles for the beautiful paving found throughout the garden.*

Joseph Needham, the great scholar of Chinese science, had once admired Versailles, but after prolonged exposure to Chinese culture he found the French palace garden gave him 'a feeling of desolation' because, unlike a Chinese garden, it seemed to be 'imprisoning and confining Nature rather than flowing along with it'. A Chinese garden historian emphasizes the importance of this impression of natural flow when he writes that the first two principles that lie behind the Chinese garden are: '1. Mankind is embedded in the Natural Order as an active though not a dominant player. 2. Man's role in the Natural Order is not to impose his will on Nature but rather to assist in the expression of that which is appropriate to the Natural Order of things.' (Quoted in Lifang and Sianglin.) This flow is an expression of the Taoist insistence on man fitting himself into nature, not bullying nature into submitting to his ideas. But a garden is always a man-made thing, so the best it can do is suggest the essence of nature's inspiration. To find this essence the visitor to the garden must look beyond the surface, perhaps imitating the Qianlong Emperor, who wrote, 'When I find pleasure in orchids, I love uprightness; when I see pines and bamboos, I think of virtue; when I stand beside limpid brooks, I value honesty; when I see weeds, I despise dishonesty.'

This representing nature and its moral lessons in miniature need be no problem if we remember the advice of another modern historian of gardens, Chuin Tung: 'The question of reality will not bother the visitor as long as he ceases to be in the garden, and begins to live in the painting.' Like Chinese painting and poetry ('Good gardens are like superb lines of verse', Chen Congzhou), Chinese gardens require some effort from the viewer and the reader; we must exercise our imaginations and our intellects, appreciating these works of art with open, but not vacant, minds. Finally, let us recall the advice of a Suzhou poet on how the visitor to a Chinese garden should behave (quoted in Osvald Siren's *Gardens of China*):

> One should enter the garden in a peaceful and receptive mood; one should use one's observation to note the plan and pattern of the garden, for the different parts have not been arbitrarily assembled, but carefully weighed against each other, like pairs of inscribed tablets . . . And when one has thoroughly comprehended the tangible forms or objects, one should endeavour to attain to an inner comprehension of the soul of the garden, and try to understand the mysterious forces governing the landscape and making it cohere.

If the Western visitor can bear some of this advice in mind, Chinese gardens will seem less disconcertingly alien and much more fascinating. But at the same time we mustn't be thinking so hard we forget to hear the Wind in the Pines or enjoy the Scent that Comes from Afar; these private gardens were made for families to live in, not just for scholars studying painting, calligraphy and enlightenment.

BELOW *The Chinese Garden, Sydney, Australia. It is rarer to find Chinese gardens outside China than to find Japanese gardens outside Japan. This was built in 1988 by Chinese artists and craftsmen to celebrate Australia's bicentenary and the friendship between Sydney and its sister city Guangzhou.*

4

THE ORIENTAL TRADITION: JAPAN

ABOVE *Ryoan-ji Temple, Kyoto. Raking the gravel into these perfect patterns is part of the duty of the Zen monks. It is impossible to see where the monk has trodden or where the rake was lifted from the stones.*

LEFT *The Japanese Garden, Seattle, USA. The garden was completed in 1960, designed by Juki Iida and Kiyoshi Inoshita. The beach made of flat stones, typically, imitates a scene from coastal Japan.*

THERE IS A STORY, perhaps apocryphal, which tells of Japanese archaeologists excavating the foundations of an ancient building in Osaka, exploring the site before it was occupied by yet another superstore. As they dug deeper, evidence came to light that the civilization revealed in the lowest strata was not Japanese but perhaps Korean. The archaeological excavations were halted; the concrete was poured. In some parts of Japanese society there is this reluctance to acknowledge that much of their culture has its origins in foreign countries. But when it comes to gardens there can be no doubting that the original influences came from China. Zen Buddhism and tea arrived in Japan from the same country, and both have given their names to a style of garden that is uniquely Japanese. One of the great strengths of the Japanese people is this ability to take foreign models, learn from them and then absorb them completely into their own culture. In the later twentieth century they did this with Western industrial and commercial practices, and, much earlier, they did it with Chinese gardens.

The components of the typical Japanese garden are thus similar to those of the Chinese, but its atmosphere is quite different. There are rocks, water and plants, but many more plants, while the rocks are less dramatically fissured and contorted. With the exception of the dry gardens, Japanese gardens are calmer and greener; and they are designed and cared for with a delicate, even fussy attention to detail. The most important difference between the two traditions is that many Japanese gardens are to be looked at, not to be walked through or lived in. They are carefully organized compositions, like beautiful pictures, and thus to be seen from a point of view dictated by the designer. They are not to be explored; indeed, the presence of humans in the garden will often upset the illusion of distance, the carefully crafted false perspective. Japanese gardens can seem almost inhumanly perfect, and the visitor will look in vain for inscribed tablets recording happy evenings spent drinking with friends. As we shall see, the Japanese stroll garden was a comparatively late development; if humans did explore earlier gardens, it was more often by boat than on foot.

The buildings in traditional Japanese gardens are more emphatically rustic than those in China, usually only a single storey high, often thatched and with none of the fanciful patterns of tracery in the windows. The light, sliding panels, covered in translucent paper, that form the walls of the Japanese house mean that interior and exterior can be united even more completely than in China, where the garden building usually has pairs of heavy doors, which can be folded back. A Japanese garden may be enclosed by a fence made of bamboo or shaggy brushwood, and this will be held together not by nails, which are too obviously man-made, but by a cord of some natural material; and, typical of a style that pays attention to the minutest detail, the knots holding the brushwood or bamboo in place will themselves be beautiful. If there is a wall around the garden, it will often be pockmarked with age, or stained with lichen, not pristine white or grey. Thus the inspiringly simple life of the countryside is brought into the town, as in Chinese gardens, but in a rather more literal way. To this day Japanese gardens are treated with a kind of reverence that the teeming multitudes of visitors to Chinese gardens seldom show; it is as if the religious origins of the earliest gardens have never been quite forgotten in Japan.

Rocks, which were worshipped in primitive Japanese religions, are weighty presences, giving a feeling of permanence and solidity to contrast with the impermanence and mutability of trees and shrubs. The stones are not piled high like the vertiginous rockeries of China; most often they are laid singly and flat, although sometimes raised to be vertical. These upright stones are never left isolated to be admired like a piece of natural sculpture, as in some Chinese gardens; rather they are grouped together, and often arranged so as to have a religious significance – for example, a large central stone supported by two lesser stones may represent Buddha and his acolytes.

From the earliest days, rocks have been immensely important in Japanese gardens; indeed, when diplomatic relations were established between China and Japan in the early seventh century, one of the first gifts the Chinese emperor sent to his Japanese counterpart was a particularly fine rock. The eleventh-century *Sakuteiki*, perhaps the earliest book in the world on the making of ornamental gardens, uses the phrase 'setting stones upright' to mean making a garden. The author issues a stern warning about how stones are to be used: 'It is unusual to set large stones in places other than beside a waterfall, on the tip of an island, or in the vicinity of a hill. In particular stones taller than 90 centimetres should not be set near any buildings. He who ignores this rule will not be able to hold onto his household; it will fall into disorder.' (Translation by Jiro Takei and Marc P. Keane.) In the eleventh century stones were still able to exert some kind of metaphysical power, it seems.

Plants, too, are treated differently in Japanese gardens. Many trees are allowed to express their own natures, the only human intervention being to prop them up when they grow old and weary; no attempt is made to disguise the props, since the age and infirmity of the trees make them more venerable. The ubiquitous pines are often delicately pruned, their downward-growing tufts of needles removed, and shrubs are sculpted into solid shapes, rounded like green boulders, or planted in billowing hedges that resemble immense green waves. Such topiary may have been a seventeenth-century import from Europe; in the earliest gardens it seems that shrubs were allowed to grow naturally. The azaleas and camellias that grow so well in Japan's acid soil are regularly subjected to extensive shaping. The result of this pruning is, of course, that many of the flowers are lost, but colour is not of the first importance in the Japanese garden, although from the earliest days the blazing but melancholy beauty of autumn leaves, especially the delicate acers, was much appreciated. Camellias were at first planted only in Buddhist monasteries where, like the fragile cherry blossom, it was the transitory beauty of their flowers that was celebrated. As a famous Japanese proverb has it: 'If it were in our power to keep the cherry blossom on the tree, we should cease so much to admire it.' Sometimes the shape of a tree is controlled in its early years so that it will later play its part in a subtle composition; for example, the lower branches may be weighted or tied down, so that they grow out flat, parallel to the surface of a nearby pool. Underfoot the damp atmosphere of maritime Japan allows a wide choice of ground-cover planting; grass grows as vigorously as in damp England, but here moss is also widely used.

Unsurprisingly water also is differently handled in a rainy country where waterfalls and streams abound. It was used in early gardens to make lakes with islands in them, following the Chinese model. But the streams in these early gardens had to flow in an auspicious direction, as the *Sakuteiki* makes clear: 'The flow of water should come from the east, pass beneath the buildings, turn to the southwest, and thus wash away all manner of evil.' It has been calculated that there are 2,488 waterfalls taller than 5 metres/16 feet in Japan, and since all oriental gardens imitate nature, we find many artificial falls in Japanese gardens. Like rocks, cascades had a religious significance; in Japan's esoteric Buddhism waterfalls were associated with Fudo, a reincarnation of the Buddha who had the power to purge evil. Allusive, metaphorical Japanese garden makers, unlike the more literal Chinese, have not always found it necessary to have real water in their gardens; raked patterns in sand or gravel, and arrangements of overlapping, flat stones, can suggest the presence of water in a garden that is entirely dry. Waterfalls also can be dry, the falling of the water suggested by the striations in the rock and the foaming stream by white pebbles. This suggestive compression seems particularly to appeal to the Japanese; the Zen priest Tessen Soki, who may have designed the famous dry garden at Ryoan-ji, wrote in his garden book of 'reducing 30,000 miles to a single foot'.

Japanese gardens are also recognizable by their furnishings, in particular stone lanterns and water basins used for washing the hands and mouth. Both of these came originally from temples, but the tea masters adopted them for the tea garden, whence they spread into all Japanese gardens.

The stone lanterns borrow their shapes from the brass lanterns used in temples; they now come in a great variety of different forms, from the snow-viewing lantern with its bowed legs and wide roof with swept-up corners, to the more sedate, compact lamps set on stone pedestals. Lamps must be of practical value, so they are to be placed in a garden where light is needed, for example at the turning of a path. They are lit in the tea garden to guide guests along the winding path to the tea house, but may also be lit on 5 February to exorcize the dark, wind spirits, and on 15 August for the Buddhist feast of the dead. Water basins were used for ritual cleansing of the hands and mouth before the worshipper entered a Shinto temple. The form of washing basin most often found in gardens is the *tsukubai*, which means 'crouching bowl', so called because the visitor had to crouch down while using it; tea masters valued this because it helped participants in the tea ceremony to achieve the necessary state of humility before they entered the tea house. Both stone lanterns and *tsukubai* are especially prized when they show signs of age, being covered in moss and lichen, or even slightly chipped, which shows their durability in the rough and tumble of the real world; some *tsukubai* are even deliberately chipped to age them, and to show the texture of the stone.

The Nezu Institute of Fine Arts, Tokyo. This museum has a lovely garden tucked away in a quiet valley below the building. The details of the garden, such as the stone lantern and the bamboo water pipe seen here, are exquisite.

This deliberate 'distressing' of garden furniture brings us to a central but abstract quality of the Japanese garden, the characteristic that the Japanese sum up in the two words – usually used in tandem – *wabi* and *sabi*. Ask any native speaker what these words mean, and they will readily begin an explanation, then pause and scratch their heads, before admitting it is almost impossible to translate everything that the phrase implies. All Japanese readily understand these words, but their meaning is so deeply embedded in the culture that it defies precise translation. *Wabi* originally meant 'isolation in rustic surroundings', often referring to the voluntary poverty and simple lives of those who took to the mountains in search of enlightenment. *Sabi* refers to the patina of age on material objects. Together these words refer to 'the beauty of things modest and humble' and 'the beauty of things imperfect, impermanent, incomplete' (Andrew Juniper).

This emphasis on the changeable, impermanent nature of the visible world, an idea central to Buddhism, is fundamental to Japanese thinking; and it is, of course, an idea more perfectly expressed in the fragile beauty of a garden than in any other art form. Everything that is alive is in a constant state of flux; only dead things are unchanging or perfectly balanced – hence the avoidance of symmetry and even numbers in classical Japanese gardens. If a group of rocks seems too complete and stable, the designer will add a *suteishi*, literally a discarded rock, to energize the composition. The solidity of rocks set against the swaying branches of trees is another way of contrasting the permanent with the transitory, but the distinction is most perfectly symbolized in the waterfall, since it is permanent only by constantly changing. This emphasis on the melancholy beauty of what is ephemeral may explain why Japanese gardens are best seen through a mist or a light rain; the dampness makes the stones shine, and adds to the composition a sombre sobriety that is an essential part of a Japanese garden's beauty.

Certainly Japanese gardens in the West are best appreciated in rainy cities – Seattle, or London, or Portland, Oregon.

Japanese culture loves to classify, enumerate and rank things; for example, the knots holding together the fence around a Japanese garden are all numbered and named. Rocks, too, have been classified into fifty-seven specific types; particularly charming is the Frolicking Bird rock. Similarly there are sixteen recognized kinds of single-trunked bonsai tree, which include the 'octopus', the 'coiled' and the 'windswept'; and ten types of waterfall, among them 'linen falling', when the water falls in a solid sheet, and 'thread falling', when the water is broken into thin streams as it falls. So it would be wrong to think of the Japanese garden as a single thing: the Japanese themselves classify their gardens into at least five kinds – the aristocratic gardens of the Heian period, the Buddhist Jodo or Pure Land (Terra Pura) gardens, the dry gardens, the tea gardens and the stroll gardens. We shall trace how these developed from original Chinese models into gardens that are distinctively and uniquely Japanese.

In the eighth-century *Nihon Shoki* (the Chronicles of Japan) we hear of a first-century emperor's delight in his garden and his pond full of carp, and the record for 612 tells of the Emperor Suiko's garden with a bridge and a representation of Mount Sumeru, the centre of the Buddhist universe, perhaps constructed by a Korean garden maker. Later a government minister was nicknamed the Lord of the Island, since he had a pond with an island in it. In these early references it is possible to detect the influence of the Chinese Islands of the Immortals, in Japanese known as Horai; like the Chinese, the Japanese believed these elusive islands were carried on the backs of giant turtles. The first official contact between China and Japan had occurred in 607, when Ono no Imoko led an embassy from the court at Nara to the Chinese capital, Ch'ang-an, and the Chinese emperor presented Suiko, his Japanese counterpart, with a particularly remarkable rock. Amazingly, one ninth-century garden still exists, the Saga-no-in, to which the Emperor Saga retired in 823. This garden, too, originally had a lake with five islands, and a waterfall which contemporary scholars think was always dry. If the theory is correct, this is the first Japanese departure from Chinese models – unless, that is, there were dry gardens in China of which no record exists. A few years earlier, Japan had moved her capital from Nara to Heian-kyo, the Capital of Peace and Tranquillity, present-day Kyoto. This city was laid out on a rigid grid pattern in imitation of the Chinese capital. A central avenue ran from the southern gate, Rashomon, to the imperial compound, and aristocrats were given rectangular parcels of land closer to or further from the imperial precinct according to their rank. Two rivers enclosed the city – to the east the Kamo River and to the west the Katsura – so there was no shortage of water in the gardens of the new capital.

Before we go on to examine the Kyoto gardens of the extraordinary Heian period, we should pause to consider the spiritual beliefs that have had an influence not only on these early gardens but on the whole tradition of garden-making in Japan, Shinto and Buddhism. Shinto is an animist religion, which encourages the worship of natural spirits, *kami*, found in rocks and trees. Sacred trees, usually of tremendous age, are identified by the *shimenawa*, the straw cord that is hung around their girth to keep away evil spirits. To this day the 1,000-year-old ginkgo tree in the city of Sendai is worshipped as a deity. The word *niwa*, which today signifies garden, originally referred to the area that had been cleansed for the arrival of Shinto *kami* – an early example of the garden being a place where humans and divinities can establish contact. It was part of the Shinto tradition to wash the hands and mouth before entering this sacred precinct, but traditional washing basins can now be found also in Buddhist monastery gardens and tea gardens. Less visible but much more widespread in its influence is the reverence for nature that Shinto encourages, which in part explains the respect still accorded to gardens in Japan.

Spreading from India, Buddhism reached China in the first century AD, Korea in the fourth century and Japan in the sixth century. One of the Sutras that became hugely influential in garden-making was the description of the Pure Land or Western Paradise of Amitabha, God of Light, whom the Japanese call Amida. The Indian text taught that Amida would welcome the spirits of those who followed him into a paradise of sensual pleasures, which included a garden with a lake, golden sands, jewelled flowers and exotic birds. Here the souls of the saved would be reborn to eternal life on a flowering lotus. Also deeply influential in Japan, as we have seen, has been the Buddhist emphasis on the insubstantiality and transience of the visible universe.

The extraordinary Heian period lasted from 794 to 1192; it was a period of comparative peace, which encouraged the flowering of a remarkable culture. This culture was almost exclusively Japanese, since the country was in one of its 'closed' periods; the last official embassy to the T'ang dynasty in China was in 894 and the last contact with Korea in 928. Thus the only foreigner mentioned in *The Tale of Genji*, a novel written in the early years of the eleventh century, is the Korean astrologer in chapter one. In theory the emperor ruled, but real power was in the hands of the chief ministers, who were members of the Fujiwara clan. The dominant religion at the court

The Japanese Garden, Seattle. This is a stroll garden; as the visitor follows the path round the lake, different views emerge. In contrast to Chinese gardens, Japanese gardens are often densely planted. The flat, seemingly rustic bridge is typically Japanese.

was Esoteric Buddhism with its elaborate rituals, often accompanied by chanting of the Sutras, and sometimes by quite violent rites of exorcism. We know about life at the Heian court not only from paintings of the period but from the books written by two remarkable women, the Lady Murasaki, author of *The Tale of Genji*, and Sei Shonagon, whose *Pillow Book* is still in print. The imperial court encouraged a cult of sensuous beauty, which was found in music, calligraphy, the harmony of colours in a woman's clothes, the scents mixed and worn by men, and in the poems improvised on the spur of the moment in response to a challenge or composed during a poem-writing competition. garden-making was also encouraged, although no secular garden of the Heian period has come down to us. The principal imperial garden was the Shinsen-en, the Garden of Divine Spring; it contained a large lake, as always to the south of the palace, with a white sand 'beach' in imitation of the Japanese coast, a spring, a stream, a hill and at least one pavilion. Its 12 hectares/30 acres were used both for social occasions and for religious ceremonies, such as the Prayer for Rain.

Noblemen, too, had extensive gardens, which often imitated natural scenes to be found in the Japanese countryside. This was paradoxical because usually courtiers disdained the country, since it was the source of everything that was boorish and uncivilized, even threatening; there was a common fear at the court of being exiled to the remote regions of Japan – something that happened even to the shining prince, Genji. Nature was beautiful in the controlled environment of the garden, but having to live for any length of time among scenes of untamed nature was more than a civilized courtier could bear. One nobleman had a sand bar laid out in his garden and planted it with contorted pines in imitation of a celebrated coastal scene on the Sea of Japan. Even more elaborate was the ninth-century imitation of the Bay of Matsushima, one of Japan's Three Scenic Wonders, which Minamoto no Toru created at his Riverbank Villa. He went to the lengths of replicating the salt kiln to be found at Matsushima, and had seawater brought from the coast which was boiled to produce salt. This was an attempt to bring the inspiration of nature into the life of the court by imitating it in a very literal way.

In the great novel *The Tale of Genji*, written in the early years of the eleventh century, the hero himself turned garden designer, aiming not to copy nature literally, but rather to create views, like a painter, which the guests in his villa would particularly appreciate. This is Arthur Waley's translation: Genji 'effected a great improvement in the appearance of the grounds [of his villa] by a judicious handling of knoll and lake, for though such features were already there in abundance, he found it necessary here to cut away a slope, there to dam a stream, that each occupant of the various quarters might look out of her window upon such a prospect as pleased her best'. Thus one of his lady friends had a garden that was at its best in autumn, her favourite season, and another a garden that was beautiful in spring. The range of plants Genji used was extensive – cherry, of course, wisteria, lespedeza, kerria, azalea, red plum, bamboo, deutzia, briar rose, tree peony and orange, 'whose scent reawakens forgotten love', a characteristically Japanese note of sombre nostalgia. He even introduced plants 'brought from wild and inaccessible places . . . so seldom seen that no one knew what names to call them'. And all this to please a lady who was a native of such an uncivilized place. The spring garden was particularly attractive to the young, especially 'the little wood on the hill beyond the lake, the bridge that joined the two islands, the mossy banks that seemed to grow greener not every day but every hour'. To satisfy these young people, Genji had boats made in the Chinese style, with prows shaped like dragons or birds, so that the garden could be explored. Paths were scarce, though we read that some were luxuriously covered in jade dust; perhaps it is legitimate to wonder how often they were meant to be walked on.

Koishikawa Koraku-en, Tokyo. This, too, is a stroll garden, the oldest in Tokyo, dating from the early seventeenth century. Waterfalls are common in rainy Japan, and they have been classified into various types; here we see the type called 'falling threads'.

Gardens of this period, when Chinese influence was still strong, were not just pictorial compositions: they were also used by the inhabitants of the villa. Genji's gardens, for example, were animated not only by boating parties but by football, the courtly form of the game, known in Japanese as *kemari*; we read that in the setting of the garden 'the rough, noisy game suddenly took on an unwonted gentleness and grace. This, no doubt, was in part due to the characters of the players, but also to the influence of the scene about them. For all around were great clumps of flowering bushes and trees, every blossom now open to its full.' Gardens were also used for music making and for poetry competitions. A form of the latter had been borrowed from China; it involved floating a wine cup down a winding stream past the players, each of whom had to improvise a set of verses before the wine cup reached him, the penalty for failure being to drain the cup of its contents.

This physical pleasure in the garden contrasts with a melancholia, much more idiosyncratically Japanese, which characters find in gardens throughout the novel: 'One autumn day when the chrysanthemums in front of the palace had wilted to the loveliest hue, and the rainy sky had a melancholy beauty of its own' are the opening words of one section. This pleasure in the beauty of dying chrysanthemums is echoed in Murasaki's diary: she tells of preparations for a visit by the emperor which included the planting of chrysanthemums, some of which were coming into bloom, but some were chosen just because they were 'fading to various hues'. Morning glory was also admired precisely because its beauty was transient, a reminder of what Murasaki calls in her novel 'the shifting fabric of the visible world'. Cherry blossom, the Japanese flower above all others, offered a similar melancholy pleasure. Murasaki's novel was enormously influential and scenes from Genji's garden were recreated in the seventeenth century by Prince Toshihito and his son Prince Noritada.

The *Sakuteiki* came out of this same sophisticated world. The author was almost certainly Tachibana no Toshitsuna (1028–94), the illegitimate son of Fujiwara no Yorimuchi, an important member of the all-powerful Fujiwara clan. The book is a strange mixture of practical advice on building gardens, geomantic superstition and aesthetic judgment. Among the ideas he lists as basics, two are fundamental themes in all Japanese garden-making. 'When creating a garden, let the exceptional work of past master gardeners be your guide' typifies the conservatism of all oriental gardening; the 'secret' learning was handed down from the garden master to his disciples. A fifteenth-century book on garden-making begins with these imperious words: 'If you have not received the oral tradition, you must not make gardens.' The second basic concept of the *Sakuteiki* is: 'Visualise the famous landscapes of our country and come to understand their most interesting points. Re-create the essence of these scenes, but do so interpretatively, not strictly.' This seems to be a direct criticism of the 'salt kiln' style, the literal reconstruction of natural landscapes, and much more in tune with Chinese emphasis on the garden's providing not an imitation of nature but the quintessence of nature itself.

Toshitsuna also insists that the garden maker should 'create a subtle atmosphere'; the word he uses in Japanese is *fuzei*, made up of two characters which separately mean 'wind' and 'feeling', which wonderfully encapsulates how fleeting and intangible is the mood of a garden. An important section of his book deals with taboos: 'If so much as one of these taboos is violated, the master of the household will fall ill and eventually die, and his land will fall into desolation and become the abode of devils.' These taboos are all connected with geomancy: for example, 'Do not set a stone that is higher than the veranda in the immediate vicinity of the house. If this rule is not obeyed, troubles will follow one after the other, and the master of the household will not live for long.' So important was this pseudo-science that there was a Bureau of Geomancy at the Heian court. If this seems naive, Toshitsuna's understanding of perspective and composition is remarkably sophisticated. In writing of waterfalls he says: 'If the main point of view is from the right side, set a good-looking stone of reasonable height above the left Bracketing Stone; above the right-hand Bracketing Stone set a shorter stone that will show the left side to its best advantage. If the main viewpoint is from the left side, the opposite holds true.' Notice the emphasis on the precise point from which the composition is to be viewed.

Geomancy dictated that gardens should always lie on the auspicious side of the house, which was the south, and that water should flow from east to west. The west was to take on greater significance with the rise of the cult of Amida and his Western Paradise. In the later Heian period more and more people began to turn to this form of Buddhism with its emphasis on individual salvation, as they rejected Esoteric Buddhism and its elaborate, court-centred rituals. The gardens of this Jodo or Pure Land (Terra Pura) style were developed from the lake gardens of the earlier Heian period. Usually the temple of Amida was sited to the west, beyond a lake, and, balancing it, to the east we often find a temple representing this world. The best remaining example of this style is the Byodo-in garden at Uji. Built in the early eleventh century by Fujiwara Michinaga and remodelled by his son Yorimichi, the Phoenix Hall, an impressively Chinese-style building, looks across the Ajiike pond. Directly in front of the room containing the Amida image a stone lantern reminds us that Amida was the god of light.

Originally the garden at Saiho-ji on the outskirts of Kyoto was also a Jodo or paradise garden with two temples, but later it was reworked by Muso Soseki (1275–1352) as a dry garden, in a period when Zen was becoming the dominant form of Buddhism in Japan. Saiho-ji is now famous for the mosses that blanket the ground, the product of neglect in the nineteenth century, but it is also celebrated because in this garden the visitor can find the elements of several Japanese garden styles. The lake with its islands is typical of the Heian aristocratic style, as is the recreation of real scenery in miniature; the peninsula with a rocky island off its tip imitates the Shima peninsula. The dry cataract in the upper garden with its mantle of moss now seems the product of nature, as does the 'island' in the shape of a turtle, swimming in a sea of moss, but in reality both are Muso's creations in the later, Zen style. As part of this development towards a minimalist, dry garden, the brightly flowering trees were allowed to die and not replaced. Muso built a pavilion here which does not survive, but which was much imitated, as we shall see. He also laid out a path around the lake, an early example, perhaps, of what was to become the stroll garden. This development of Saiho-ji from a Heian aristocratic garden to a Western Paradise garden, and then into a Zen-style, dry garden, is symptomatic of what was happening in Japan during the post-Heian period.

As the influence of the effete court and the Fujiwara clan began to decline, civil war broke out between various warrior families. For a time the capital was moved to Kamakura, before Ashikaga Takauji moved it back to Kyoto in 1334 and gave himself the title of shogun. Zen Buddhism with its lack of ritual and emphasis on quiet, individual meditation in the search for enlightenment was well suited to this period of turmoil and social disorder. Zen teachings had been brought back from China by the priest known as Yosai or Eisai (1141–1215), who founded the Japanese Zen sect Rinzai. The new shogunate was keen to promote this form of Buddhism to emphasize its difference from the imperial court with its rituals of Esoteric Buddhism.

Muso Soseki was not only a garden maker; as the leading Zen monk of his period, he also developed a nationwide network of Zen monasteries, which wielded considerable political influence. Many gardens are ascribed to him, but it is doubtful if a man so busy with teaching, running his monasteries and acting as an adviser to the government would have had time for much garden design. He had studied with Chinese teachers, including one sent over to Japan by Kublai Khan as a peace offering after the Chinese ruler's failed attempt to conquer the country. It is no surprise, then, to find renewed Chinese influence in these gardens, with outdoor corridors (*lang*) connecting one building with another, and the buildings themselves were often of two storeys, unlike earlier Japanese buildings with their modest, single storey. Muso was criticized by contemporary Zen priests for being too worldly, and too interested in gardens: a monk at the Toji temple wrote: 'People practising Zen should not construct gardens . . . for how can one remain in a deep state of Zen if one cannot detach oneself from the daily sorrows that disturb the heart' – sorrows fostered, of course, by the ephemeral pleasures of a garden. Despite such opposition Muso's influence was so great that he was given the title *kokushi*, teacher of the nation.

Muso was appointed first abbot of Tenryu-ji, the Temple of the Heavenly Dragon. This building had begun life as the palace of the Emperor Gosaga, who had retired there in 1256, but in 1339 it was turned into a Rinzai Zen monastery and the Shogun ordained that prayers should be said there

Tenryu-ji Temple, Kyoto. This villa was turned into a Rinzai Zen monastery in 1339 with the famous garden maker Muso as its first abbot. On the far side of the pool, to the right, the dry waterfall and the contrastingly horizontal stone-slab bridge can be seen.

for the soul of the Emperor Go Daigo, who had died in exile. Muso had chosen the site, and he was ordered to redesign the garden in the dry style, as he had done at Saiho-ji. In several ways this garden breaks decisively with the Heian tradition: the lake is too small for boating, and it is not to the south of the main building, the abbot's quarters; nor does it contain a central major island. The remarkable features of Tenryu-ji, which are still visible, are gathered at the far side of the lake, where a horizontal stone bridge makes a striking contrast with the vertical accent of the dry waterfall. In the midst of the lower part of the dry fall there is a pointed rock, which has been identified as a carp stone. This refers to the belief (Chinese in origin) that if a carp could leap to the top of the waterfall, it would be transformed into a dragon, a metaphor for spiritual striving intended to inspire the monks in their attempts to achieve enlightenment. In China the leaping carp had also been a metaphor, but for a more mundane form of success, passing the civil service exam; the humble candidate would be thus transformed into a powerful mandarin.

The rocks for this dry work at Tenryu-ji are blue/black and brown/black schist from Kishu, which must have been brought by boat along the coast and up the river. Their stripey colours are intended not only to suggest falling water but also, perhaps, to remind the viewer of the inks used in Chinese landscape painting of the Song period. In front of this dry fall is another fine composition, a rock island made up of one tall, pointed stone and several attendant stones with flat tops. The view from the abbot's quarters is composed in three planes, foreground, middle ground and distance, which may suggest further influence from Song landscape painting. The planting includes azaleas and irises, pine, for the resilience of the evergreen, contrasting with maple, whose dramatic autumn colours last only a day or two; the maples of this area were already famous at the time of the *Tale of Genji*. The Emperor Go Daigo had been exiled to Yoshino, so cherry trees from that district, which he had admired, were included in the planting. The trees grew tall, but when a storm blew them down the 'borrowed' landscape (in Japanese *sakkei*) of the surrounding hills was revealed as part of the composition.

By the time the third Ashikaga shogun, Yoshimitsu, grandson of Takauji, came to power, the state was at peace, so he could devote himself to the arts and philosophy. He was a serious student of Zen and an admirer of all things Chinese. On retirement from his official position in 1394, he took the vows of a Zen monk and moved to an old palace that had been built in the style typical

Tenryu-ji Temple, Kyoto. The simple, single-stone bridge connects the mainland to the eastern island. Koi carp are found in many monastery pools, and are often very tame.

of the Heian nobility, with the house facing a lake. Yoshimitsu's building, however, did not face the lake, but stood in it, although the lake has now shrunk, so the building today stands at its edge. And his building was a swaggering three storeys high, in the Chinese style. The ceiling of the top storey was gilded and for this reason it was called the Kinkaku-ji or Golden Pavilion. In 1950 the original building was burned down and its replacement is gilded, perhaps rather too opulently, on the outside of the upper two storeys. This opulence is hardly appropriate for a Zen monastery, but we should remember that the original building was used not only for meditation but for parties, plays and poetry competitions, in conscious imitation of the high culture of the Heian period.

The lake, which dates from the thirteenth century when it was celebrated by the poet Teika, is known as Kyokochi, the Mirror Lake, and its shore line, perhaps to suggest the seashore of Japan, is crowded with rocks; many of these were given by nobles seeking to gain favour with the Shogun, and the names of the donors are still preserved. There is a path around the lake but many of the rock compositions on the islands, which are concealed when looking from the pavilion, are best seen from boats, as in Heian gardens. A long, stony peninsula divides the composition into foreground and background; the former is crowded with islands, many in the shape of turtles, recalling the mythical Islands of the Immortals held aloft on the backs of giant turtles. The perspective is carefully controlled by crowding the nearer part of the lake, while the further part is empty; also the pines on the main island are pruned to a size that adds to the effect of distance. At the base of the hill there are two springs, from which it is said Yoshimitsu took the water for his tea; these seem to imitate Muso's treatment of the spring at Saiho-ji. One of the pools is fed by the Dragon Gate Cascade, again with a carp stone, but here the fall contains real water.

Heian splendour returned briefly to this garden in 1408 when the powerless emperor deigned to visit the newly completed estate with his retinue; there were boating parties, poetry competitions, music and feasting. After Yoshimitsu's death, and in accordance with his wishes, the Golden Pavilion estate was turned into a memorial temple, and its correct name is now Rokuon-ji, the Temple of the Deer Park – a reference not to animals but to the place where the Buddha first preached to his disciples after his enlightenment. It is worth noticing also that this is a Zen temple with no dry garden.

Yoshimitsu's grandson, Yoshimasa (1435–90), who became the eighth shogun of the Ashikaga dynasty, was also a great patron of the arts and a passionate admirer of the garden at Saiho-ji, which he visited several times each year. Thus when he came to build his retirement garden it is no surprise that the main building, the Silver Pavilion, was an imitation of the Ruri-den, one of Muso's buildings at Saiho-ji, which has since disappeared. Myth has it that the building was to be covered in silver leaf, though no evidence of this intention has been found. As a devotee of Zen, he would rather have prized the simplicity of the building in its present state, nestling among trees. The Silver Pavilion is much more modest than the Golden Pavilion; it shows the Chinese influence in the bell-shaped windows of the upper storey, but the lower is more Japanese, with screens that can be removed to allow an uninterrupted view of the garden. The hillside spring is again an almost exact reproduction of the one designed by Muso 150 years earlier at Saiho-ji. The lake is comparatively small, with a series of small islands joined by bridges, so it seems this garden was to be explored on foot, following a twisting path from whose surface random stones protrude to ensure that the visitor walks slowly. The waterfall is similar to that at the Golden Pavilion, but is here called the Moon Washing Spring. One of Yoshimasa's pleasures was waiting for the moon to rise over the neighbouring hills, although, as a devoted Zen student, he might have argued that the waiting is better than the fulfilment of expectation.

Originally there were twelve buildings on the site, but only two have survived, the Silver Pavilion (perhaps so called as it was silvered by the moonlight) and the Togu-do, which now contains an image of Yoshimasa dressed as a monk and, more significantly, a room for taking tea. This is one of the earliest surviving examples of a room dedicated to tea drinking, but at this period the formalized rituals of the tea ceremony had not been developed; tea was taken simply as an aid to concentrated Zen meditation. Today, in the lower garden, there is a white, gravel sea, raked into wavelets, and a cone of the same gravel with a flat top. These attempts at a dry garden do not harmonize with the composition as a whole and were almost certainly added later. Some say the garden was designed by the famous painter Soami, who was certainly one of the many artists encouraged by the Shogun, but it may be that it is the work of Yoshimasa himself. Certainly the garden we see today, merging with the forest and with its azaleas only gently pruned, seems more natural than many Japanese gardens. When he died, Yoshimasa, like his grandfather, willed that his estate should become a Rinzai Zen monastery, in which the garden played an important part; for a Zen adept, nature itself was a source of inspiration, since the Buddha himself was immanent in every natural object.

The simplicity and restraint of Jisho-ji – the correct name for the Silver Pavilion since Jisho was Yoshimasa's Buddhist name – may also have been a response to the turmoil of the time. In 1466 civil war broke out between two powerful families; these struggles are usually called the Onin Wars, after the place where they began. For ten years the country was divided against itself and cities sacked. In the end Kyoto was in ruins; even comparatively distant places, like the temples at Saiho-ji and the Golden Pavilion, had been burned to the ground and their gardens ransacked. After such a traumatic period it was perhaps felt inappropriate to build luxurious pavilions and expensive gardens. It may be such a feeling that explains, too, why the last part of the fifteenth century saw the creation of many of the most famous dry gardens. The samurai warrior class found

BELOW *Daitoku-ji Temple, Kyoto. The Zen monastery was founded in the early fourteenth century by Kokushi, whose honorific title was 'teacher of the nation'. It was much damaged during the Onin Wars, but was rebuilt in the fifteenth century.*

a particular appeal in the teachings of Zen Buddhism with their direct path to enlightenment, unmediated by any priest, and their emphasis on unsparing self-discipline, total self-reliance and direct action. One famous samurai garden, built far from the capital in the eighteenth century, has come down to us – the dry garden at Hofu made by Katsura Tadaharu. Simple, plain, dry gardens – the Japanese expression *kara sansui* means literally 'dry mountain water' – are often associated entirely and exclusively with Zen, but this is wrong; as we have seen, the Saga-no-in may have contained a dry waterfall in the ninth century, well before Zen had taken such a hold in Japan. And books on Japanese gardens written in the eighteenth and nineteenth centuries make no connection between dry gardens and Zen. This garden style is rather the ultimate expression of the ascetic minimalism so dear to the Japanese heart; we find it also in bonsai plants and haikus. In the early fourteenth century Muso had written a poem praising this kind of garden, entitled 'Echoes of a Mock Landscape':

> Not a grain of dust is raised
> Yet soar the mountain ranges.
> Not a drop of water is there
> Yet falls the cataract.

With the slenderest of means the imagination of the viewer is stimulated.

The most famous dry garden in Japan is certainly Ryoan-ji, the Garden of the Peaceful Dragon. Before the construction of the Zen temple this had been a twelfth-century Heian lake garden; the scarlet *torii* or gate of a Shinto shrine can still be seen on the island. The Zen temple was built in 1450, almost immediately burned down in the Onin Wars and rebuilt in 1488, at which time

ABOVE *Daitoku-ji Temple, Kyoto. This abstract dry garden contrasts with the famous dry garden of Daisen-in, a sub-monastery of Daitoku-ji, which is more pictorial.*

a dry garden was created to the south of the monastery's main hall. The 30 by 10 metre garden/ 98 by 32 feet we see today cannot date from this period; early eighteenth-century prints show cherry trees growing in the garden, and a composition of nine stones, not the present fifteen. The cherry trees may have been expelled from the dry garden, but in blossom time they still tempt the eye to stray from the ascetic purity of rocks and sand, waving their beautiful flowers just outside the wall that encloses the garden, thus emphasizing all that the dry garden lacks, or, more precisely, has turned its back on. The wall itself, made of clay boiled in oil, may not be original either; the site may once have been open, with long views down the slope and away to the wooded hills. The monastery was again destroyed by a fire in 1779 and the garden with the fifteen rocks we see today was probably constructed after that date; certainly a print of 1799 shows the present layout of stones. Another possibility is that the rocks were rearranged after the 1779 fire, with only the great stone at the back left in its original place; this stone is signed with the names Hikojiro and Kotaro, the foremen of the fifteenth-century stoneworkers who had made the original garden. A signed garden is a rarity in any culture, at any time.

And what does this garden mean? For a Zen monk that is the wrong question, since Zen seeks to disable the rational intellect, which constantly fills the mind with ideas and questions, thus distracting the student from the path to enlightenment. A much more positive step towards enlightenment is to empty the mind, in itself no easy task. The very emptiness of this garden is its point. Here there are none of the sensuous pleasures we expect in an ordinary garden; there are no sounds, no smells, and we may not touch the rocks. As in the Muso poem quoted above, everything must come to us through our eyes and then our minds. But there is nothing: just fifteen rocks,

ABOVE *Ryoan-ji Temple, Kyoto. The most famous of the dry gardens, composed of fifteen rocks, raked pebbles and moss. The whole is surrounded by a wall of boiled clay. On the right are visitors absorbed in viewing this empty garden.*

with eddies of moss around some of them, pleasingly arranged in raked sand. There is no point from which we can see the whole composition, so we must explore, as in any good garden; but here only with our minds and eyes. Some see the pattern of rocks as miniature islands poking up out of an ocean; the sand raked into swirls around the rocks certainly nudges the visitor towards the idea of moving water. Others see a movement from left to right, from the five-rock group to the smaller groups. Whatever this garden may mean, it is certainly not an aid to meditation, though the raking of the gravel may form part of the monks' self-discipline. Zen monks needed no external, physical object on which to meditate; such an object would only be a distraction. The 'bearded barbarian', Bodhidharma, who brought Zen from India to China, summed up his teaching as:

A special transmission outside the scriptures;
No dependence upon words and letters;
Direct pointing to the soul of man;
Seeing into one's own nature.

Seeking to derive meanings from fifteen stones, some moss and sand can only divert the mind from this 'direct pointing'.

Some have suggested that the garden at Ryoan-ji was designed by the painter Soami, and the same ascription has been made for another dry garden, that at Daisen-in. There is no decisive evidence that he designed either garden. In 1513 Kogaku Soku retired as abbot of the Zen monastery of Daitoku-ji and founded the sub-temple of Daisen-in. His residence was decorated with landscape paintings by Soami (this is certain), and his dry garden is surely an imitation of a landscape painting. In an area of 100 square metres/119 square yards, nowhere more than 3 metres/10 feet deep, we see miniature mountains, a dry waterfall and a white gravel stream pouring down into a placid, pebbly ocean. All this is to be viewed from a low, sitting position either on the wooden terrace or inside the residence. The 'waterfall' is created by a remarkable rock with white, quartz striations and, as at Tenryu-ji, its vertical makes a striking contrast with the flat horizontal of a slab bridge. In 1961 the garden was restored and a corridor-bridge (probably replacing one found in the original garden, though there is much discussion) divides the garden into two; this offers views of the garden through bell-shaped windows like the ones seen in the upper storey of the Silver Pavilion. Where the 'water' flows into the flat of the 'ocean', a boat-shaped rock floats at anchor; this may have come from Yoshimasa's garden at Ginkaku-ji. After the destruction of Kyoto during the Onin Wars, many of the gardens were abandoned and fine stones were easily removed.

These dry gardens were cheaper to construct and more durable than the luxurious gardens of the earlier Muramachi period – two advantages not to be overlooked in times of political uncertainty. During the sixteenth century, though, the disorders that had plagued Japan since the Onin Wars were finally brought under some kind of control by two great warlords – Toyotomi Hideyoshi and Tokugawa Ieyasu; the latter founded a dynasty that ruled Japan until the mid nineteenth century. They devised a social system that was in many ways feudal; at the top was the emperor, powerless but the source of the shogun's authority; then came the shogun; below him were the local lords, the daimyo, and then the samurai.

BELOW *Sanpo-in, Kyoto. One of Japan's six most famous gardens. Many of its stones were brought here from Hideyoshi's Palace of Accumulated Pleasures. As the path makes clear, this is another example of a stroll garden.*

Hideyoshi was a remarkable character; because he was born a peasant, he could never assume the title of shogun, but there was no doubting his power. In 1588 he invited the Emperor to visit his newly finished palace and garden called Juraku-dai; quite deliberately this had been built on the site of a Heian-period imperial palace. The visit lasted five days and included the usual poetry competitions, music, dancing and feasting. Hideyoshi was something of a megalomaniac; his garden had to be larger and more opulent than any other. To this end he ransacked the gardens of others to bring together a remarkable collection of stones. But Juraku-dai lasted only four years and many of these stones were subsequently transferred to the garden of Sanpo-in (sometimes in English written Sambo-in). This temple was also used by Hideyoshi for his lavish parties, and the garden we can visit today is still stuffed full of the remarkable stones he collected. He wanted no one to be in doubt that he was the most powerful man in Japan, with the result that the garden is overwhelming and overcrowded. The designer was Yoshiro, whose gifts were recognized in his honorific title Kentai, excellent gardener. Sanpo-in is made up of the usual lake, islands and a waterfall; the last caused many problems and had to be remodelled three times before Kentai and the abbot were satisfied.

During the late fifteenth and early sixteenth centuries tea drinking began to take on a new significance; it was a secular, social activity which allowed members of different classes – merchants and scholars, daimyo and samurai – to meet and talk peacefully about their non-political, often aesthetic interests. Secular it may have been, but that did not mean that it was devoid of moral or spiritual significance. Tea had originally been imported from China, where it had been taken by monks to keep them awake while meditating. But for the Japanese, with their love of ritual and regulation, it was not enough merely to drink: there had to be rules governing how to prepare oneself for the ceremony, how to make the tea (using powdered leaves and a whisk), how the guests

Ginkaku-ji Temple, Kyoto. The Silver Pavilion was built in 1482 by Yoshimasa as a villa; it became a monastery after his death. The natural landscape of hills and woods is incorporated into the garden. The Silver Pavilion is on the left, projecting into the lake.

should behave and so on. Thus the tea ceremony was born. At Ginkaku-ji the tea room was, by contrast, a simple, small room named Shuko-an, the retreat of Shuko, the Zen monk who led the unceremonious tea drinking.

It was the sixteenth-century master Sen no Rikyu (1522–91) who formulated the rules that govern the ceremony to this day. The tea house, he said, should be small, rustic in design, with a low doorway, so that those entering have to humble themselves by bending. Inside there would be no decoration, but a small alcove in one wall, called the *tokonama*, should contain a single beautiful object. Outside there was to be a stone where samurai would stand to take off their swords, a basin where hands and mouth could be washed, a stone lantern to light the way and a winding stone path – to be negotiated slowly – leading from the rustic gate to the door of the tea house, or to the hut where guests wait until they are invited to enter. All these elements help to induce the right state of mind in the participants – peacefulness, concentration, humility and courtesy.

The garden of the tea house also contributed to this psychological preparation. It was designed to be walked through, slowly, and not to be admired; rather it acts as an airlock between the disorderly, grubby workaday world and the calm beauty of the tea house. Usually the tea-house garden is divided into two parts by a simple bamboo fence, the outer part containing the hut where the guests wait until the tea master invites them to the ceremony. In a seventeenth-century tea manual Chasho Senrin writes of the tea house garden: 'Trees should not be planted, nor stones arranged, nor sand scattered, nor gravel designed – such things distract a person's mind; they confuse and destroy the spirituality of the ceremony itself.' As another seventeenth-century manual has it, the tea garden should 'look like the hermitage of a recluse found in the shadow of an old forest in the countryside. A thicket should be planted, a narrow path should be laid out, a gate of plaited bamboo or a garden wicket be constructed. In appearance it should be simple and calm.' Clearly there is something here of the urban myth that all country life is simple and pure. Also there should be few flowers in the garden of the tea house.

Despite which the tea master Rikyu grew fine morning glories in his garden, and one day the dictator Hideyoshi asked to come and see them. He was furious when he found not one flower remaining in Rikyu's garden. On entering the tea house, however, he found one perfect blossom displayed in the *tokonama*. This is another example of the minimalism and concentration of Zen; a single flower will demand and be given total attention, when a garden full of flowers might be given only a cursory glance. A final example of the artful naturalness, or the natural artfulness, of the tea garden: one day Rikyu asked his son to sweep the garden before guests arrived for the ceremony. His son swept the garden with the greatest care, but Rikyu was not satisfied. The son swept it again, but still his father was not happy. Rikyu came into the garden, looked at the perfectly swept ground and, reaching up to a tree which was in the full glory of its autumn colours, he shook the branch until a scattering of jewel-like leaves lay on the ground. Finally, he was satisfied.

Tea gardens were the first Japanese gardens to be designed by lay people; earlier garden designers had all been monks, known as *ishitate-so*, priests who place stones. The most celebrated designer of the early seventeenth century, however, Kobori Enshu (1579–1647), was an aristocrat, a daimyo, tea master and commissioner of public works. As with other famous garden makers, many gardens are ascribed to him on the basis of no evidence at all. But we know he was closely involved with the garden at Konchi-in, a sub-temple of perhaps the most powerful Zen temple in Japan, Nanzen-ji. The influential abbot of the monastery, Suden, had served as a knight under the first of the Tokugawa shoguns, Ieyasu, and it was he who called in Kobori Enshu. The garden was begun in 1611, but not finished until 1632 when Kentai, the outstanding gardener, took only two weeks to place all the rocks that had been selected for the garden.

The pond garden is divided from the dry garden by a simple Shinto *torii* or gateway. The dry garden is an oddity, as it is laid out in a narrow, long strip, not unlike Daisen-in; this lack of depth is emphasized because the garden is seen from the terrace of the main hall across a wide, very long belt of raked, white gravel. The main axis of the composition runs through the centre of the temple's main hall, out into the garden, through a stone square and between two mounds.

These mounds represent two islands, the turtle island on the left and the crane island on the right. And if we have missed the references to the Islands of the Immortals, there is an arrangement of rocks representing Mount Horai for good measure. The garden is not walled but bounded by a slope, thickly planted with trees; on the right stands a small shrine dedicated to prayers for the soul of Ieyasu. The programme of the whole garden is a kind of prayer that the first Tokugawa shogun has achieved a place among the Immortals. And, for the first time in a Japanese garden, we are aware of a certain symmetry in the layout.

In 1615 the Shogun issued the Edict for the Conduct of the Nobility, which included these clear instructions for the emperor and his court: 'The imperial court shall keep to the arts, and, above all, pursue learning.' garden-making was clearly one of the arts that was permitted them, and two notable gardens were constructed by members of the imperial family, under the influence of Enshu, and perhaps with his help. One of these was the garden at the Katsura detached palace, the first stroll garden (note the relaxed verb), in Japan, completed in 1659; some have ascribed it to Enshu, who was dead by the time of its completion, but almost certainly it is the work of Prince Hachijo no Miya Toshihito and his son Noritada, who were Enshu's friends.

Many earlier Japanese gardens had included paths as one means of exploring them, but this was the first time the path deliberately controlled the views the visitor has of the garden, using a technique the Japanese call *mie-gakure*, which means 'seen and hidden'. The main path at Katsura twists and turns, enticing the visitor into a leisurely exploration; the variety of different surfaces adds to the pleasure of visitors, while controlling the pace at which they move. Perhaps the fact that the hero of *The Tale of Genji* had a country retreat in the Katsura area inspired the designers,

ABOVE *Nanzen-ji, Kyoto. This was one of the most powerful Zen monasteries, and has several sub-monasteries such as Tenju-an, whose garden we see here. The formal topiary may only date from the nineteenth century and be an imported fashion.*

for this garden deliberately recalls scenes from the novel, and thus it may, in some ways, seem quite old fashioned. The lake contains islands joined by bridges, all of which are high enough to let a boat pass underneath; so even if the visitor does not explore the garden by boat, it is possible to imagine a boat, perhaps with musicians on board, passing along the canals. In other ways, too, Katsura is conservative and backward looking: there is an imitation, necessarily in miniature, of one of Japan's most famous pieces of natural scenery, the sand bar at Ama-no-hashidate. A promontory covered in smooth stones adds to the illusion of the seaside, though the stone lantern at the end, which may represent a lighthouse, is perhaps a step too far. But in other ways the garden breaks with tradition; the house faces not south, as a Heian palace would have done, but south-west, perhaps to have a better view of the rising moon. One of the five tea houses, the Geppa Ro, was specifically sited for watching the moon rise. Most surprising is the curious hint of European influence in the straight paths, lined with trees or trim hedges; the walk leading to the Sumiyoshi pine and Miyuki-michi Lane are two examples. We are not used to straight lines in an oriental garden.

In 1629 the Emperor Gomizuno-o retired at the early age of thirty-five, worn down by constant tensions with the Shogun Iemitsu – tensions which were not eased when the Shogun insisted the Emperor marry Ieyasu's granddaughter. Gomizuno-o first created a garden in central Kyoto with the help of Kobori Enshu, and later a country retreat on the lower slopes of Mount Hiei, just outside the city. If it is not dry, a Japanese garden must have a lake, but it was no easy matter to build one on such a steeply sloping site; the problem was solved with a huge earth dam, 200 metres/218 yards long and 15 metres/49 feet high. Originally there were three villas and gardens at Shugaku-in, but the lower two have been neglected and now it is the upper garden,

BELOW *Shugakuin Imperial Villa, Kyoto. The seventeenth-century garden is built on the lower slopes of Mount Hiei to take advantage of the views. But building a lake on a slope was no easy matter. The Turret-Shaped Lantern was used to light the old path beside this stream.*

restored in the 1820s, that the visitor sees. The villa and the garden merge gently with the woodland and, with the exception of the dam, the hand of man is little visible. This, too, is a stroll garden with a footpath round the lake and bridges linking the islands, but, as in Chinese gardens, there are pavilions along the way to draw attention to the best views; from the Rinun-tei, the Cloud Touching Pavilion, the views of the garden and away to the Kitayama hills are breathtaking, and give the impression that the garden is merely an incident in the unfolding beauty of the natural landscape. Again unexpected straight lines make us wonder about European influence – for example, the path along the dam with its carefully sculpted triple hedge, and the pine alley, almost an avenue, that links two of the villas. But the detail that is most strikingly un-Japanese is that the edge of the lake is not lined with rocks; instead the grass slopes directly to the water's edge.

What is the explanation for these 'European' touches – the symmetry at Konchi-in, the straight avenues and paths at Katsura, the grass banks surrounding Shugaku-in's lake? Europe had only 'discovered' Japan in 1542, when some Portuguese sailors were shipwrecked on its coast. However, under the rule of the remarkable Hideyoshi, Japan had been open to European trade; commercial contacts were established with Portugal, Holland and England. To ingratiate themselves, the Spanish even presented Hideyoshi with an elephant. Portuguese, Spanish and Italian Jesuits were active in the country also and it may be that they brought with them European ideas of what made a garden beautiful. Certainly Luis Frois, a Portuguese missionary, who in 1585 published a book on the cultural differences between Europe and Japan, noticed how 'With us the lawn is valued as a place to sit, while in Japan it is intentionally removed.' Was it along the channels of trade or through Christian missionaries that some knowledge of the formal, Italian garden style had percolated into Japan? Certainly gardens do follow trade: in the twentieth century Japanese gardens were exported in the wake of the trade that Japan so successfully established with the West, which is one reason why we are much more familiar with Japanese than Chinese gardens.

Whatever the source of European influence, this openness to the outside world was about to change. Under the Tokugawa shoguns of the early seventeenth century xenophobia was encouraged; edicts were passed against Christianity in 1612 and again in 1614. The Tokugawa clan moved the capital from Kyoto to Edo (modern Tokyo), where they had built their castle; castles, too, may have been suggested by European example. Finally, in 1633, the Edict on Closing the Country was promulgated, after which foreign contacts became extremely difficult, if not impossible; only the Chinese were still allowed to travel in Japan, although the Dutch kept open a small trading post on an island off Nagasaki. Japan was re-opened to the outside world only in the 1860s. When Commander Perry, with four US battleships, arrived to begin trade and diplomatic negotiations in 1853, he showed the astonished Japanese models of a railway and a telegraph system. Stuck as they had been for 230 years in a pre-industrial age, they were, naturally, amazed.

During this closed period the laws established by Hideyoshi to stabilize the country after a time of civil war became the means to stifle all change. No one could move out of his or her class; samurai were forbidden to farm, but had to live in castles as retainers to a lord, and they alone were allowed to bear arms. The lords had to support these samurai, even though there were no battles for them to fight, and this led to the impoverishment of the nobility. The result was that few gardens were made in this period, since the upper classes could not afford it, and the lower classes, however great their prosperity, would not have been permitted to express themselves in works of art, in the same way that they were forbidden to wear silk.

While the Shogun established himself in Edo/Tokyo, the Emperor remained in Kyoto. But Kyoto was no longer the centre of power and little work was done on the gardens there for more than two hundred years. In Tokyo, however, some of the Tokugawa clan attempted to make secular gardens in the traditional style, often with details copied directly from historic Kyoto gardens. The Koishikawa Koraku-en was begun by Tokugawa Yorifusa (1603–61) and completed by his successor, Mitsukuni. The designer was the Confucian scholar Shu Shunsui, and the garden's name, literally 'pleasure after', refers to a Confucian saying that the conscientious ruler should only relax and take pleasure after he has made his country peaceful and prosperous. The designer's problem in flat, marshy Tokyo was that rock had to be brought a long way, and only with great difficulty could

Koishikawa Koraku-en, Tokyo. Hermann von Puckler-Muskau called paths 'the silent guides to a garden'. In a Japanese stroll garden they control the order in which we see the views, and the speed at which we move. Who could hurry over stepping stones such as these?

it avoid looking artificial; lakes were easily dug, but natural waterfalls were out of the question. The Koraku-en is a stroll garden including imitations of famous Chinese and Japanese scenes; for example, the dam recalls the west lake at Hangzhou. Part of the garden is now a public park.

Rikugi-en, an eighteenth-century Tokyo garden, has also become a public park and is a good example of a large Tokyo lake garden. At Mito, too, the Tokugawa clan constructed a fine nineteenth-century garden, the Kairaku-en, and opened it to their subjects as an inspiration to the artists among them. The brushwood and bamboo fences, in particular the knotwork, throughout this garden are immensely beautiful, but the pruning of the shrubs is perhaps excessive. At Kanazawa the Maeda clan, the most powerful *daimyo* family under the Tokugawa shogunate, created a private garden for themselves in the shadow of their castle. The site is only 53 metres/ 173 feet above sea level, but the garden is full of fast-flowing water, and the Midori Taki, the Green Waterfall, is 6.6 metres/21.6 feet high. The explanation for this water pressure is that a river has been tapped 10 kilometres/6 miles from Kanazawa, and the underground pipe system, laid in 1632, still feeds the garden. The house of one of the Maeda clan's samurai retainers, Tsuda Genba, has been preserved, though not in its original place. These gardens of the nobility are rare exceptions in a period when much of the country was suffering from desperate poverty, and survival was the highest priority for most people.

The opening up of Japan to the outside world resulted in an explosion of European and American interest in all things Japanese, almost equal to the excitement stimulated a century earlier by the discovery of Pompeii. This fascination was spurred on by Japanese participation in the International Exhibition of 1862 and the World's Columbia Exhibition in Chicago in 1893. In England Baron Redesdale published *Tales of Old Japan* in 1871, and filled his garden at Batsford

BELOW *Kairaku-en, Mito. A nineteenth-century garden built by the ninth Lord of Mito, Nariaki Tokugawa. The garden was always intended to be open to the vassals of the Tokugawa clan for their entertainment and inspiration.*

ABOVE *Shinjuku Park, Tokyo. The celebration of the cherry blossom is a festival that involves the whole country. The nineteenth-century Shinjuku Imperial Garden shows unmistakeable signs of European influence – rolling English lawns and French formality, for example.*

in Gloucestershire with Japanese plants. Others added a Japanese touch to their gardens – a stone lantern here, a pagoda there, even a tea house, satisfying the English addiction to tea – but there was usually little understanding of the ideas lying behind the classical Japanese garden. In America Lafcadio Hearne explained Japan to his fellow countrymen in *Glimpses of Unfamiliar Japan* (1894), while in the same year G.T. Marsh created a Japanese garden that has since been incorporated into San Francisco's Golden Gate Park. At Giverny in France Monet surrounded himself with Japanese prints and built one of the most celebrated 'Japanese' bridges in his water garden. Even Whistler's mother seems to have placed her chair on a Japanese *tatami* mat. Many twentieth-century European architects found that Japanese garden minimalism harmonized well with their spare, undecorated buildings. The American-Japanese sculptor Isamu Nogachi, for example, designed a garden for the UNESCO headquarters in Paris that is clearly Japanese in inspiration, though he admitted that it was not authentic.

And how did Japan cope with the flood of foreign influences that followed the end of the shogunate and the restoration of the emperor? In 1903 Hibya public park in Tokyo was laid out on the site of two daimyo estates; every daimyo had been obliged to spend half his time in Tokyo, where the Shogun could keep an eye on him, but after the restoration of the emperor they were free to return permanently to their country estates. There were no designers in Japan, so the park is a collage of details borrowed from German public parks. At Hibya it is also possible to see how Japanese architects were challenged by the new influences from abroad; in the park there

is a strange brick building, in the Gothic style, which used to house the state telegram service. Shinjuku park, also in Tokyo, was created in 1906 and includes Japanese, English and French gardens. This park may bow to some foreign influences but the planting includes seventy-five species of cherry, under which office workers in trim suits still picnic, to celebrate the coming of spring and the transitory beauty of the cherry blossom. The garden is also famous for its chrysanthemums, whose symbolism is as important to the Japanese as to the Chinese. Even Kyoto finally saw a revival of garden-making. From 1894 to 1896 Yamagata Aritomo created his garden at Murin-an, not far from Nanzen-ji, where the house was built in a blend of Western and Japanese styles. The garden, too, shows some English influence in the extensive lawns, but in this complex stroll garden much is traditionally Japanese – the pebble beach by the pool, the three-tier waterfall and the stepping stones which imitate the path in a tea garden. The garden at Murin-an is only 3,000 square metres/3,587 square yards but within this space Aritomo has included all these traditional details without any sense of crowding.

In the twentieth century Japanese garden designers and architects were, predictably, divided between Westernizers and traditionalists. But one artist tried to cut across these divisions: Mirei Shigemori (1896-1975). When he became interested in gardens, he made a detailed examination of many of the historic gardens in Japan; the results of this research were published in the twenty-six volumes of *Nihon Teienshi Zukan* (1939), an illustrated history of the garden in Japan. Shigemori designed more than a hundred gardens, in each of which he tried to marry the Japanese tradition to contemporary sensibility, always bearing in mind his view that 'A garden which can be admired by anyone at any time is a garden that is infinitely contemporary.' At the very end of his life he designed the remarkable Garden at the Dawn of History for the Matsuo-taisha, one of the oldest

ABOVE *The Kyoto Garden, Holland Park, London, This garden was made in 1991 by design experts from Kyoto. We see here an example of the 'shishi odoshi' or deer scarer. One end of the lower bamboo fills with water, until it overbalances and tips the water out; the other end then falls back on a piece of rock, making a sharp sound to frighten the deer.*

Shinto temples in Kyoto. This collection of pointed rocks, set at odd angles among rough grass, represents the coming of the gods, but, like the much earlier garden created by the Chinese Emperor Wudi it is also a place that beckons the gods to descend.

Shigemori's most celebrated garden is at Tofuku-ji, the chief temple of the Rinzai Zen Buddhist sect, again in Kyoto. In 1939 he was commissioned to design a new garden for the abbot's house, in fact four gardens for the building's four sides. The rocks in the south garden recall the Islands of the Immortals in a sea of sand, and to the right the five sacred mountains are reproduced in miniature – although rather than miniature mountains these are metaphors for the Go-zan or five leading Zen monasteries in Kyoto. Much here is traditional, but the rocks are massive, while the miniature mountains, covered in moss, are not literal representations of the countryside. In the west garden moss and azaleas, cut into flat-topped cubes, alternate in an irregular pattern of squares. This pattern is continued in the north garden, but here the pattern is lower, created out of moss and stepping stones. Here, as one moves through the garden, the moss slowly absorbs the stones, and in the end the moss is itself absorbed by the gravel. This theme of mutability, of something changing into something else, is brilliantly caught in a garden that hardly changes at all. The final garden, to the north, is made of seven foundation stones, taken from earlier temple buildings, arranged in a sand sea to imitate the pattern of the Great Bear constellation. The stars move, of course, but here their movement is frozen into a work of sculpture, although alteration and development is suggested by the way the sand sea flows into the moss and trees that surround the garden.

Perhaps the most celebrated Japanese garden designer at work today is the Zen monk Shunmyo Masuno. He has designed gardens all over the world, taking elements of the traditional Japanese

BELOW *The Japanese Gardens, the Curragh, Ireland. It may seem improbable to find a Japanese garden in Ireland's National Stud, but this shows how the craze for all things Japanese spread to all corners of Europe in the early twentieth century.*

garden and reinterpreting them. When he came to design the garden of the Canadian embassy in Tokyo, it was the landscape of the two countries that was his inspiration – as usual, the Japanese designer begins with nature itself. In Tokyo's Kochimachi Kaikan he has used real water, but in other gardens water is suggested by raked sand or gravel. He says that he is a student of Muso Soseki, the early fourteenth-century maker of Saiho-ji, and clearly his roots are deeply traditional. This is how he sums up the philosophy that guides his garden design: 'I think the most important thing in executing a design is to talk to the plants and the stones, and hear what they themselves have to say about how they wish to be laid out.' This submission of the designer to the natural elements that are his material is characteristically Japanese, and, consciously or not, Shunmyo is echoing the words of the eleventh-century *Sakuteiki*, in which the writer tells the aspiring garden maker to 'follow the requests of the stone'.

Nothing could be more traditionally Japanese than Shunmyo's humility in the face of nature and Shigemori's emphasis on process – creation and development, mutation and decay. For a Japanese, eternity is an endless pattern of constant change, not something fixed; this is an idea alien to most Western thinking, which is dominated by dualism – good or bad, alive or dead, nature or man, permanent or temporary – and sees mutation, particularly the ultimate change of death, as a cause of regret. For the oriental thinker, humans, like nature, are imbued with the energizing *ki* (*ch'i* in Chinese); therefore, to think of man and nature as separate, as entirely different kinds of entity, is a fundamental fallacy. A Japanese writer says that an occidental gardener feels complacently 'like a deity who has crafted order from chaos, and thus somewhat god-like'. Oriental gardeners, by contrast, feel themselves part of the nature that is the material of their work of art, though few feel as close as the twelfth-century Chinese poet Mifei, who used

to bow to a particularly fine rock in his garden and call it brother. The miniaturization dear to the Japanese heart is a concentration of this *ki*, whether in a bonsai tree or a haiku.

In both Chinese and Japanese cultures the past, the elderly, the experienced, the worn are revered, which is in striking contrast to the American admiration for the new, the bright, the innocent. But this reverence for the past can be a trap; as Shigemori argued, it can hamper the development of new ideas, and the imitation of ancient examples can become a sterile exercise, often dominated by 'rules' for garden-making. In this Shigemori is echoing the words of the *Sakuteiki* written nearly a thousand years earlier, which emphasized the balance that needs to be found between the traditional reverence for nature and individual inspiration in making the work of art called a garden: 'Recreate the essence of those scenes [from nature] in the garden, but do so interpretatively, not strictly.' In Japan the artists, the garden makers, have an almost priestly role to play, as interpreters between divine nature and the human race.

Jonangu Shrine, Kyoto. The gardens here are of different periods, from the Heian to the present day. The pruning of the trees is ubiquitous, and enhances the beauty of the weeping willow (above). It is said that Japanese gardens are best viewed in the rain: the rocks shine, and the melancholy beauty of the garden is at its most intense.

5
THE ITALIAN TRADITION

ABOVE *Villa Gamberaia, Settignano. The fifteenth-century villa was enlarged in the eighteenth century, and the gardens have been much altered, most recently in the early twentieth century. The villa's position looking out over the roofs of Florence is uniquely beautiful.*

LEFT *Villa Allegri Arvedi, Verona. This seventeenth-century villa is still the heart of a working estate. The box parterre dates from the seventeenth century; its pattern has not been changed, and some of the box hedges survive from the original planting.*

IN THE MAKING OF PLEASURE GARDENS, as in so many other arts, the Italians taught the whole of Europe a lesson, and set the standards by which civilized gardens were to be judged. With the Renaissance and its fascination with all aspects of classical Rome, Italy became the country that inspired every other. In eighteenth-century England the Grand Tour continued this tradition, but by then England was beginning to develop a garden style that challenged the artifice and the straight lines, the architecture and the fountains of the classical Italian garden. Then in nineteenth-century England, as the pendulum of fashion swung again, Italian gardens became all the rage, or rather an English version of them, with heavy balustrading and without the brilliant light of Italy.

As far back as the imperial era wealthy Romans (there were no Italians then) were dedicated garden makers, and inaugurated a great period of construction not only in Italy but in all parts of the empire. Of course, they had to modify their style somewhat to suit local climates and growing conditions, but the Roman gardens at Fishbourne in England, at Side in Turkey and at Volubilis in Morocco are strikingly similar in layout and detail. Much of our knowledge of these domestic Roman gardens derives from the excavations at Pompeii, where no fewer than 450 have been found. Usually such urban gardens were created in courtyards, but also sometimes behind the house, occupying one end of the rectangular lot on which it was built. In the latter case the visitor would enter the house directly from the street, cross the atrium (open courtyard) and catch a glimpse of the garden behind the private sleeping quarters of the owner. As house builders became more ambitious they enlarged this second open courtyard, behind the atrium, and beautified it with plants and perhaps a pool in the middle, and usually surrounded it with a colonnaded walk; this became known as the peristyle garden. All these gardens were rectangular, so they fitted easily into the rigid planning of densely populated Roman towns. Two Pompeiian houses are particularly interesting from the garden point of view: the House of the Vettii with its complete peristyle and the House of Loreius Tiburtinus, which has a long central canal and reconstructed pergola, not in the middle of the house but behind it.

We know from pollen samples what plants were blooming in the gardens of Pompeii in August AD 79, and they prove that these gardens were made for pleasure, not merely for produce. Such plants as southernwood, cerastium (familiarly known as snow in summer), campanula, lychnis, asters and pinks must have been grown for decoration. Evergreen shrubs such as *Arbutus unedo* and oleander would also have been grown for their flowers, although Pliny the Elder records that the latter had an additional practical value as a cure for snake bites. There were climbing plants trained over pergolas to create shady bowers, vines certainly, but also ivy and, in later times, roses. The inhabitants of Pompeii grew myrtle and box for their scent and to be pruned into topiary shapes; branches of these were also woven into coronets to decorate statues or the brows of an honoured guest.

Water added to the pleasure of these gardens. The Romans were experts in hydraulics, as we can see in the pipework at the House of the Vettii. Rainwater was collected from the roof of the house in an *impluvium* and thence directed to where it was needed; brass taps would regulate the supply to different parts of the garden. In towns water had to be paid for if it was drawn from a public aqueduct, so its generous use also demonstrated the wealth of the householder. We find pools of many designs, sometimes fed by water cascading down a water stair. Fountains were fed from cisterns raised above the level of the garden; water would spout from statues into raised round or rectangular basins. At Herculaneum a complex first-century fountain in brass represents the Hydra, each of its heads squirting water. The flowing water would cool the air and its sound would refresh the inhabitants of the house.

In the House of Ancora Nera at Pompeii a sunken garden was reached down a flight of stairs; here the plants would benefit from the ready supply of water, while humans could enjoy the cool air and the prospect of greenery. Not surprisingly such sunken gardens are found also in the Roman colonies of North Africa, where their coolness must have been much prized. These gardens were used for dining, as were nymphaea; originally these last were caves or grottoes where springs sacred to the nymphs bubbled up, but they developed into sophisticated subterranean chambers adapted for the entertainment of guests. At Sperlonga, on the coast south of Rome, a cave was extended and used as a dining room. Here the Emperor Tiberius was dining one day when part of the roof collapsed; Tiberius was unhurt.

The gods were not forgotten in Roman gardens; in his *Natural History* Pliny the Elder even writes of there being something sacred in the experience of merely entering a garden. Smaller nymphaea in the gardens at Pompeii were decorated with mosaics and sometimes with shells, which would remind the religious of Venus, supreme goddess of gardens. Shrines to the gods of the household, the *lares*, were often painted with frescoes; on solemn occasions they were garlanded and offerings laid in front of them. Other gods often celebrated in gardens were Flora, Bacchus, Pan and Priapus, the fertility god, son of Aphrodite and Dionysus. Statues of these were commonly both cult objects, to be decorated with garlands on festival days, and decorative, a nude Venus being especially popular. Christian iconography has taken on some of the plants and imagery common in Roman gardens; Venus' dove and rose are both common symbols in Christian art, while Pan, god of the wilder side of nature and the spreader of panic, has been transmuted into the devil.

As the economy of Rome flourished, some private citizens began to accumulate the surplus cash that is the necessary condition for the creation of more ambitious gardens, and with that cash came the leisure to enjoy their new creations. In Rome many nobles made gardens on the slopes of the Pincio, which was known as the Hill of Gardens. The most famous of these were the gardens of Lucullus, whose legendary wealth and appetites have made him notorious. A successful general, he had returned from Persia completely converted to the Persian style of gardening, to such an extent that he was known as 'Xerxes in a toga'. He was not the only invader of Persia to be converted to

LEFT *The House of the Vettii, Pompeii. This is a typical Roman peristyle garden. The water system has been well preserved, and the lead piping that takes the water from storage tanks to different parts of the garden is still visible.*

ABOVE *The House of Loreius Tiburtinus, Pompeii. This garden lies behind the house, on either side of a central canal, not in a courtyard. The reconstruction of the pergola has been based on the position of the original post holes.*

its ways and its garden style, as we have seen. Lucullus was probably responsible for introducing the cherry and the peach to Rome in about 60 BC. Terracing steep hillsides to plant vines and other crops was a well-established agricultural practice, but Lucullus was perhaps the first to create a pleasure garden on terraces, and his example was followed by the wealthy Maecenas, who made his garden on the Esquiline hill. A beautiful fountain, in the form of a giant drinking horn, from this garden is preserved in the Capitoline Museum. Tacitus tells the story of how the gardens of Lucullus descended to the possession of one Valerius Atticus, who suffered a fate similar to that of the unfortunate Fouquet at Vaux le Vicomte. His gardens were much too desirable; Messalina, terrifying wife of the Emperor Claudius, forced him to commit suicide so that she could have them for herself.

The best picture we get of a Roman of the early empire in his garden comes from the letters of Pliny the Younger. A successful lawyer in the capital, Pliny had property in many parts of Italy but he usually lived in two villas, in one near the sea during the winter, just outside Rome, and one in the Tuscan hills during the heat of summer. His winter villa at Laurentinum, complete with centrally heated bedroom, was so close to the sea that he describes hearing the breakers roaring and the spray created problems in the garden; as he explains, his box hedge was damaged by the salt and he had to fill the gaps with rosemary. The garden here seems to have been planted with useful fruit trees – mulberries and figs, for example; presumably in winter there was less temptation to spend much time outside. His Tuscan villa, by contrast, was on a hillside, well away from the fetid air of the coast; building on a slope meant not only healthy air but also extensive views. He describes a formal garden with topiary figures of animals carved out of box, and an oval path inside which were more box figures and other clipped shrubs. But his great pride was his riding-ground, shaded by plane trees, which were hung with ivy swags and planted with laurel and acanthus, while roses grew in the centre. Here he had a marble dining bench with a pool of water in front of it, also edged in

polished marble; the main dishes were placed on the rim of this pool, while lighter dishes floated on the surface of the water. Further away a fountain flung its jet into the air. There was a bedroom near by for the post-prandial nap; this had windows in all its walls, but they were curtained by a vine that grew over the roof; even here, inside the building, there were springs of water.

Pliny is clearly very proud of the innumerable shapes into which box trees were cut in his Tuscan garden; the most elaborate spelled out his own and his gardener's names. The latter would probably have been his *topiarius*, meaning the gardener in charge of the ornamental garden, as opposed to one in charge of the vegetable or fruit garden. Such men were often of Greek birth or descent, and it seems they were celebrities in their time, since we find many named on gravestones. Cutting shrubs and bushes into shapes, which we know as topiary, would have been only one part of their work; they were also painters of murals, landscape architects and place makers (the term which Lancelot 'Capability' Brown used to describe himself), their title deriving from the Greek word *topos* meaning 'a place'. The *topiarii* seem to have been men, but work in smaller domestic gardens would probably have been done by women; at least that seems to be the conclusion to be drawn from the hairpins found in the Roman garden at Frocester Court in England.

While the wealthy were creating their own gardens, more public-spirited individuals were founding public gardens. The first was Pompey's Portico garden, laid out in 55 BC; it was planted with avenues of plane trees so that citizens could take the air in the comfort of their shade. In his 'Ars Amatoria' Ovid points to another advantage of these trees and of public gardens in general: they were good places to pick up a lover. He tells those in search of love:

> Do you but saunter gently in the shade,
> At summer's height, of Pompey's colonnade

and you can't fail; though a ticket to the theatre, he admits, will be an even surer guarantee of success. The Empress Livia also founded public gardens, and Julius Caesar left his gardens to the public when he died, a fact emphasized by Shakespeare's Mark Antony in his funeral oration. Many public buildings, such as temples and baths, had gardens attached to them; those attached to libraries must have been particularly appreciated, since reading manuscripts would have been much easier by daylight than by the light of candles, oil lamps and tapers.

ABOVE *Villa Poppaea, Oplontis. Only part of this villa has been excavated, but plaster casts of tree-root holes reveal that mature plane trees once grew in its large garden.*

Hadrian's Villa, the Villa Adriana, just below Tivoli to the east of Rome, was both a private and a public space, since it was the seat of the imperial government when Hadrian was in residence. Here we find many of the typical features of a Roman garden but on a monumental scale. The Poikile was an enormous peristyle garden, while the Canopus, a long, narrow stretch of water in a shape called an *euripus*, had a dining grotto at its southern end through which water flowed into the canal. An advantage of flowing water was that its noise would cover the Emperor's conversation, so he could talk more intimately and perhaps more indiscreetly; in Islamic gardens we find splashing water used for the same purpose. The Canopus is supposed to be a representation of the canal that linked Alexandria to the city of Canopus in Egypt, where there was a famous temple dedicated to Serapis. This reminder of Egypt must have been somewhat painful to Hadrian, since his youthful lover, Antinous, had died in the waters of the Nile. There is evidence that the steep sides of the canal were terraced and planted, sometimes using half an amphora as a planting pot. Another part of the villa gardens was landscaped to represent a happier scene, this time Greek, the idyllic Vale of Tempe. In the Piazza d'Oro it is just possible to make out the remains of the ingenious underground irrigation system that was used to water the plants without disturbing the Emperor when he was entertaining guests there.

It is clear that growing plants was an important activity for the Romans. Even those who had no gardens made use of their windowsills; pedestrians were warned about flowerpots falling from them. And when they did not have real gardens, the wealthiest had gardens frescoed on the walls of their rooms; a magnificent example is Livia's dining room, the frescoes from which are preserved at the Palazzo Massimo in Rome. As the empire expanded and wealth accumulated in Rome, the gardens became more and more elaborate, with ostentatious competition between neighbours; in the time of Nero a certain host even spent 4 million sesterces on rose petals for a dinner party. These excesses were deplored by many, the poet Horace included, who felt that the ancient republican virtues of moderation, restraint and self-sufficiency were being undermined.

By now it is possible to identify many features of Roman gardens which became typical of Italian gardens – the formal layout, the topiary shapes, the use of water, the narrow range of flowering plants and the preference for hillside sites. With the Renaissance came a revival of interest in every aspect of the classical Roman civilization, including its gardens, with the result that in many of the most celebrated Renaissance villa gardens Roman influence is paramount. But before leaping ahead to the Renaissance it is important to consider some of the things that were happening in Italy during

RIGHT *Villa Adriana, Tivoli. This was more like a small town than a villa. At the northern end of the Canopus, seen here, there was an open-air dining room with water running though it; this both cooled the air and made the emperor's conversation inaudible to spies.*

what used to be called 'the Dark Ages'. The most important development was the dominance of all aspects of Western European life by the Christian Church. At first there was no Christian architecture and so the early fathers borrowed from the Romans; two examples are the basilica form used in the design of churches and the atrium courtyard, which was reborn as the monastery cloister. In the sixth century St Benedict established his order of monks among the Roman ruins of Subiaco; later at Cassino he laid out a garden described as 'a paradise in the Roman fashion'. In many cloisters we find formally patterned gardens in which the monks grew herbs for medicine and the kitchen.

The development of the monastic garden is found throughout Christendom, but in Andalucia and southern Italy the influence of Islamic culture was also strong, particularly in the Kingdom of the Two Sicilies; the architecture of Palermo still bears witness to this influence. After their conquest of Sicily in the ninth century the Muslims built many pleasure gardens; often these were enclosed courtyards with fountains and colonnades, but we also hear of pleasure parks. Some disappeared under Norman rule, and others were modified. During the reign of Roger, King of Sicily, who was crowned in Palermo cathedral on Christmas Day 1130, Arabs, Lombards, Greeks, Jews and Spaniards lived in peace together under the rule of a Norman knight. This remarkable court was one of the channels through which Islamic culture and science flowed into the mainstream of European thought. Roger built an enormous park, which surrounded Palermo 'like a necklace that ornaments the throat of a young girl', as an Arab poet described the scene in the late twelfth century. In gardening terms the Arabs must also be celebrated for the introduction into Italy of the orange and, perhaps, the lemon. The Romans had had a fruit called a citron, which was sweeter than a lemon with thick, knobbly skin. Pliny referred to citrons as apples from Media, so they must have originated in the Middle East, and may even have been the legendary golden apples of the Hesperides; but they were not lemons, nor oranges, both of which fruits were to play a central role in Italian gardens from the Renaissance onwards.

The proud republics of late medieval Italy, Florence for example, had public gardens and in 1333 the Venetian republic sponsored the establishment of a medicinal herb garden. Perhaps the most celebrated garden of late medieval Italy is that described by Boccaccio in his *Decameron*, begun in 1348; it belonged to the villa where a group of young storytellers found refuge from the plague in Florence. This garden is described as containing shady arbours covered in vines, jasmine and roses, a meadow encircled by orange and cedar trees, and at the centre a beautifully carved fountain, a garden detail found in much medieval European courtly literature. Boccaccio's friend,

LEFT *Villa Medici, Fiesole. This hugely influential villa was built by Michelozzo for Cosimo de' Medici in the mid-fifteenth century. The hillside site made it necessary to lay out the garden in terraces, but these terraces are not directly connected to each other.*

the poet Francesco Petrarca (Petrarch), was also a passionate gardener, but not a very successful one; he records his plantings and their failures with great candour in his notebooks. He was one of the first scholars to withdraw from the court in search of *otium*, thoughtful ease, contrasted by Roman writers with *negotium*, the involvement in civic affairs. When Petrarch retired from the turmoil of the papal court at Avignon, to the surprise of his friends, who had foreseen a brilliant public career for him, he found in the Vaucluse a country house with two gardens, one of which he dedicated to Bacchus, the other to Apollo. On moving to Parma in 1348, he added a pleasure garden to the existing vegetable garden. For Petrarch, as for many early humanists, gardens were intimate spaces for study, philosophical reflection and debate, just as they had been for the younger Pliny.

Pliny's influence is paramount also in the work of Leon Battista Alberti, whose *The Villa*, probably written about 1438, anticipates the fashion for building country seats that was about to begin around Rome and Florence. In his major work *The Ten Books on Architecture* (1452) he draws heavily on classical sources, recommending hillside sites because of their healthy exposure to sun and wind. He follows the ancient practice in suggesting that porticoes should be positioned to the south-east of the house, where the low winter sunlight can enter, but not the scorching sun of summer, because it stands much higher in the sky. Many of his precepts seem to have been in the mind of Michelozzo Michelozzi when Cosimo de' Medici commissioned him to design a villa for his son, Giovanni, at Fiesole.

Giovanni was a learned man as well as a banker and diplomat: in his library he had a copy of *De Re Rustica* by the first-century Roman writer Columella, and

ABOVE *Villa Medici, Fiesole. This was one of the first villas to take advantage of the healthy air of the hills; earlier villas had been built on the flat, at the centre of the farmland they controlled. Cecil Pinsent redesigned the garden in the early twentieth century, but preserved the Renaissance atmosphere.*

Theophrastus' treatise on plants. Earlier Medici villas, Il Trebbio for example, had been built in the valley, so the choice of a hillside site at Fiesole was a radical departure. The garden of the Villa Medici was partially redesigned by Cecil Pinsent in the early twentieth century, but the general layout is almost unchanged from the time when Lorenzo de' Medici, Cosimo's grandson, used to meet there to discuss ideas with his Platonic Academy. Its two parallel terraces give wonderful views over Florence, and there is a small *giardino segreto* on the other side of the house for more solitary contemplation. But the visitor will notice that a characteristic feature of Italian gardens is missing here: the two terraces are not linked by a flight of steps, which was to be a major feature in the dramatic gardens of the high Renaissance. This may be because the upper terrace, with its shading pergola, was for guests and learned conversation, while the lower was for the gardeners, working at growing fruit and vegetables for the house.

Two other magical gardens near Florence, although of a later date, spurn the potential drama of their hillside settings, making no use of terraces and flights of steps. The almost flat garden of the Villa Gamberaia protrudes from its hillside into the Arno valley, so that the visitor looks down on the distant roofs of Florence as if from the deck of a battleship. Beside the house a straight, flat, narrow lawn, known as the Bowling Green, stretches the full length of the garden,

ABOVE *Villa Gamberaia, Settignano. The pools are early twentieth-century alterations, carried out by the Princess Ghyka of Serbia; they replaced earlier planting beds, but are laid out in the same pattern. This is a good example of how a historic garden can be improved by sympathetic development.*

LEFT *Villa Giulia, Rome. The villa was built in the mid-sixteenth century for Pope Julius III. The subterranean nymphaeum we see here would have been used for dining during the torrid days of the Roman summer.*

225 metres/246 yards, linking the belvedere, which hangs over the valley, to the Ninfeo (nymphaeum) excavated out of the steep hill and surrounded by shading trees. This green space provided an area close to the house for healthy outdoor exercise, as Alberti had suggested. The garden of the Villa Capponi, like that of the Villa Gamberaia, has naturally and properly evolved over the centuries, as new owners had new ideas and made new demands on their outdoor space. But here also one can see a perfectly preserved *giardino segreto*, lying below the house and now entered by a narrow staircase. Originally this garden, which is totally surrounded by high walls and hedges, could be entered only from the house by a subterranean passage; it was a later owner who added the set of external steps. Here the proprietor of the villa and his guests could enjoy the winter sun while being protected from the bitter tramontana, the wind that whistles over the surrounding hills – a pleasure that would surely have appealed to Pliny the Younger.

With the Villa Medici the great period of garden and villa building in central Italy begins, first around Florence and then Rome. It was not only the revival of interest in things Roman that spurred the nobility into developing their gardens away from the towns but also the fact that law and order were now better established, and there was surplus cash to invest in a country property. Florence was the banking capital of Europe, while in Rome the princes of the Church were able to draw on money generated by the pilgrim trade and, if they were lucky enough to belong to a family one of whose members was elected pope, there was almost no limit to the resources that were available. In 1516 Pope Leo X and his cousin Cardinal Giulio de' Medici ordered the overworked Raphael to design a villa on the slopes of Monte Mario, where eminent guests could be entertained before they made their ceremonial entrance into Rome. The villa, now known as the Villa Madama, was laid out across the slope of Monte Mario, with its garden stretching flat from the house along

RIGHT *Villa Capponi, Florence. This is one of the most delightful and best-preserved fifteenth-century villas around Florence. The sunken garden, once accessible only from the house, provided sun in winter and protection from the wind.*

the same contour, so that opportunities for dramatic flights of steps were again ignored. Work on the villa was interrupted by Raphael's death in 1520 and his complete plan for the garden was never realized. In a letter describing his project Raphael shows how he has been influenced by Alberti and by the example of the ancients, Vitruvius in particular. For example, he explains how the villa was sited so that it was protected from the unhealthy winds, a point emphasized by Alberti: 'I have sited the villa along the axis north-west to south-east, so that no windows open towards the sirocco, but only towards healthy winds.' In the middle of the garden he placed a pool, fed with spring water, which reminds us of the pool in Pliny's Tuscan villa. And outside the beautiful loggia (which still exists) he laid out a *xystus*, 'called thus by the ancients, a place full of trees planted in regular patterns'.

Shortly after Raphael had begun work on the Villa Madama, the imperious Julius II, who liked to be known as 'pontifex maximus et imperator', commissioned Bramante to design a courtyard to link the Vatican palace with the hill of the Belvedere, a building in which he planned to exhibit much of his collection of classical sculpture. This work had not been completed when Sixtus V ruined the design by building a wing of the Vatican Museum across one of the terraces; nevertheless, Bramante's courtyard was to have enormous influence. He showed how it was possible to reshape the land to suit the demands of the designer. The ascent of the Belvedere hill was to be accomplished in two stages: the first terrace was reached by a central flight of steps, the second by a pair of ramps on either side. In the wall supporting the upper terrace, and opposite the head of the flight of steps, was a giant niche with a fountain. He also designed a new façade for the Belvedere to harmonize with his composition. A recent, ill-informed art critic writes: 'Bramante would have had little in the way of physical remains of antiquity to use as a model, but he was doubtless inspired by the literary sources.' Of course Bramante knew his Pliny, his Vitruvius, and he was familiar with the ideas of Alberti, but he had probably also visited the great

LEFT AND ABOVE *Villa Madama, Rome. Originally designed by Raphael, the work on this hillside garden (left) was never completed. Raphael was much influenced by Pliny the Elder's description of his own country estates. The flat garden stretches along the hillside with niches in the wall on the left; Giovanni da Udine's delightful elephant fountain (above) occupies the central niche.*

Sanctuary of Fortuna Primagenia at Palestrina, some 40 kilometres/24 miles from Rome, with its ramps and steps ascending the hillside, and this might well have provided him with a physical example from antiquity.

The whole Belvedere courtyard was planned to be the pope's private garden, but it also served as a theatre for papal ceremonies, and for jousting matches. At the Vatican end a set of semi-circular steps, reminiscent of a Roman amphitheatre, gave the audience fine views of the proceedings in the courtyard and on the two terraces. And the garden was made more dramatic by the presence of fountains, not the placid, round pools so often found in the centre of medieval gardens: Bramante's fountains had water gushing from walls and out of statues, a detail which impressed a visitor of 1523. This flow of water must have recalled the dining area of Hadrian's Villa, of which Bramante had made careful drawings, where water cooled the air as it rushed down the rocky slope into the calm of the Canopus basin. Following classical precedent Bramante also set up statues to decorate the garden, some in niches; the same visitor of 1523 noticed a Venus, an Apollo

BELOW *The Vatican Gardens, Vatican City. These gardens are a hodge-podge of different periods and styles. But it is worth visiting them to see the exquisite casino Pirro Ligorio built for Pius IV, and to get a close-up view of the dome of St Peter's, built by Michelangelo and Giacomo della Porta.*

and the Laocoon. The layout was symmetrical and the planting formal, of course, again following classical precedent. In Bramante's revolutionary, but also deeply retrospective, design we have the elements of the garden style the world has come to know as 'Italian': the theatrical use of a hillside site, steps, balustrades, statues, moving water, a symmetrical layout and formal planting. It is a paradox that Bramante invented – or perhaps it would be truer to say he rediscovered – the Italian style 350 years before the political entity known as Italy came into existence.

The Sack of Rome in 1527 shook the confidence of the Church and the whole of the Catholic world: how could God allow his own city to be laid waste by barbarians from the north, and Protestant barbarians at that? But it was not long before some confidence returned and the second half of the sixteenth century was a great period of garden-making. In the 1560s Cardinal Gambara, bishop of nearby Viterbo, decided he needed a garden at his summer retreat in Bagnaia. Having decided to turn part of his hunting park into an elegant garden, he summoned a designer, probably Vignola, who was already working on the Farnese palace and garden at nearby Caprarola, where the Cardinal was a frequent guest. Gambara didn't need a house (he already had a palace in the town), just a garden, with a pair of pavilions for picnics. But this was a time of reform in the Church, following the crisis of 1527, and critical voices were heard attacking the luxurious lives of many leading churchmen. One of the foremost reformers was Carlo Borromeo, and it was probably he who insisted the money for the second pavilion at the Villa Lante, as the garden at Bagnaia came to be known, be diverted to building a hospital. Thus the symmetrical second pavilion was only completed after Gambara's death.

LEFT AND BELOW *Palazzo Farnese, Caprarola. The main gardens lie in the shadow of the bulky fortress that Vignola transformed into a villa for Alessandro Farnese in the mid-sixteenth century. Further up the hillside, hidden in the woods, lies the more private, and more delicate, casino. The river gods (left) bear a strong resemblance to those at Villa Lante, where perhaps Vignola also worked.*

Like many high Renaissance Italian gardens, the garden of the Villa Lante has a programme that can be interpreted like an elaborate metaphorical poem; it is laid out to convey a series of ideas to the visitor who is learned in classical myth. The garden should be entered from the top, if this meaning is to become clear. Today we enter from the bottom, nearest the town, and are immediately struck by Giambologna's great Pegasus fountain, which stands outside the garden but clearly announces the pagan inspiration of this whole site, garden and park. The winged horse of classical legend was a symbol of artistic inspiration, creating a channel of communication between the mundane world and the divine world; not only did he ascend from earth to a place among the stars, but where his foot touched the ground a magical spring would emerge, around which the muses would gather – Hippocrene was a famous example. It is a striking fact that that the religious leaders who created some of the finest high Renaissance gardens drew their inspiration almost entirely from classical mythology; thus we look in vain for Christian symbols at the Villa Lante.

Reading from top to bottom, the garden tells the story of nature tamed by art. Thus on the top terrace the twin pavilions are rusticated, and decorated with fruit and flowers – nature as the inspiration of art, bountiful but untamed. The first fountain is the Fountain of Deucalion, a reference to the flood that showed Nature in all its destructive majesty, preparing the world for the new age. Next comes the Fountain of the Dolphins, symbols of intelligence and artistic creativity, creatures who can flourish in the water and were said to save humans from drowning. Further down we find the river gods, Tiber and Arno, but now water is not a threat but a benefit to man, as we can see from the cornucopias the gods cradle and from the presence of the goddesses Flora and Pomona, the deities of fertility and bounty. As we descend the slope we find water increasingly tamed, in this case by the art of the virtuoso hydraulic engineer Tommaso Ghinucci; water sculpts the scales of a crayfish (*gambero* in Italian), the ubiquitous,

ABOVE *Villa Lante, Bagnaia. This jewel of a garden was completed in 1573 for Cardinal Gambara. The Fountain of Pegasus, by Giambologna, at the entrance, announces the theme of the garden's programme – how art can work in harmony with nature.*

punning symbol of Cardinal Gambara, and at one point is channelled down the centre of a marble dining table to cool the wine. Finally, on the lowest level of the garden, we emerge from the shade of the great plane trees on to an almost square, flat, sun-bathed terrace. Clearly this is the conclusion of the story; here water calmly takes its placid place among the topiary shapes of the brightly lit box parterre. Man and nature are harmoniously reconciled in the high art of this very formal garden.

The garden at the Villa Lante is not large, but it is wonderfully satisfying. The essential elements of the Italian garden – light and shade, terraces descending a steep hillside, water moving and still, sculpture, elegant pavilions, balustrades and steps – work together in a modest, unceremonious way. The absolute symmetry of the layout, with the fountains marking the central axis, gives a feeling of repose. But there is no boredom, as the garden has to be explored; it cannot be seen as a whole from any single point. We may no longer be able to follow the garden's programme as an educated sixteenth-century visitor might have done, but we are led on and up to see what the water can be made to do next; we hear its sound above us and are enticed to explore further. On a hot day the fountains and falls cool the air while from the shade of the aged plane trees we look out

ABOVE AND LEFT *Villa Lante, Bagnaia. The programme of the garden begins at the top of the slope (left), where a pair of pavilions, bearing the crayfish of Gambara, flank the Grotto of the Deluge. From this threatening beginning the water descends the slope, performing a series of virtuoso manoeuvres until it reaches a placid conclusion in the sunlit parterre (above).*

on to the brightly lit lowest terrace, which is now decorated with a pattern of box hedges like a French parterre, but would originally have been planted with citrus trees, and the twelve squares might well have contained herbs and flowers. As we see it today the garden at the Villa Lante is almost without flowers; the flabby hydrangeas and stiff camellias added in the twentieth century do nothing to enhance the magic of the place.

At the Villa Lante it is possible to appreciate how a sixteenth-century prince of the Church organized nature into a garden for his private delight and the pleasure of his classically educated friends. At the Villa d'Este in Tivoli we see how another churchman made his garden a much more startling, more public testimony to his own and his family's power and wealth. Owing not a little to his parentage (his mother was Lucrezia Borgia), Cardinal Ippolito d'Este had risen rapidly in the Church – so rapidly that he was appointed Archbishop of Milan at the tender age of ten. By 1550, however, he had realized that he would never achieve his great ambition – to become pope; he was thought (rightly) to be too worldly. Thus when, as a sop to his ambition, he was offered the governorship of Tivoli, with its notoriously recalcitrant population, he accepted. One reason he was perhaps not too reluctant to accept this post is that the Villa Adriana, the huge complex built by the Emperor Hadrian, lay near at hand, and Ippolito was not slow to take advantage of the store of classical statuary that it provided. The theft (or should we say recycling?) was made easier because he employed as garden designer Pirro Ligorio, who was already his private antiquarian and soon began excavations at the Villa Adriana.

BELOW *Villa d'Este, Tivoli. This mid-sixteenth-century garden was created by Pirro Ligorio for Cardinal Ippolito d'Este. The river Aniene has been tapped to draw huge quantities of water into the garden under enormous pressure. Here we see the Organ Fountain, one of the garden's tallest.*

The garden that Ligorio designed at the Villa d'Este can be seen in a fresco in the palace, and its layout has been little changed, although many of the original statues have been removed. The flights of steps and ramps may have been influenced by Bramante's work in the Belvedere courtyard, but Ligorio had also worked at the Temple of Fortuna Primagenia at Palestrina, so he would have seen how the ancients tamed a hillside site. As at the Villa Lante we now enter the garden from the wrong end – from the house, as Ippolito d'Este himself would have done, not from the gate at the bottom of the garden where any plebeian visitor would originally have entered. In this garden we are given a lesson in what water can be made to do: it spurts up, splashes down, fans out sideways, cascades down a fall, burbles down the banister of a stair, drives the movement of automata, even powers an organ, although when Montaigne visited the garden in 1581 the Organ Fountain could raise only one quavering note. It has now been restored to its full splendour.

Educated visitors to this garden would not only have admired the layout and the hydraulics but also have pieced together the garden's meaning, because here, as at the Villa Lante, there was an iconographic programme at work. We can still appreciate something of this, although the garden has been robbed of many statues that would have made interpretation easier. The first theme is the relationship between Rome and Tivoli; on the first terrace down Tivoli is represented by the Fontana di Tivoli to the right, while to the left is La Rometta, an ensemble that recalls the Isola Tiberina in Rome. Ligorio designed both the statue of Roma Vittoriosa and the statues of the nymphs around the Fontana di Tivoli. A second theme in the garden is, again, the relation of nature to art; above the Tivoli fountain the statue of Pegasus shows the winged horse at the moment when he touches the ground of Mount Parnassus, causing the eruption of the spring Helicon, the source of all poetic inspiration. And, of course, another theme is the glory of the d'Este family; their white eagle can be seen everywhere and references to Hercules are explained by the fact that the d'Este family claimed descent from this hero.

The unsung heroes of these gardens of the high Renaissance are the water engineers, the *fontanieri* in Italian. Tommaso Ghinucci, who had brought water to the town of Bagnaia and to the hunting park of the bishops of Viterbo, is seldom mentioned in accounts of the Villa Lante garden, though his fountains, falls and rills are essential to the delights the garden offers. But in their day the rare skills of these men were highly prized, as we can see from two events in the career of Curzio Maccarone, perhaps the most celebrated *fontaniere* in Rome. So essential was his

LEFT *Villa d'Este, Tivoli. In this garden the visitor is given a masterclass in what water can be made to do. It goes up, down, sideways, in sprays, jets and fans; it even plays an organ, and once provided the power for mechanical, singing birds.*

ABOVE *Palazzo Piccolomini, Pienza.*
This tiny, mid-fifteenth-century garden has
remained largely unaltered. It lies under
the palace Rossellino built for Pope Pius II.
The views from here over the sun-scorched
Val d'Orcia are spectacular.

expertise that work on the fountains at the Villa d'Este had to be delayed until he had completed his work at the d'Este palace in Rome. The Farnese cardinal, transforming his castle at Caprarola into a summer residence befitting his status, also wanted to employ Maccarone, but he had an even longer wait. It was not until Ippolito d'Este died in 1572 that Maccarone was able to begin work on the fountains at Caprarola; the result of this delay was that Cardinal Farnese had to show Pope Gregory XIII, his guest in 1578, a shamefully incomplete garden.

The water mechanisms at the Villa d'Este, the Owl Fountain and the Water Organ, were designed by a Frenchman, Luc Le Clerc, in imitation of classical originals, but there was also some influence from the world of Islam; travellers to Constantinople and to the court of Timur (Tamburlaine) had brought back reports of such hydraulic devices. Another detail of the Villa d'Este garden that may be the result of Islamic influence is the water running down the handrail of the stairs. In 1556, just at the time the gardens at Tivoli were being planned, a letter by the Venetian ambassador to Spain, Andrea Navagero, was published; in this he describes in detail the Islamic gardens of the Generalife in Granada, including the stairway with water flowing down its handrail.

Few gardens of the Italian high Renaissance have come down to us in such magnificent condition as that of the Villa d'Este at Tivoli. The Giardino Giusti in Verona, which was made in the 1570s, is also in excellent order, although it has been extensively remodelled and replanted. This is a garden that reminds us of Stendhal's characterization of the typical Italian garden as the place 'where architecture is married to the trees'; it is precisely the architecture of the garden that is so striking – the avenue of towering cypresses, which Goethe described as soaring 'into the air like awls', the rigorously symmetrical, box-edged parterres with their fountains, statues and lemon trees in ancient terracotta pots. And terracotta and lemon are the only colours apart from the different shades of green. Here the presence of water is less dramatic, less emphatic,

ABOVE *Giardino Giusti, Verona. This late sixteenth-century garden is a composition almost entirely in green. The only colour comes from the terracotta pots holding lemon trees, and the sparkle of the water in the few, small fountains.*

LEFT *Villa della Petraia, Florence. Buontalenti laid out this late sixteenth-century garden for Ferdinando de' Medici. The garden has since been considerably altered.*

RIGHT *Villa Lancellotti, Frascati. Many later Renaissance gardens had parterres laid out in elaborate patterns, sometimes reproducing the coat of arms of the proprietors, all best appreciated from the windows of the palace. Here the garden is sixteenth century, but the nymphaeum in the background is later.*

BELOW *Villa Cicogna Mozzoni, Varese. This garden was created in about 1600; the largest part lies on a steep slope behind the villa, where the water descends a water stair and plays water games. Here we see the peaceful formal garden, with its fishponds, which lies directly outside the villa.*

but the movement it gives to the garden provides a satisfying counterpoint to the sculptural stillness and rigidity of the evergreens and the topiary. Again the garden uses a hillside site, but here there are no terraces; instead the visitor is led up a steep slope to a balcony from which the symmetrical pattern of the parterre below can be appreciated to the full.

Not all garden makers followed the fashion for terraces, fountains and symmetrical planting. At Bomarzo, in the Cimini Hills to the north of Rome, Vicino Orsini turned his back on these garden elements when in 1552 he began creating his Sacro Bosco (Sacred Grove) with its stone monsters, grotesque animals and bizarre leaning house. And in a stone inscription he emphasized that this garden was created 'sol per sfogar il cor', only to unburden his heart. He was related by marriage to the Farnese, who were creating the great palace in Caprarola at much the same time, and he was a friend of Cardinal Gambara, who was working on the Villa Lante, but he decided, splendidly, to go his own way. The site of his sacred grove was not cleared, terraced and set in order; rather, many of the trees were left and the great outcrops of volcanic rock were carved where they were found. Winding, narrow paths connected one group of carvings with another; there is no focal point, no climax to the whole composition. And the statues represent characters not

Il Sacro Bosco, Bomarzo. This is a curiosity among Italian Renaissance gardens. It was created by a retired soldier, Vicino Orsini, in the mid-sixteenth century, and lies in a valley far below his palace. The iconographic programme of the garden remains obscure – if there was one. Orsini teases the visitor with references to 'Orlando Furioso' and Dante, but in an inscription suggests he was merely 'unburdening his heart'. What single explanation can possibly unify the leaning house (above), the dragon (left) and Echida, mother of Cerberus (right)?

from classical myth but from the Italian epic *Orlando Furioso*, and from the work of Dante. The whole creation seems aimed at teasing and disconcerting the visitor – both intellectually, as it is very hard to decipher the iconographic programme behind the work, and emotionally, because some of the statues are horrifyingly energetic and others are amusingly quaint. The inscription beneath the statue of the Sphinx catches this teasing tone exactly: 'You who enter here, consider it part by part, and then tell me if all these extraordinary things are made as a trick or as a work of art.'

Vicino Orsini was a soldier, but he must have been an idiosyncratic individual; certainly his park continues to baffle and intrigue the twenty-first-century visitor.

His daughter, Ottavia, is one of the few Renaissance women garden makers whose work we know about and can still appreciate. In 1574 Ottavia Orsini married Marcantonio Marescotti, the lord of Vignanello, a small town south-east of Viterbo; he was a man whose violent temper led to his assassination in 1608, after which Ottavia was left to run the estate on behalf of her two young sons, Sforza and Galeazzo. She was an intelligent and educated woman who turned her small court into a creative community where all the arts were encouraged. Her castle was a dour, practical, defensive building designed by Antonio da Sangallo the Younger, so it was no easy business to transform it into the Renaissance palace she had set her heart on. To create a garden she first bridged the moat that defended the castle's walls and then levelled the hilltop that stood next to the castle. On this totally flat canvas she laid out a design of twelve rectangular compartments, each of which contains its own elaborate pattern, with modest fountains at the major intersections of the paths. The frames for the compartments were probably originally created in rosemary; now they are planted in a mixture of myrtle, *Viburnum tinus* and laurel, but the intricate interior patterns are all in box. She must have been proud of her creation for she signed it; the central compartment nearest the house has her initials, O.O., enclosing those of her sons, S. and G. Her parterre is entirely screened from the town by walls and two rows of *Quercus ilex*, and it can be best appreciated only from the upper floors of the castle. This garden, which Georgina Masson called 'the most magnificent box parterre in Italy', is severely rectilinear in plan, with no elaboration of fantastical curlicues such as we find in French *broderie* parterres, which became the fashion in a later century. An example of this elaborate, imported style still exists at the Villa Allegri Arvedi, just north of Verona, where it has been proved that not only the layout but some of the box plants themselves date from the late seventeenth century.

BELOW *Castello Ruspoli, Vignanello. Georgina Masson wrote that this is 'the most magnificent box parterre in Italy'. The formal arrangement of rectangles, bounded by low hedges, would originally have been filled with rare plants.*

ABOVE AND RIGHT *Castello Ruspoli, Vignanello. In the early seventeenth century the daughter of Vicino Orsini, Ottavia, had this parterre (above) laid out on a specially flattened hilltop. Ottavia Orsini signed the garden with her own initials (right), enclosing those of her sons, Sforza and Galeasso.*

ABOVE *Villa Doria Pamphili, Rome. Much of this garden is now a public park, but this sunken garden is not open to the public. The original pattern of geometric beds was replaced in the early seventeenth century by the 'broderie' parterre we see today.*

LEFT *Castello di Celsa, Siena. The sixteenth-century garden was designed by Baldassare Peruzzi, whose circular chapel still stands in one corner of the garden. In the seventeenth century the gardens were altered, and this formal garden with a hanging pool created. The views to distant Siena are delightful.*

RIGHT *Villa Carlotta, Lago di Como. The villa was built in 1745 and given as a wedding present to Carlotta, Duchess of Saxe-Meiningen. The gates marked the original landing place from the lake. This entrance garden is very formal, but behind the house there is an English-style garden, more typical of nineteenth-century Italian taste.*

BELOW *Villa Corsi Salviati, Sesto Fiorentino. On a flat site outside Florence, this garden has gone through many changes. The present design was carried out in the early twentieth century, but its aim was to recreate the eighteenth-century layout of the garden.*

The vocabulary of what we know as the Italian garden had by now been firmly established – few flowers, rectilinear plan, elaborate use of water in reflecting pools and fountains, terraces, statues and balustrades, symmetrical planting and, supremely, the architecture of light and shade. At the Villa Garzoni in Collodi the seventeenth-century garden has been overlaid by eighteenth-century taste; typical of that period are the playful terracotta figures on the balustrades of the terraces and stairways. Above this elegant set of steps the water cascades down a water stair that makes it flash and sparkle. The water seems to be descending even more steeply than it really is, because Ottavio Diodati, who renovated the garden in 1786, used a technique from the theatre to alter the perspective: he widened the upper steps of the water stair to make it seem closer to the spectator. Fanciful also are the arabesques of the *broderie* parterre, which can best be appreciated from the top of the stair. The slope below the steps has partitions of glaring flowers and coloured pebbles. Here the architectural sobriety and the limited colour palate of the high Renaissance gardens have been left behind; there is more artful whimsy, more flamboyance, and less controlling intelligence. More traditional, however, are the narrow paths that lead into the *bosco* (wood) on either side of the water stair; these are laid out with rigid symmetry.

At Cetinale, near Siena, many of the traditional elements are treated in a much more sober, indeed penitential way, and there is no water to enliven the scene. The garden was laid out by Carlo Fontana in the late seventeenth century for Cardinal Flavio Chigi, a member of the celebrated Sienese banking dynasty, and its theme is penitence. The Cardinal is said to have done away with a rival in love and he came to Cetinale to repent. The long, narrow axis behind the villa, marked by sombre cypresses, leads the eye inexorably to the flight of steps that ascend the hill to the hermitage – and it is indeed a penitentially steep climb. The figures and the cross on the distant façade are

ABOVE *Villa Allegri Arvedi, Verona. This view shows how gardens made only a small impression when a villa was seen from a distance. This is particularly true of this villa, which has always been the hub of a working estate.*

RIGHT AND BELOW *Villa Garzoni, Collodi. This seventeenth-century garden is necessarily detached from its villa, since the latter was, for reasons of defence, built on a clifftop. From the top of the stairs (right) the visitor looks down on the flat circular space (below), while further up an eighteenth-century water stair leads to the hilltop.*

LEFT AND ABOVE *Villa Cetinale, Sovicile, Siena. From the formal garden near the house it is possible to get a distant glimpse of the Romitorio, the hermitage, on the hillside (left). The theme of this garden is repentance, as the statue, wringing his hands (above), makes clear.*

gigantic, so that they can be easily seen from the garden below. The *bosco* here is also interpreted in terms of repentance; the walks take the visitor past chapels and statues that recall the austere lives of the Desert Fathers. The sparkling gaiety of water would be out of place in this sober setting, as would the bright colours of flowers. But an early twentieth-century Chigi married an Englishwoman; she, of course, could not imagine a garden without flowers, so they reworked the delightful *giardino segreto* to the south of the villa into something very close to an English garden, complete with herbaceous borders.

French influence has been detected in the layout of the wonderful garden of the Villa Barbarigo at Valsanzibio near Padua, although it was started in 1669 ten years before Le Nôtre made his influential Italian journey. The garden that we see today has all the purity of line and harmony of

BELOW AND RIGHT *Villa Barbarigo, Valsanzibio, Padua. This late seventeenth-century garden is divided into four by firm axes (below), but each quadrant contains a different kind of garden – a maze, a rabbit island and so on. Just inside the entrance a bearded sea god relaxes in the rain (right).*

proportion that typify the Italian garden at its best. In the main part of the garden there are almost no flowers, although in the early eighteenth century the garden was famous as the home of many rare plants; these were gathered in a parterre immediately in front of the house, where they were planted in small box-edged beds. Two great cross axes lead the eye away to the gentle, wooded slopes of the Eugean hills, and they divide the garden into equal sections of shaded walks. Fountains and *giocchi d'acqua* (literally 'water games'), now magnificently restored, enliven the scene. Near the entrance the replanted hedge maze, with its central mound, perhaps symbolizes the path to perfection, both a Christian and a Platonic concept. 'On a huge hill/Cragged and steep, Truth stands, and he that will/Reach her, about must, and about must go', as John Donne puts it. By the exercise of their intelligence humans should be able to make their way straight to the mount of perfection, but sin and error have made it necessary to follow a winding track. Originally the intention had been to crown the central hill with a square temple, but it seems this was never built. The hedge maze was a seventeenth-century development of an ancient garden motif; examples of labyrinth patterns are found in several Roman gardens. It is perhaps significant that the maze is near the entrance, for mazes also signified initiation, a necessary testing before the visitor was allowed to experience the delights that the garden had to offer.

In the great Italian gardens water was not only used to delight the visitor with fountain displays: it also drove mechanical devices such as the Screech Owl Fountain at the Villa d'Este, where birds would be heard singing until a screech owl appeared and silenced them with his own piercing call. Water-driven automata had been described from the earliest period in the gardens of eastern palaces; the singing golden birds of Byzantium that so caught the imagination of W.B. Yeats were also probably water driven. Perhaps less appealing were the *giocchi d'acqua* that became popular in seventeenth-century Italy; these consisted usually of hidden jets of water, controlled by the owner or his gardener, which could be switched on to souse the unwary visitor. An elaborate example that is still partly working can be found at the Villa Torlonia near Lucca; visitors were driven by jets of

LEFT *Villa d'Este, Tivoli. To enjoy the cooling effect of the water to the full it is possible to walk behind the Oval Fountain. The sound of the water echoes around the walls of the enclosed courtyard.*

ABOVE *Villa Torlonia, Frascati. This imposing palace had numerous noble owners before it was demolished by Allied bombs on 8 September 1943. The park, which is now open to the public, and its elaborate waterworks have been restored.*

water down the length of the sunken garden, until they were forced to take refuge in the grotto – and, thus corralled, they were given a final, thorough soaking. The *giocchi d'acqua* in the benches at the Villa Barbarigo have been restored and switch themselves on when the visitor crosses an electric beam; this happens before we prepare to sit, and thus we are spared the drenching that so amused our forebears. Most *giocchi d'acqua* are no longer in working order, but they can be found in operation at the perfectly preserved early eighteenth-century garden of the Villa Buonaccorsi near Macerata. Perhaps in the heat of the Italian summer such games were tolerable, but the elaborate clothes of the period must have been unbearably heavy when soaked in water, so one wonders if everyone enjoyed the joke.

At the far end of Ottavia Orsini's garden at the Castello Ruspoli in Vignanello a pair of stately gates opens into the hunting park. As hunting became a less popular activity of the upper class, the only wild area of a garden was usually the *bosco*, which provided shady walks for the inhabitants of the villa, where noble ladies could take the air without risking the fair complexions which set them apart from the peasantry, the *contadini*. At the Villa Rizzardi near Verona the *bosco* was originally laid out in formal straight lines, but after its destruction during the Napoleonic occupation it was planted in a more informal English style, and it has been made more romantic with a pair of stone pumas that crouch on either side of the winding path, their thrilling wildness safely transformed into art. In this garden there is also a fine green theatre, more open than the example at the Villa Reale near Lucca but lacking the terracotta figures of the *commedia dell'arte*. The garden of the Villa Rizzardi, created by Luigi Trezza between 1783 and 1791, is a brilliant rethinking of how to use the typically Italian hillside site. Here the house is situated not at the top of the slope; instead it looks along the lowest of three, long parallel terraces, marked by lines of well-grown trees.

ABOVE AND LEFT *Villa Reale, Lucca. The Baroque Green Theatre still has its cast of* three *commedia dell'arte* characters. *Paganini sometimes performed here for Napoleon's sister Elisa Baciocchi.*

ABOVE AND RIGHT *Isola Bella, Lago Maggiore. The main part of this seventeenth-century garden (above) rises from the lake shore in tiers, like a giant, square wedding cake. From its summit ten terraces descend to the water (right), each formal but differently designed.*

Trezza's organization of space is masterful, and has all the elegance of the architectural Italian garden at its best. But it is here we say goodbye to the Italian garden proper; the taste for so-called 'English' gardens was soon to sweep away many formal gardens throughout the peninsula, just as in England 'Capability' Brown's landscaping destroyed so many fine formal gardens of an earlier period.

Which is not to say that great gardens were no longer created in Italy, but they were largely created by foreigners, many of them English, who have never been able to resist the lure of exotic, colourful plants. Two Englishmen made wonderful gardens in Italy, Sir Thomas Hanbury at La Mortola in the mid nineteenth century, and Ernest Beckett, Lord Grimethorpe, at Ravello in the early twentieth century. In 1868 at La Mortola, just outside Ventimiglia, the Quaker Thomas Hanbury began to make a remarkable garden, initially much influenced by his brother Daniel, a botanist with a particular interest in medicinal plants. The steep site beside the sea was terraced and plants were collected from all over the world, so that by the end of the century the director of Kew could write that the garden 'had no rival among the principal collections of living plants in the world'. But it was not just a collection of plants: it was also a garden where the plants were arranged for aesthetic effect, and its beauties were much admired by Queen Victoria on her two visits. After many vicissitudes and a long period of neglect La Mortola has been taken over by the University of Genoa and is being developed as a botanical garden. It is good to see that the place is being cared for, but regrettable that a great garden is becoming no more than a collection of plants arranged by genus, for the convenience of scientists.

BELOW *La Mortola, Ventimiglia. Sir Thomas Hanbury bought the site in 1867, and it was developed as a botanical garden under the guidance of Ludwig Winter. After a long period of neglect the garden now flourishes under the care of the University of Genoa.*

ABOVE *Villa Cimbrone, Ravello. The site was bought in 1904 by Ernest Beckett, soon to become Lord Grimthorpe. The courtyard of the villa imitates the Moorish style of the nearby Villa Rufolo.*

Much further south and forty years later Lord Grimethorpe bought a ruined farm and a piece of land with a superb view over the Amalfi coast; it is said he paid only 100 lire for the lot. With the help of a local tailor, who clearly had some talent as a designer, he created the villa and the garden of the Villa Cimbrone at Ravello. This garden is a wonderfully idiosyncratic blend of traditional Italian and late nineteenth-century English taste: no terracing, but many statues, a rose garden, winding paths through the woods, straight paths in the formal part of the garden, a lawn, an avenue of cypress, a temple, a tea pavilion and, of course, that hallmark of an Edwardian garden – a pergola. The tradition of creating great botanical collections was continued by the Scot Neil MacEarchern at the Villa Taranto near Lake Maggiore, where the microclimate makes it possible to grow an astonishingly wide range of plants. Parts of this garden manage to become beautiful as miniature works of art, but some remain just the framework in which to display a collection of plants. He began his garden in 1931 and, with huge generosity, in 1951 gave it to the Italian state.

Totalitarian government means that all aspects of life become politicized, including the making of gardens. During the twenty years of the Fascist era the emphasis was on the glory of the traditional Italian garden: in April 1931 Mussolini ordered an exhibition on the subject in Florence. Aristocrats and town councils were encouraged to restore their historic gardens, although the word 'restoration' was not applied with scholarly accuracy. More often a highly decorated style thought to be typical of the high Renaissance was invented for the occasion. And when an Anglo-Italian family, the Caetani, began to create one of the great gardens of the world at Ninfa in the 1920s, they demonstrated their opposition to the regime by designing the garden in a deliberately relaxed, romantic, English style.

In 1297 the Caetani family had paid 200,000 gold florins for the town of Ninfa, which lay, profitably, on the road from Rome to Naples. The place was destroyed by papal troops in 1382, when the family took the 'wrong' side during the Great Schism. Then the malaria that was endemic in the Pontine marshes began to drive out the remaining inhabitants, so that by 1680 the town was deserted. But in the early twentieth century the Caetani family used to visit Ninfa for picnics, and in 1922 Ada Wilbraham Caetani, an Englishwoman, and her son Gelasio began to make a garden here. Their progress was made harder because Italian nurseries at this period had a very limited range of plants. Some of the roses that Ada planted still survive at Ninfa, curling their way up the rose-brick walls of the ruined medieval town and poking their heads out of the empty windows. Gelasio's brother Roffredo married an American, Marguerite Chapin, and together they continued the development of the garden. But it was to their child, Lelia, and her English husband, Hubert Howard, that we owe the splendour of the garden we see today. These two were great plant collectors and added many of the 10,000 species that still flourish at Ninfa. Lelia was also an artist and, not satisfied with painting garden views, she used to paint pictures of what she wanted the garden to look like, in this way creating some of the great compositions that still enchant the visitor.

Everything grows at Ninfa with enormous speed and to enormous proportions because of the abundant water and the high temperatures. This luxuriance of growth and the informality of the layout make it seem such a relaxed garden, but in reality it is a work of art of the greatest subtlety;

the relaxation must be allowed to go just so far and no further, in the same way that the ruins must be allowed to decay but not to fall apart completely. Wild flowers are welcomed into the garden but not allowed to become dominant; the grass is left unmown, but not everywhere. Today the director of the garden, Lauro Marchetti, is responsible for treading this fine line between chaos and order, and he is supremely successful. And for visitors brought up on eighteenth-century views of the Roman *campagna* with ruins and wild flowers, and for those who are worshippers of Sissinghurst in England, the combination of carefully relaxed planting and ruins is irresistible. This is the very antithesis of an Italian garden, but neither is it an English garden; Ninfa is unique and one of the glories of the world.

The influence of wives cannot be overestimated in the creation of Ninfa. Two other lady gardeners have made interesting twentieth-century Italian gardens, both on hugely challenging sites. In 1956 when the Marchesa Lavinia Taverna started gardening at La Landriana, she and her husband had first to remove unexploded bombs and shells from the sandy soil over which the Allies had advanced only twelve years before. She was a great plant collector but, realizing the need for more structure in her garden, in the late 1960s she asked for the help of the celebrated English designer Russell Page. From all accounts their relationship was productively argumentative; the marchesa didn't always follow his advice, but the elegant proportions and formal planting that typify Page's work are still a dominant note at La Landriana. The division of the garden into thirty-two rooms allows for a rich mixture of formality and informality both in layout and planting. In the Orange Garden mop-headed acers stand at the centre of six rectangular beds, lording it over the glistening orange trees, whose heads are also clipped into balls, the shape being echoed beneath by clipped box, myrtle and *Myrsine africana*; this elegant simplicity is as successful as it is original,

BELOW *Ninfa, Latina. Ninfa was a prosperous town on the road between Rome and Naples, but in 1382 the ruler, Onorato Caetani, took the wrong side in the Great Schism and the town was sacked. In the 1920s the Caetani family began to make a garden among the ruins of the medieval city.*

ABOVE *Giardini della Landriana, Tor San Lorenzo. The Marchesa Lavinia Taverna and her husband bought the site after the Second World War. With the help of Russell Page they designed a wide variety of linked gardens, some formal, some informal. Here globes of* Myrsine africana *echo the roundness of the oranges.*

a fine example, it would seem, of Page's very un-English style. In fact, however, this garden was created by the marchesa when she grew tired of the roses with which Page had originally filled the beds. Elsewhere paths ramble through a dell under blossoming cherries, down to a lake; there is a delightful garden room under ancient olive trees, where the predominant colours are grey and yellow, and there is a white garden. Since the marchesa's death the garden has not always been maintained to the highest standard, so that the sharp lines of the formal plantings have become blurred. But La Landriana remains a most interesting blend of English and Italian taste; paradoxically the English informality was supplied by an Italian and the Italian formality by an Englishman.

At La Biviere in Sicily the Principessa Borghese and her husband also had a challenging site to cope with when they began their garden. The site was originally a small harbour on a lake, sacred to Hercules, that had had to be drained when the threat of malaria became too severe. On such unpromising, flat terrain the Borgheses have created an extraordinarily original garden. The jetties of the port have been used as a home for gigantic succulent plants, collected from all over the world, and their grotesque shapes make this almost another Bomarzo, but a park of natural not sculpted monsters. As Miki Borghese writes in her account of the garden, 'Anyone who had learned to love the strange world of "succulent plants" knows that with them . . . nature unleashed her imagination, giving almost architectural shapes to these odd inhabitants of the planet.'

ABOVE *Giardini della Landriana, Tor San Lorenzo. In another part of the gardens the topiary is more formally Italian.*

BELOW *Le Balze, Fiesole. The garden was made in the 1920s by Cecil Pinsent on a narrow, hillside site. His design contains many echoes of the Italian Renaissance garden.*

But here there are not only succulents: roses flourish lavishly and there is colour as well as form. This is another original garden, neither Italian nor English but an idiosyncratic garden where the strong personality of the owners is expressed at every turn.

An Italian garden has always been a theatrical space waiting to be populated; a solitary individual will always seem isolated and out of place in such surroundings. Italian culture in general has little room for the solitary individual; visits to the supermarket and the hospital, picnics, eating in restaurants, etc. are all communal, and usually family, activities. Thus the Italian garden needs to

RIGHT *Villa Borghese, Rome. These gardens were begun by Scipio Borghese in the early seventeenth century. The gardens around the casino were laid out by Girolamo Rainaldi, and include an elegant aviary. They have recently been restored.*

be populated; it is the people, not flowers and shrubs, who add the colour and glamour that are otherwise lacking. And little is hidden; there is no mystery; these gardens are for display and require actors and an audience, just like the Bramante courtyard.

The Italian garden style is apparently easy to imitate; you just lay out a pattern of low box hedges with larger hedges behind, bung in a few statues, a handful of steps and a length of balustrade, and, if the budget will stretch to it, add a fountain or two. But in late nineteenth-century England when Italian gardens were all the rage, it was apparent to all that this imported style was a kind of pastiche; beds filled with blazing geraniums could not supply the effect created by the Italian sun. Another problem is that when the garden is carelessly planned, with little attention to the proportions of the spaces into which it is divided, the result is a disaster, particularly when the beds are filled with shapeless, garish annuals. Then there is the different light: in Italy the strong light creates dramatic contrasts between light and shade; the shade has an architectural impact, it seems so dense and solid; fountains sparkle brilliantly in the sun; and the white of statues stands out sharply against the sombre background of ilex, yew or box. In the mistier light of England these contrasts are much less dramatic, and the architectural character of the garden is less easily appreciated.

At Trentham Park Sir Charles Barry laid out an elaborate Franco-Italian garden for the Duke of Sutherland; what is left can give us an idea of how little suited is such a style to the flatness of Shropshire. And at Shrubland Park in East Anglia Barry, working closely with the owner, Sir William Middleton, created what he called 'the Villa d'Este descent', a breathtaking flight of steps with transverse terraces. Many of the great houses of Victorian England sit on a flat podium and it became traditional to treat this flat space in an Italian or French style with formally patterned beds full of exotic annuals, surrounded by balustrades and sets of steps. In late Victorian England, as taste began to change, William Robinson led the attack on such Italian-style gardens, calling them 'stone gardens', and, in a brilliantly chosen phrase, he described gardens full of symmetrically arranged topiary as 'posing grounds', which takes us back to the theatricality of the quintessential Italian garden.

Italian gardens were more successful in the southern states of the USA, and, of course, in California in the early years of the twentieth century. Many landscape artists came from the US to study at the American Academy in Rome, Ralph E. Griswold and Edward G. Lawson being among the more celebrated. They borrowed details and even whole designs to take back to America. This is why green theatres, modelled often on that of the

BELOW Villa Capponi, Florence. In 1882 when Lady Scott purchased the fifteenth-century villa, she added another walled, lower garden, below the sunken garden (see page 127). Later still, in 1928, Cecil Pinsent was called in to design a swimming pool in the lowest part of the garden. However, these changes have not altered this garden's period charm.

Villa Gori, near Siena, were to be found as far apart as Groton, Connecticut, and the Wattles Garden in Hollywood. Another detail, popular in America, was the *catena d'acqua* (literally 'water chain', a water channel with protrusions from the sides that make the water swirl and eddy), a fine imitation of which was created at the Culbertson garden in Pasadena, California. How well the Italian garden style suits the bright light of California can be seen at the J. Paul Getty Museum in Malibu, where the garden seeks to reproduce the courtyard of the Villa dei Papiri near Herculaneum.

Today the Italian gardener is as proud of his or her topiary as ever was Pliny the Younger; few trees escape the orderly, annual shaping that Italians love in their gardens, though elsewhere disorder is one of the multiple charms of the country. For centuries the Italian garden maker showed little interest in flowers or in colour, but today colour, sometimes of the most violent hue, is admired, and many historic parterres, which would have had their box compartments outlined in coloured sand or gravel, today are planted with garish, shapeless annuals – 'because the general public like them'. Worst of all are the begonias that affect the historic Italian garden like a spotty plague.

Italian music, painting, sculpture and architecture set the standards for artists throughout Europe; in gardens too the Italian model was dominant, until challenged by the innovations of the English landscape style in the eighteenth century. The Tudor and Stuart gardens of England, with their formal lines, fountains and gravel walks, derive from Italian example, modified sometimes by French interpretation. Dutch baroque gardens, Spanish patios and French parterres are typical of the garden cultures of those countries, but if we look for their roots we shall find them all in Italy, and often in ancient Rome.

ABOVE AND LEFT *Villa Torrigiani, Lucca. In the seventeenth century the front of the villa would have been laid out as parterres around the two pools. Today (above) the pools survive, but the parterres have given way to an 'English' park. The sunken garden (left) has survived too, together with the grotto where guests would have been soaked by jets of water.*

BELOW AND RIGHT *Villa Balbianello, Lago di Como. The first villa was built here in 1540, the owner being attracted by the glorious views down the three arms of the lake. In the later eighteenth century Cardinal Durrini built the present casino (below). The garden (right) is not terraced but has sweeping lawns and informal paths.*

6

THE ENGLISH LANDSCAPE PARK

ABOVE *Wrest Park, Bedford. The garden buildings provide a record of changing taste in eighteenth-century England. They range from Thomas Archer's Baroque banqueting house (1711) to this later eighteenth-century Chinese pavilion, built for Jemima, Marchioness Grey.*

LEFT *Buscot Park, Faringdon. The house dates from the late eighteenth century, but the garden was developed in the twentieth century, Harold Peto's elaborate water garden being one of the most successful additions.*

Did it ever strike you as odd to find so many imitations of classical Roman buildings scattered over the face of England? Here a pantheon, there a nymphaeum; here a Temple to Flora, there to Neptune – and all these temples to pagan gods in supposedly Christian England. Then there are triumphal arches, exedra (patterns of convex and concave steps meeting at a circular centre), celebratory columns – a whole mass of alien, classical clutter. What is it doing in the gentle English landscape? Most of these buildings are to be found in what is known as a landscape park, a revolutionary style of gardening that has spawned a host of distant European imitators known as *giardini inglesi*, *jardins anglais*, *englische Garten* and so on. The curious thing is that the fashion for the landscape park, at its peak of success, almost led to the elimination of the flower garden, for which the English deserve to be equally famous. It has been said: 'The "Jardin Anglais" refers to a time when the English lost their heads and scrapped their gardens.'

So how and why did the landscape park with its imitation classical buildings become the dominant style in eighteenth-century England? After the return of Charles II from his exile in France in 1660, the nobility began remaking their gardens, or creating new ones, in the French style following Le Nôtre; Charles even invited the celebrated designer to England, although there is no record of his ever having crossed the Channel. The French style emphasized a single viewpoint. At Versailles it was that of the King; he could stand on his terrace and see the avenues cut through his woods radiating (as was appropriate for *le roi soleil*) in a *patte d'oie* or goosefoot pattern; everything seemed to derive from him. The central avenue disappeared over the horizon, giving his majesty the flattering sensation that his power had no limit. To lay out your English grounds in this style was not easy if you had a small estate of a mere few hundred acres, so it was with some relief, after 1688 and the arrival of William and Mary, that garden makers turned to the Dutch style, which could be imitated in more confined spaces.

Parks in the French style are now few and far between, but at Hampton Court Palace in Surrey with its radiating avenues of limes, arranged in the familiar *patte d'oie* pattern, it is possible to appreciate the majestic effect they aimed at. The same pattern of alleys on a smaller scale can be seen at Inkpen Old Rectory in Berkshire. The best extant evidence of the wholesale influence of the French style are the prints made by Knyff and Kip in the late seventeenth and early eighteenth centuries of eighty-two palaces and country seats. Two things are immediately striking about the parks illustrated in these engravings: the dominance of the straight line, and the symmetry of their design.

The park at Longleat in Wiltshire is typical of its period; it had been designed for Lord Weymouth in 1685 by George London, who in 1681 had founded the famous Brompton Park Nursery where Henry Wise began work in 1688. The broad central avenue stretches from the house between a series of symmetrically arranged smaller gardens, all rectangular in outline, although some of the rectangles contain circular shapes. The central avenue leads to a fountain on a distant hillside, whence straight rides radiate through the woods. Nearer the house there is evidence of a *broderie* parterre, elaborate patterns of beds edged in box which the Mollet family had made fashionable in seventeenth-century France. Charles II had employed André and Gabriel Mollet at St James's Palace, and, the King's taste was imitated by English nobles throughout the land.

Just as the *patte d'oie* design at Versailles focused all the avenues on a single point, the King, so garden design in Restoration England drew its inspiration from one centre, the court. But all this was to change.

In 1688 the English disposed of a second king, this time less bloodily than forty years earlier. With his successor, William III, came a taste for Dutch gardens whose intricate patterns, still largely rectilinear, could be imitated on a smaller scale. At Westbury Court in Gloucestershire it is possible to appreciate something of the Dutch style. Maynard Colchester created the gardens between 1694 and 1705; his account book survived and made possible an accurate restoration of the garden in the mid twentieth century. Unmoving water is a dominant feature, with two rectilinear canals in this modest, flat, walled garden; the first is long and narrow (135 metres by 6.5 metres/ 442 feet by 21 feet), enclosed by yew hedges; it stretches from a two-storey pavilion to a *clairvoyée*, a gap in the wall, beyond which there would originally have been a long view down an avenue. The second canal was added by Maynard Colchester's successor. Typical of the period is the topiary and the formal parterre, which has been recreated from Kip's engraving of 1707. The dominance of art and the human hand is stressed where *Prunus lusitanica*, shaped into sturdy umbrellas, is arranged in the pattern of a quincunx. The design of this garden probably owes little to court influence, and much more to the fact that Maynard Colchester had Dutch neighbours.

Within fifty years such intricate, labour-intensive gardening had gone out of fashion; the straight lines of Westbury's canals and of Longleat's avenues were things of the past. Trees pruned into formal shapes were detested for their artificiality. Thus a whole tradition of Continental gardening, all deriving ultimately from Italian example, was rejected, as a newly self-confident England began to discover an English style of park and garden-making. Many of the elaborate gardens of Tudor and Stuart England with their fountains, grottoes, statues, balustrades and steps disappeared for ever

BELOW *Westbury Court, Westbury-on-Severn. A rare example of a Dutch-style garden, created in about 1700 by Maynard Colchester, whose account books, together with an engraving by Kip, have enabled the National Trust to restore the garden accurately. The yew hedges enclose a canal.*

ABOVE *Wrest Park, Bedford. Another rare garden, an early eighteenth-century design, perhaps by Bridgeman, very much in the French style. Here we see the Long Water with woods on either side. 'Capability' Brown worked here later, but spared the earlier layout.*

under the rolling swell of grassland, the lakes and the clumps of trees designed by Lancelot Brown.

After the trauma of the Cromwellian rebellion the English were determined to avoid another civil war and that meant fostering a kind of social cohesion based on tolerance. They had avoided the religious extremes of Catholicism under James II and of Puritanism under Cromwell; the Church of England was seen to represent a kind of golden mean between those two extremes. The Act of Toleration, which was passed in 1689, gave freedom of religion to all but Catholics and Unitarians. At the same time on the field of battle Marlborough was winning victory after victory against the overweening French. The English felt themselves different from their Continental neighbours, and in many ways superior; they were free in a way that no other European country was, particularly since the monarchy established after 1688 had severely limited powers. There was a new awareness of national identity and a self-confidence bred of military and economic success; it manifested itself partly in a new interest in the national past led by the Royal Society, which was granted a royal charter in 1662; Anglo-Saxon documents were published, the ancient language was studied and the antiquities of the English countryside were examined.

The gardens of the late seventeenth century, however, still followed foreign models, and they came to be seen as too opulent, too socially divisive, too showily extravagant in their artifice and in the engineering required by their mechanical devices; the seventeenth-century garden at Wilton House in Wiltshire, for example, contained a grotto where three artificially created rainbows could be seen simultaneously. They were the gardens of a court-centred nobility who, by the early eighteenth century, were no longer the force in the land they had been.

At the Restoration about 250 people, 160 of them peers of the realm, owned estates of more than 4,046 hectares/10,000 acres, and upon them John Evelyn urged a sense of responsibility. They needed to replace the severely depleted timber stocks of the nation by planting trees and avenues.

ABOVE *Wrest Park, Bedford. Allées are cut through the woods, and at their intersections there are temples, columns or, as here, a bridge to add variety. There are even the 'remains' of a bath house, built as a romantic ruin.*

Charles himself set an example by planting 6,000 elms at Greenwich in 1664. At this time trees were often 'plashed' (or pleached) – that is to say their sides were pruned so that they looked like a kind of hedge on stilts; Horace Walpole criticized this French style of pruning trees, removing all the lower branches, so that their groves 'seem green chests set upon poles'. Evelyn did not approve of this style of pruning either, and wrote of the elms in St James's Park, which had been opened to the public in 1661, 'I did much prefer the walk of elms at St James' Park as it lately grew, branchy, intermingling their reverend tresses.' He was anticipating a taste for allowing natural growth that was to become all the rage in the next century. Some took Evelyn's urging to plant timber too much to heart; the Duke of Montague, who between 1684 and 1705 laid out his garden in the French style at Boughton in Northamptonshire, planned an avenue that would link his estate with London, 112 kilometres/70 miles away.

The early years of the eighteenth century were a period of economic prosperity, a necessary condition for garden-making. After 1707, when the parliament of Scotland was merged with that of England, these two countries plus Wales formed the largest free-trade area in Europe, and it was a vigorous trade, usually carried on by water as the roads were still so bad. As Daniel Defoe wrote: ''Tis our great felicity in England that we are not yet come to a gabelle or tax upon corn, as in Italy, and many other countries.' During the eighteenth century the pace of enclosure increased and with it the productivity of the land. It has been estimated that 1,011,700 hectares/2.5 million acres of open field and 809,000 hectares/2 million acres of common land were enclosed, with the result that sheep produced twice as much meat and three times as much wool as previously. Corn was exported so successfully that the rise in prices caused unrest in the Gloucester coalfields, and wool continued to be a major source of export income. Merchants who invested in this trade often spent their profits on the purchase of land, for only land gave a person social consequence.

And their newly purchased, often newly enclosed, land had to be profitable, so they were anxious to make improvements to it. The Royal Society also concerned itself with agricultural improvement, and there was a thirst for new devices to make agriculture more profitable; Jethro Tull's seed drill and horse hoe were typical products of this initiative. These newly rich, newly landed country gentlemen would read Addison and Steele's *The Spectator* to learn how to behave politely and how to think correctly.

Addison was to play a significant part in forming the new English taste for a more relaxed, less formal style of gardening. In 1699 he was awarded a bursary of £300 to enable him to study on the Continent, before beginning his career as a diplomat. He was to lose the bursary with the death of William III, but by then he had had time to travel widely in France and Italy. While still on his way through France he wrote to his friend, the dramatist Congreve, about the gardens he had seen: he says he preferred Fontainbleau because there 'The King has Humoured the Genius of the place, and only made use of so much Art as is necessary to Help and regulate Nature without reforming her too much.' We shall hear much of this kind of language in early eighteenth-century writing about gardens: 'the genius of the place' is, of course, a straight translation of the Latin *genius loci*, while the debate about whether art or nature should be given precedence in garden-making was not new and has yet to reach a conclusion. Addison in the same letter seems to come down in

BELOW *Hampton Court Castle, Leominster. The present owners are not restoring the seventeenth-century Baroque garden: instead they are making something excitingly new. But they have kept the parkland as the setting for the house and Paxton's fine conservatory.*

favour of nature; just after the passage quoted above, he writes: 'For my part I think there is something more charming in these rude heaps of Stone than in so many Statues, and would as soon see a River winding through Woods and Meadows, as it does near Fontain-bleu, than as when it is toss'd up in such a Variety of figures at Versailles.' Rude heaps of stone preferred to the sculpted smoothness of statuary, and a river winding thought more beautiful than a straight, orderly canal or a fountain! Something radical is stirring in the undergrowth!

As the hugely influential editor of *The Spectator*, Addison continued to promote the view that something more 'natural' was to be preferred to the highly wrought artifice of French and Dutch gardens. In his famous essay, number 414, dated 25 June 1712, he writes that contemporary English gardeners 'instead of humouring Nature, love to deviate from it as much as possible. Our trees rise in Cones, Globes and Pyramids. We see the Marks of the Scissars [sic] upon every Plant and Bush. I do not know whether I am singular in my Opinion, but for my own part, I would rather look upon a Tree in all its Luxuriancy and Diffusion of Boughs and Branches, than when it is thus cut and trimmed into some Mathematical Figure.' In the same essay he praises the extensive gardens of France and Italy, but fears that the pragmatic English might dislike devoting so much land to non-profitable purposes. He suggests that it may be possible for the land to be beautiful and profitable, posing a question to the thrifty English landowner that was to find a rapid and widespread response: 'But why may not a whole Estate be thrown into a kind of Garden by frequent Plantations, that may turn as much to Profit as the Pleasure of the Owner?' And he illustrates what he means: 'A Marsh overgrown with Willows, or a Mountain shaded with Oaks, are not only more beautiful, but more beneficial, than when they lie bare and unadorned. Fields of corn make a pleasant Prospect, and if the Walks were a little taken care of that lie between them, if the natural Embroidery of the Meadows were helped and improved by some small Additions of Art, and the several Rows of Hedges set off by Trees and Flowers, that the Soil was capable of receiving, a Man might make a pretty Landskip of his own Possessions.'

The word 'landskip' (this is the original form of the word, borrowed from the Dutch) originally meant a painting that took as its subject a view of the countryside, in contrast to a 'seascape'. But gradually the word came to mean also the rural scene itself, which could, of course, be improved and altered until it resembled a painting. And it was in the paintings of Gaspard Poussin and Claude Lorrain that the British found another model for their new kind of gardening. The landscapes to be seen in the background of these painters' works seemed a kind of idealized, Italian landscape, hints of which the privileged youth of late seventeenth- and eighteenth-century England had seen on the Grand Tour – hints only, because it was Roman ruins that they had seen, and from these the traveller had to reconstruct in his imagination the great monuments and gardens of the Roman republic and early empire.

Stephen Switzer, who had worked with Wise and Vanburgh at Blenheim in Oxfordshire, in his *Ichnographia Rustica* (1718), following Addison, argued for what he called 'rural gardening', a kind of gardening which no longer draws strict boundaries between the pleasure grounds, the park and the farm, but treats the whole estate as potential landscape. He traces this style of park and garden-making back to the Romans; 'the Romans had doubtless the same kind of extensive gardening', 'their Elysium being none other than the happy and regular Distribution, and cheerful Aspect of pleasant Gardens, Meadows and Fields'. He shows how the British could become the heirs of this great tradition of gardening, and ''Tis then we shall hope to excel the so much boasted Gardens of France.' He rejects the finicky, fussy Dutch style – 'those crimping, diminutive, and wretched Performances we everywhere meet with . . . The Top of these Designs being in Clipt Plants, Flowers and other trifling Decorations'. National pride called for a new, British gardening style and Switzer, by grounding this new style in classical precedent, gave it an added impetus.

It was not necessary to own a huge estate to begin gardening in the new style. At Twickenham to the west of London the great poet Alexander Pope had a mere 2 hectares/5 acres, and they were rented. As a Catholic he was subject to many kinds of legal discrimination; he could not, for example, live within 16 kilometres/10 miles of London. Since the main road from Hampton Court to London divided the house from the garden and the river, Pope had to create a tunnel, or, to use the severe words of Dr Johnson, whose taste in gardening was formed by a later age, 'Vanity produced a grotto where necessity enforced a passage.' This grotto became famous and Pope worked on it until his death in 1744. It was walled with unusual fragments of crystal and coral, and fitted with mirrors to reflect the daylight into unexpected corners. An alabaster lamp shed a romantically dim light, and water was engineered to produce a 'little dripping murmur'. Here the savage satirist, the leading writer of the Age of Reason, allowed his imagination to rampage. His garden was an anthology of garden styles; there were mounts as in Tudor gardens, there were statues but no topiary, there were straight allées but also winding paths, and the views to the Thames were left open. Pope even found room for a vineyard, a bowling green, a kitchen garden and an orangery.

This fierce polemicist had firm views on many things, gardens included. In his *Epistle to Burlington* Pope describes just the kind of garden he deplores:

> His Gardens next your admiration call,
> On every side you look, behold the Wall!
> No pleasing Intricacies intervene,
> No artful wildness to perplex the scene:
> Grove nods at grove, each alley has a brother,
> And half the platform just reflects the other.
> The suff'ring eye inverted Nature sees,
> Trees cut to Statues, Statues thick as trees.

Pope loathed not only the way this walled garden repulses the landscape outside its boundary, and its artificial formality, but also the vast cost of the whole showy enterprise:

> 'Tis Use alone that sanctifies Expense,
> And Splendour borrows all her rays from sense.

He admired the man who can balance beauty with utility:

> Whose ample Lawns are not ashamed to feed
> The milky heifer and deserving steed.

In an age when civil war was still a recent memory, the absence of dogmatic extremism, was a supreme virtue, and Horace, poet of the Golden Mean, was one of this age's favourite authors. It was an age that called itself Augustan to underline the links they felt with the late Roman republic and the early empire. Polished behaviour was emphasized and the enlightened circle of writers and painters felt they were living in a time when civilization had reached one of its peaks. Pope had written imitations of Horace, translated Homer and Virgil, making them 'speak good English', and rewritten some poems by Donne, giving them the polish that Donne would have given them had he lived in a more enlightened age!

Some even liked to see Britain as in a sense the heir of Rome; in what James Thomson called 'the matchless constitution, mixed/Of mutual checking and supporting powers' many found parallels with the consuls (the king), patricians and plebeians of ancient Rome. One even wrote that London might become 'a new Rome in the west'. So when Switzer saw the English as Rome's heirs with their new taste for 'extensive gardening', he was far from alone. The classical authors were the reading of every country squire: in Somerville's ideal vision

> A rural squire, to crowds and courts unknown
> In his own cell retired, but not alone;
> For round him view each Greek and Roman sage,
> Polite companions of his riper age.

The country squire or nobleman retired on his estate (perhaps because he was a Whig and thus out of power) could see himself imitating Horace's retirement from the thronging streets of Rome, a common theme of late seventeenth-century verse. And when Horace Walpole, later in the eighteenth century, came to praise the new style of gardening that England had invented, he echoed Horace in his encomium: 'We [the English] have discovered the point of perfection. We have given the true model of gardening to the world; let other countries mimic or corrupt our taste; but let it reign here on its verdant throne, original by its elegant simplicity ['simplex munditiis' was Horace's phrase], and proud of no other art than that of softening nature's harshnesses and copying her graceful touches.'

So when we find temples, rotundas, exedras, triumphal arches, celebratory columns and the rest decorating the English countryside, we are intended not simply to recall the paintings of Gaspard Poussin, or sketches made on the Grand Tour, but also to see a political statement in these buildings; Britain, like Rome, had freed itself from the tyranny of an absolute monarchy, and founded an empire. It is not surprising, therefore, that on the highest point on Hawkwell Field at Stowe in Buckinghamshire, in a place visible from almost any point of the compass, stood a Gothic temple, which was originally called the Temple of Freedom. Temples abounded in this nominally Christian country, but the rational, middle-of-the-road English aristocracy, some of whom were deists like Addison, saw nothing shocking in these pagan structures.

At Stowe the references to Rome and to contemporary politics are too obvious to be missed. William Kent had spent ten years in Italy as a young man and had there met Lord Burlington,

BELOW *Stowe, Buckingham. One of the most influential landscapes in the country, and one on which almost every famous eighteenth-century British designer worked. The buildings and layout are full of classical and political significance. The Palladian bridge was copied from an earlier example at Wilton House.*

ABOVE *Kingston Lacy, Wimborne Minster. Stowe boasted one of the earliest ha-has in England. The example here shows the sloping bank, leading to the vertical wall, which made it impossible for animals to enter, while the view into the park was uninterrupted. Most ha-has were not equipped with cannons!*

who was to be his first patron. Kent trained as a painter, but his lack of talent in that field made him turn his painter's eye to architecture and landscape. At Stowe Lord Cobham, one of the many Whig peers condemned to life on their country estates after 1710 when the Tories came to power, employed first Charles Bridgeman and then Kent to release the garden from its formality and to unite it with the park, so that his lordship might, in Addison's words, 'make a pretty landskip of his own possessions'. While Kent designed the buildings, Cobham himself seems to have laid down the iconographical programme for the Elysian Fields. This area near the house took its name from the paradise inhabited by the souls of classical heroes; the whole tone is elegiac, a mournful paean to past glory. The Temple of Ancient Virtue was modelled on the Temple of Vesta at Tivoli, but Kent placed it in such a way that it invited comparison with the Temple of Modern Virtue – a ruin, naturally, with a headless bust at its apex, supposedly representing Robert Walpole. The composition included the Gothic parish church and the Temple of British Worthies; the Gothic had its own particular political significance, as we shall see later. The Temple of British Worthies is built in an exedral shape, possibly an imitation of the Villa Mattei in Rome, but instead of the pedimented aedicule at the centre Kent designed one of his favourite pyramids. The temple contains busts of English heroes, such as Drake, Milton and Newton, all dead, and the visitor exploring behind the monument will find a memorial to one Signor Fido, whose exemplary virtues stir our admiration, until we realize Signor Fido was a dog.

Stowe provides us with a perfect example of what was happening in the early years of the eighteenth century. The old formal gardens, clearly separated from the park beyond, were pulled apart and the land was reshaped into flowing forms. What remained of the garden was opened up to the park, and beyond the park Cobham followed Pope's dictum to 'call in the country'. The garden is to be explored, not seen from one point of view, and as visitors follow the tour (Stowe was the first garden for which a guidebook was produced) they are presented with new compositions and see the buildings in new combinations, which provoke new thoughts and reactions.

The unbroken line of sight from the formal garden into the park was made possible by the ha-ha, a ditch with one vertical and one sloping wall, which prevented animals from invading the area near the house, while giving the impression, from a distance, that there was no barrier at all. This device, which became essential to the picturesque unity of the landscape park, was developed from military models, perhaps invented by the seventeenth-century French military engineer Vauban. Bridgeman had designed a primitive kind of ha-ha at Stowe, but this was more of a wall with horizontal stakes preventing animal incursions. At Claremont in Surrey Kent used the more sophisticated double-sided ditch in a great curving line. It was thanks to the ha-ha that Kent, in Horace Walpole's famous sentence, 'leaped the fence and saw that all nature was a garden'. Few more fatuous words have gained such celebrity; whatever nature is, it is not a garden, and never was so, even in the improved parks and farms of early eighteenth-century England.

When Kent returned from Italy, he complained about England, calling it this 'Gothick country', meaning by the adjective all that was rough, uncivilized, unpolished, unimproved. But he was soon designing in the Gothic as well as in the classical style, because the Gothic also had its political

ABOVE *Audley End, Saffron Walden. The magnificent Jacobean house is surrounded by a nineteenth-century parterre garden, and beyond that by a 'Capability' Brown landscape park. Brown was an architect and landscaper, or, rather – as he styled himself – a 'place maker'.*

implications. At Cirencester Park in Gloucestershire Lord Bathurst, Pope's great friend, asked Stephen Switzer to help him with improvements to the park, although his lordship perhaps decided much of the layout himself. One of the improvements was the restoration of Alfred's Seat; Alfred was a national hero, who had resisted the Danish invader and ensured British freedoms which were only lost at the Norman Conquest. At Stourhead in Wiltshire there is an Alfred's Tower, designed in 1765, a companion in architectural style to the Gothic parish church and the fourteenth-century Bristol Cross. When Kent worked for Queen Caroline in Richmond Park in Surrey, he was required to provide several buildings in the nationalist, Gothic style, which were to underpin the emphasis on the intellectual giants of England's past such as Newton, Locke and Boyle, who were celebrated in the Hermitage. Here again there was an implied counterblast to the French with their Cartesian system of thought. The Hermitage was classical in inspiration, though the pediment is deliberately incomplete and the lack of a turret upsets the symmetry. But when he came to design Merlin's Cave something more fantastically 'British' was appropriate, a Gothic doorway, dumpy, thatched roofs and the interior decorated with tree trunks and branches. The Gothic was a popular style as it spoke with a more thoroughgoing English accent; it also allowed designers bored with the sobriety of classical and Palladian architecture some fun.

Kent often found himself reworking a landscape created by the unfortunate Bridgeman – unfortunate in the sense that his landscapes were almost entirely submerged under the later work of Kent and Lancelot Brown. This happened at Claremont, although Kent spared the splendid amphitheatre Bridgeman had created, not as a theatre for plays but as a place from which to view the beauties of the landscape. This amphitheatre was designed in the exedral shape, with a set of concave steps leading down to a circular stage, from which convex steps lead to ground level, but in England it was not paved in stone but created entirely of grass. This exedral design was borrowed from Italian models, and 200 years later revived on a smaller scale by Lutyens in what he called his 'in and out' steps. At Claremont Kent redesigned the lake in a more informal shape and added a grotto. Later in the century Brown also worked at Claremont, modifying and removing some of Kent's work.

Perhaps Kent's most celebrated composition, and a garden where we can still experience his shaping hand, is at Rousham, just north of Oxford. He began work there in 1737, and again he kept some of the alterations Bridgeman had made twenty years earlier – the great flat bowling green lawn outside the garden front of the house, for example. At the end of this elevated, open space there are extensive views over the river Cherwell winding below and then out to the fields on its other bank. To tempt the visitor to the edge, Kent placed there a statue which General Dormer, the owner, had collected on his Grand Tour. The statue of a lion attacking a horse is a copy of one at the Villa d'Este.

Another stronger echo of Italian originals is the Praeneste Terrace, where Kent created a set of arches with a walk in front; the name recalled the great Temple of Fortune at Palestrina, the modern name for Roman Praeneste. It, too, stands on a hillside offering wonderful views over the countryside. A quite different emotional experience, and a quite different, more mysterious, enclosed picture, is offered by the Vale of Venus, the Roman goddess of gardens. Here Kent brings the stream down a series of falls built in a kind of rustic-classical style; the stream is made to disappear underground and then re-emerge, which all adds to the drama. Horace Walpole praised the 'opening and retiring shades' of this part of Rousham, which he thought might have been copied from Pope's garden. The feeling of enclosure here contrasts strongly with the openness of the view from the bowling green, and such variety is typical of the pleasures Rousham offers the visitor.

BELOW *Claremont, Esher. Another hugely influential landscape where Bridgeman, Kent and Brown worked, often destroying the work of their predecessors.*

But Kent had not finished when he had reshaped the garden itself; the country had to be called in, as Pope had put it. To do this Kent built an eye-catcher on the furthest hill. This was a great success, since it was British in its Gothic architecture, but visitors interpreted it as a triumphal arch, which made it also Roman. As we can see from his drawings, which almost always contain people (and dogs), Kent loved to animate a scene; at Rousham he did so by altering the route of a road, which made it necessary to build a bridge over the river at a point where it could be seen from the garden.

For Horace Walpole, in his famous essay *The History of the Modern Taste in Gardening* (published in 1780, although certainly written much earlier), Kent was the instigator of the great transformation of taste, and his great innovation was that 'The living landscape was chastened or polished, not transformed.' Others detected what was happening even earlier; in 1734 Sir Thomas Robinson wrote in a letter: 'There is a new taste in gardening just arisen . . . a general alteration of some of the most notable gardens in the Kingdom is begun, after Mr Kent's notion of gardening, viz. to lay them out, and work without level or line.' This absence of 'level or line' signified Kent not imposing straight lines on the sites where he worked but rather consulting the genius of the place. He saw with the eye of the painter but also appreciated what Sir Frederick Gibberd put so clearly, that making a garden 'is like making a series of pictures . . . but if you step into the picture it dissolves and other pictures appear; from two dimensions it becomes three, a flat plane becomes a space.' Kent's compositions were full of classical and political references, but were never dull or predictable; he knew the importance of drama and variety in a garden.

It was not only professional artists who were making gardens of the new type: the zeal for creating landscape pictures which one could walk into and explore began to affect the whole nation. As in imperial China it was comparatively common for members of the government to retire, not to spend more time with their families as is the modern way, but to spend more time on their gardens. John Aislabie was Chancellor of the Exchequer from 1714 to 1718, but his involvement with the South Sea Bubble financial scandal led to his imprisonment in the Tower of London, and the end of his political career. In 1722 he retired to his estate at Studley Royal in Yorkshire, and began work on a garden of his own invention, a kind of water parterre with classical overtones. He must have known the garden created by his wife's father-in-law (by her first husband), the poet Edmund Waller, at Hall Barn in Buckinghamshire, a garden that had a classical temple reflected in the waters of a substantial canal. In a narrow valley, between well-wooded hills, Aislabie dammed the river Skell to create a long canal and two moon pools, one circular and one

LEFT *Rousham House, Oxford. William Kent designed (or rather redesigned) the grounds here in 1738, and they have been little altered. Kent designed a series of scenes, one of which, the Praeneste Terrace, is seen here. Praeneste is the ancient name of Palestrina, where the Temple of Fortune provided classical examples of how terraces, steps and ramps could tame a steep hillside.*

ABOVE AND RIGHT *Studley Royal, Ripon.*
John Aislabie created this water parterre
between 1722 and his death in 1742. The
components of the scene are grass and water,
with the classical buildings as focal points.

the shape of a half moon, set on a specially flattened grass parterre. Behind the moon ponds stands the Temple of Piety (1728) and on the opposite side of the valley the Banqueting House, from which the garden features can be appreciated. There is also a walk through the woods from which different views of the valley are allowed, and a later Gothic temple (1745–50). But the supreme moment arrives at the top of Tent Hill; the eye is led down into the next valley and to the ruins of Fountains Abbey, surely the greatest eye-catcher of all time. The ruins were purchased by John's son, William, in 1768.

The idyllic landscape at Studley Royal was in no way related to the house, which burned down in 1946; it was a composition complete in itself. The same is true of another great landscape picture created by Henry Hoare at Stourhead in Wiltshire in the mid eighteenth century. The house (1718–24) followed the Palladian style made fashionable by Kent's friend and patron Lord Burlington. Here again England saw itself as the true inheritor of Roman taste: the restraint of Palladio's elegant buildings was much more in tune with the English spirit, and, as they claimed, with the Roman ideal of moderation praised by Horace, than the rapturous excesses of the baroque which held sway in Italy at this time. It was Henry Hoare's son, another Henry, who began to lay out the grounds. As at Studley Royal he began by damming a river, here the Stour, but instead of formal pools he created a series of lakes of irregular shape. Around the lakes Hoare laid out a path, which led to a series of buildings, where the educated visitor could 'read' the story of Aeneas and his visit to the underworld. The Temple of Flora was built in 1745, the Grotto in 1748, both by Henry Flitcroft, an associate of Kent; inside the latter the statue of the river god by Cheere is probably influenced by Salvator Rosa's picture *The Dream of Aeneas*. And both these buildings originally had quotations from the *Aeneid* inscribed over their doors. The main eye-catcher is the Pantheon or the Temple of Hercules, built in 1754, also by Flitcroft. Stourton church, the village and the Gothic Bristol Cross, erected here in 1765, form another pictorial composition, this time more British than Italian; Hoare himself called it 'a charming Gaspard [Poussin] picture'. Mythical Hercules and Aeneas were not the only heroes commemorated at Stourhead: on a distant hilltop Alfred's Tower reminds us that England had her heroes too. Both Stourhead and Studley Royal are in the care of the National Trust, and as a result we can still see how the eighteenth century managed to domesticate the Arcadian, Italianate landscapes of Claude Lorrain and Poussin in the English countryside.

The planting at Stourhead was originally austere – beech and larch, underplanted with cherry laurel (*Prunus laurocerasus*) – but gardens change with fashion and the taste of new owners. The exotic trees and pines were added in the nineteenth century and most of the rhododendrons in the early twentieth. Thus the scene we see today is more colourful and botanically varied than that Henry Hoare would have experienced. But still there was no room for flowers in such a 'learned' landscape. In *Iconographica Rustica* Switzer had written 'Clipt Plants, Flowers, and other trifling Decorations [are] fit only for little Town-gardens, and not for the expansive Tracts of the Country', although elsewhere he writes less severely about flowers, admitting they may have their place provided they are 'planted promiscuously . . . not in regular Lines as has been the common Way'.

BELOW *Studley Royal, Ripon. The ruins of Fountains Abbey were purchased by John Aislabie's son William in 1768. They provide a magnificent climax to the drama of the Studley Royal gardens.*

ABOVE AND RIGHT *Stourhead, Warminster. A beautifully conserved example of an idyllic, mid-eighteenth-century landscape, inspired by painters such as Salvator Rosa. Henry Hoare had the river Stour dammed to create the lakes. The Pantheon (above) is typical of the classical buildings that help create this ideal landscape, but (right) the late fourteenth-century Gothic cross also takes its place in the composition.*

If Stourhead turned its back on flowers, it also turned its back on the realities of country life. The creators of *fermes ornées* recognized that the countryside must be productive, but that was no reason why their properties should not also be beautiful. Though the term is French, the phrase *ferme ornée* was first used by Switzer in *Iconographia Rustica*; the first use in French was thirty years later. In 1732 the 35-year-old Philip Southcote married the Duchess of Cleveland, a woman nearly twice his age. Like Pope, he was a Catholic and so excluded from public office, but he could become a country gentleman. With this aim he bought (no doubt employing his wife's ample fortune) Woburn (sometimes Wooburn) Farm in Surrey, a property he eventually extended to some 60 hectares/150 acres. His aim from the first was utilitarian as well as aesthetic: 'from my garden I could see what was doing in the grounds, and by the walk could have a pleasing access to either of them where I might be wanted'. This walk was where Southcote concentrated his gardening attention, and the planning of it was a demanding business: in a letter he described how 'I walked the ground above a hundred different times before I could fix the whole line of the walk from the Temple to the Octagon.' It will be observed that even here, down on the farm, classical buildings were not lacking.

Almost nothing remains of Woburn Farm, but luckily Horace Walpole visited and left us a typically vivid description. He describes how the walk 'is conducted in a waving line, sometimes close under the hedge, sometimes at a little distance from it; and the turf on either side is diversified with little groupes of shrubs, of firs, or the smallest trees, and often with beds of flowers; these are

LEFT *Ragley Hall, Alcester. The grounds may have been designed by the ubiquitous 'Capability' Brown, but little is known of the history of the gardens before the nineteenth century. The rose garden near the house has been redesigned in recent years.*

ABOVE *Sheffield Park, Uckfield. Brown designed the grounds with their T-shaped lakes for the Earl of Sheffield in 1776, and later Humphry Repton also worked here. The fine collection of trees is celebrated for their autumn colour.*

rather too profusely strewed, and hurt the eye by their littleness; but then they replenish the air with their perfumes, and every gale is full of fragrancy'. Notice the 'waving line of the path': Hogarth, the leading satirical artist of the day, had recently declared the serpentine to be 'the line of beauty'. Walpole's sharp eye detected that not all the flowers were what you expected to find in a garden: 'if the parterre has been rifled for the embellishment of the fields, the country has on the other hand been searched for plants new in a garden', though he found their mixture too 'licentious' for his taste. And everywhere 'the lowings of the herd, the bleating of the sheep, and the tinklings of the bell-wether, resound through the plantation; even the clucking of poultry is not omitted; for a menagerie of very simple design is placed near the Gothic building; a small serpentine river is provided for the water-fowl; while the others stray among the flowering shrubs on the banks, or straggle about the neighbouring lawn'. Here pleasure and profit went hand in hand, a combination dear to a practical Englishman's heart.

Another celebrated *ferme ornée* was The Leasowes in the West Midlands, created by the poet William Shenstone between 1745 and 1763. Shenstone was not a rich man, like the banking Hoares or the wisely married Southcote, but he created 'a place to be visited by travellers and copied by designers', in the words of Dr Johnson. So great was The Leasowes' fame and so generous was Shenstone in allowing public access that on one Sunday in 1749 no fewer than 150 people visited his garden. Again the visitor followed a path that led round the property. Here it was the dramatic variety of scenes that was most striking. Thomas Whately described, for example, how the walk plunged into a dell from the glooms of which the visitor emerged to enjoy a 'pretty landskip'. He was delighted by the whole place: 'The variety of The Leasowes is wonderful; all the enclosures are totally different.' He was much struck by the urns and numerous carved inscriptions to be found along the way: 'The elegance of the poetry and the aptness of the quotations, atone for their length and number.' This description of quotations decorating a garden may well remind the reader of an equally wonderful and idiosyncratic garden created in the late twentieth century by Ian Hamilton Finlay at Little Sparta, south of Edinburgh. Whately notices the contrast between references to native history and those to the classical, Arcadian tradition: 'The Priory and a Gothic seat, still more particularly characterized by an inscription in obsolete language and the black letter, belong to the one; the urns, Virgil's obelisk, and the rustic temple of Pan, to the other.' Shenstone made it clear he was merely enhancing and revealing the beauties of nature: 'the shape of the ground, the site of trees, and the fall of water [are] nature's province. Whatever thwarts her is treason.'

Flowers made something of a comeback at the *fermes ornées*, but they were again under threat with the next development of the English landscape park. By the middle of the century everyone was improving their park, or in Horace Walpole's characteristically waspish words: 'There is not a citizen who does not take more pains to torture his acre and a half into irregularities, than he formerly would have employed to make it as formal as his cravat.' And 'the omnipotent magician', as the poet Cowper called him, was waiting in the wings to lend them his aid. Lancelot Brown was not born a gentleman; he had not been on the Grand Tour, nor felt a great debt to the classics, and thus he did not usually feel it incumbent upon him to include temples, rotundas and the other paraphernalia of the Italian landscape in his parks. His materials were hills, woods and water, the elements of the English countryside, which is why perhaps his work is sometimes hard to identify; it looks too natural.

Brown was born in Northumberland in 1716, but in 1739 he came south and by 1740 he was employed in the kitchen gardens at Stowe. We can get an idea of what Bridgeman's work at Stowe was like from a letter of 1724: Lord Percival writes that the garden 'consists of a great number of walks terminated by summerhouses, and heathen temples, and adorned with statues cast from the Antique. You think you have no more to see, and of a sudden find yourself in some new garden or walk, furnished and adorned as that you left. Nothing is more irregular in the whole, nothing more regular in the parts.' Kent was at work softening these regularities, and it seems that Brown became his assistant. Where the work of one ends and the other begins it is hard to establish. In his last years (he died in 1748) Kent was a famous designer and architect, much in demand, so Brown, by now head gardener at Stowe, must have been left in charge. The fame of Stowe meant that it was not long before Brown was consulted on the improvement of other parks; perhaps his first commission was from the Duke of Grafton, whose Wakefield estate bordered Stowe. Here we see at once the components of Brown's art: the great lawn that sweeps up to the house, with no intrusive flower garden to impede its flow, and in the other direction the lawn sweeping up to the sinuous border of the woods; at the bottom of the valley a lake whose serpentine form is dictated by the surrounding hills.

Brown was asked to design gardens in many parts of the world, but never left Britain; the story goes that he was asked to work on an estate in Ireland, but felt unable to begin there 'as I have not yet finished England'. In a letter to Thomas Dyer of 1775 giving advice to a French friend he outlines his aims,

> which will supply all the elegance and all the comforts which Mankind requires in the Country, and (I will add) if right, be exactly fit for the Owner, the Poet and the Painter . . . there wants a good plan and infinite delicacy in the planting etc. so much Beauty depending on the size of the trees and the colour of their leaves to produce the effect of light and shade so very essential to the perfecting a good plan.

This delicacy in planning clumps of trees was not always well understood; Brown often included 'nurse' trees, whose sole function was to protect the major trees in their infancy; often these were conifers. Some owners neglected to remove the conifers so the clump became overcrowded; others, with even less understanding of Brown's ideas, planted whole clumps of conifers.

At Castle Ashby in Northamptonshire he planted his signature clumps, more natural in form than Kent's clumps, but he also removed three of the four avenues that radiated from the house; he left one to be the main drive. He threw down the garden walls and built a ha-ha to open the garden to the countryside. As elsewhere the ha-ha kept animals away from the house, for the park was a thing of use as well as of beauty, providing pasture for horses, cattle, sheep and deer. But it should not be thought that Brown was a total enemy of all flowering plants; in the letter quoted above he writes of the pleasure to be had 'getting shade from the large trees and sweets from the smaller sort of shrubs etc.'. At Longleat in Wiltshire he planned a flower garden, and for the wilderness at Petworth in West Sussex he ordered more than a hundred roses as well as jasmine, lilacs and flowering fruit trees. But often the house was left isolated in a great meadow, starkly standing out in the landscape; this must have been aesthetically ugly and have drawn attention to the separation of the owner from his workers and tenants. The more utilitarian buildings on the estate were usually hidden, and inconveniently placed villages were removed. Bridgeman had set the precedent in this radical reordering of the landscape, but Brown and his employers followed enthusiastically in Bridgeman's footsteps. At Milton Abbas in Dorset the village was moved and Brown put on his architect's hat to design a new model village. When the tenants were reluctant to move into their new model homes, Lord Milton opened the dam, which Brown had designed to create a lake, and flushed away their objections.

That Brown was an artist with a wonderful eye for the 'capabilities' (hence his nickname) of a site there can be no doubt. In his contract with the Earl of Scarborough dated 12 September 1774 he agreed to interpret the earl's ideas 'with Poet's feeling and with Painter's eye'. In an anonymous poem published in 1767 Brown's work at Blenheim (Oxfordshire), Croome (Worcestershire) and Caversham (Berkshire) was set side by side with the work of the greatest painters and writers in the eighteenth-century pantheon:

Blenheim, Woodstock. The gardens and palace were a gift from a grateful nation to a great general, the 1st Duke of Marlborough. Henry Wise laid out a suitably 'military' garden, but Brown altered a great deal, landscaping the park and creating the two lakes on each side of Vanburgh's heroic bridge.

But your great Artist, like the source of light,
Gilds every scene with beauty and delight;
At Blenheim, Croome and Caversham we trace
Salvator's wilderness, Claud's enlivening grace,
Cascades and lakes as fine as Risdale drew,
While Nature's varied in each charming view.
To paint his works would Poussin's Powers require,
Milton's sublimity and Dryden's fire.

At Blenheim, in particular, we can clearly appreciate Brown's genius. In the early years of the century Vanbrugh and Wise had created a great formal park and garden to set off the massive new palace; the park might have been enlivened by the romantic ruins of Woodstock Manor if Vanbrugh's plan had been followed, but the Duchess of Marlborough squashed that idea, which was too far ahead of its time. There was a great formal parterre near the palace, a straight avenue with square clumps of trees marshalled along its edges, and a 'Roman' bridge over the thin thread of the river Glyme. Blenheim was the royal gift to the hero of the wars against the French, so everything had to be on a heroic scale, including the bridge. But the two-tier structure looked overweight above the little brook; no wonder the Duchess referred to it as 'that ridiculous bridge'. In 1764 the magician Brown arrived at Blenheim; with a wave of his wand he destroyed the great parterre of Wise and Vanbrugh, and then in a masterstroke dammed the stream to create two lakes, one above and one below the bridge. Now it looked no longer ridiculous but in proportion to the large body of water; all that had been lost were the rooms in its lower storey, which were flooded.

Brown's eye for the contours of hills led his patrons into much expense; he wanted the best possible setting for his woods and his lakes; he wanted variety and surprise, which meant that hills had sometimes to be moved to block one view because it might have distracted from another. Luckily the digging of the lakes produced great quantities of earth, which had to be used somewhere. In the end a Brown landscape looked so like the work of nature that his hand was invisible – *ars celare artem*. But even the great man sometimes erred; he adored planting the tops

of his new hills with tufts of trees, although the sloping sides were bare, an unnatural absurdity that his successor Humphry Repton had to correct. To achieve the predominant position he held and to charge the fees he did, Brown must have been a man of great charm as well as an efficient businessman. Lord Coventry was clearly a satisfied customer; he wrote to Sanderson Miller: 'Mr Brown has done very well by me, and indeed I think he has studied both my Place and my Pocket, which are not always conjunctively the Object of Prospectors' – by the last word he means landscape designers.

Italian art and gardens had at one time been the model on which every civilized gentleman's taste was formed not only in England but in the whole of Europe. However, in a letter from Tobias

Painswick House, Stroud. When Kent leaped the fence and found 'all nature is a garden', he did so in cultivated, manicured England. Only the parallel hedges, neatly trimmed, give an idea that here we are looking at part of a garden (the famous Rococo garden), not the English landscape.

Smollett dated 5 March 1765 we see how far English taste had now swung against the Italian model and Italian practice (we also hear the unattractive, smug tone of the Englishman abroad):

> In a fine extensive garden or park, an Englishman expects to see a number of groves and glades, intermixed with an agreeable negligence, which seems to be the effect of nature and accident. He looks for shady walks encrusted with gravel; for open lawns covered with verdure as smooth as velvet, but much more lively and agreeable; for ponds, canals, basins, cascades, and running streams of water; for clumps of trees, woods and wildernesses, cut into delightful alleys, perfumed with honeysuckle and sweet-briar, and resounding with the mingled melody of all the singing birds of heaven; he looks for plats of flowers in different parts to refresh the sense, and please the fancy; for arbours, grottos, hermitages, temples and alcoves, to shelter him from the sun, and afford him means of contemplation and repose; and he expects to find the hedges, groves and walks, and lawns, kept with the utmost order and propriety. He who loves the beauties of simple nature, and the charms of neatness will seek for them in vain amidst the groves of Italy.

There is a new confidence here: the Englishman now feels he is in a position to assess foreign gardens, even the gardens of revered Italy, with a connoisseur's cool judgment.

Brown's art was not, of course, nature, though it seemed natural, and for this reason the great painter John Constable protested, 'A gentleman's park . . . is my aversion. It is not beauty because it is not nature.' And Brown had some severe contemporary critics; one of them hoped he would die before Brown, so that he might get to heaven before Brown had improved it. But none was more severe than Sir William Chambers, who wrote: 'No appearance of art is tolerated, our gardens differ little from common fields, so closely is vulgar nature copied in most of them.' He was scathing about 'the want of judgement and poverty of imagination', and indignant at the destruction of so much fine timber: 'The ax had often in one day laid waste the growth of several ages; and thousands of venerable plants, whole woods of them, have been swept away to make room for a little grass and a few American weeds. Our virtuosi have scarce left an acre of shade, nor three trees growing in a line, from Lands End to the Tweed.' It is fine rhetorical stuff, and not without a grain of truth, for Brown had destroyed a great deal; but he had also planted huge numbers of trees – for example at Fisherwick in Staffordshire he planted 100,000 trees for Lord Donegall. Brown's influence in England was extraordinarily widespread; he is estimated to have worked on between 120 and 140 estates during his extremely energetic working life. And his influence was not confined to Britain; it would be no exaggeration to say it was worldwide. The wonderful Botanical Garden in Melbourne shows his influence in its use of water and clumps of trees; in Russia the Tsarina Catherine the Great created a landscape park in the English style at Tsarskoye Selo, and in America Jefferson, who had visited Blenheim, Chiswick (his comment was 'the garden still shows too much of art'), Painshill in Surrey and Stowe, followed some of Brown's ideas in his garden at Monticello.

The book in which Chambers savaged 'Capability' Brown was entitled *A Dissertation on Oriental Gardening*. As early as 1685 the Chinese example had been adduced by Sir William Temple as evidence of a more informal style of garden, although he warned that such gardens 'were too hard an achievement for any common hands'. Lord Burlington had owned a book on Chinese gardens, and now (1772) Chambers again used their example to criticize current English garden design. Chambers had visited China, but the taste for things Chinese that swept Europe in the middle years of the eighteenth century had been stimulated earlier by the French missionary and painter Jean-Denis Attiret, who while resident in Peking was given permission to visit the Imperial Gardens. In a letter published in English in 1752, he described the many irregular details he found there, which he summed up as 'a rustic and natural countryside'. Chambers attacked Brown for the too cultivated, too smooth finish of his work, which he ascribed to the poverty of his imagination. His essay gives us an idea of how he would have liked gardens to stimulate the imagination (it sounds more like the Hammer House of Horrors):

Their scenes of terror are composed of gloomy woods, deep vallies inaccessible to the sun, impending barren rocks, dark caverns, and impetuous cataracts rushing down the mountains from all parts . . . Bats, owls, vultures, and every bird of prey flutter in the groves; wolves, tigers and jackalls howl in the forests; half famished animals wander upon the plains; gibbets, crosses, wheels and the whole apparatus of torture, are seen from the roads.

It must be admitted that Brown's parks are not strong on gibbets or jackals! What Chambers admired in Chinese gardens he makes clear later in the essay: 'Their surprising, or supernatural scenes, are of the romantic kind, and abound in the marvellous; being calculated to excite in the minds of the spectators, quick successions of opposite and violent sensations.' He wanted gardens to be super-natural, not merely imitative of the natural; they should stimulate the imagination, like a Gothic novel, with startling, horrid images (the Latin word *horridus* means 'rough' or 'bristly': one of the favourite words of the devotees of this new taste was 'shaggy').

In 1793 the Reverend William Gilpin published an essay in which he wrote that man-made landscapes are 'never picturesque. They want the bold roughness of nature. A principal beauty in our gardens, as Mr Walpole justly observes, is the smoothness of the turf; but in a picture this becomes a dead and uniform spot, incapable of light and shade.' Sir Richard Payne Knight took this idea and used it to attack Brown and his followers in a didactic poem, 'The Landscape' (1794):

> To improve, adorn, and polish, they profess;
> But shave the goddess whom they come to dress;
> Level each broken bank and shaggy mound,
> And fashion all to one unvaried round;
> One even round, that ever gently flows,
> Nor forms abrupt, no broken colours knows;
> But, wrapped all o'er in everlasting green,
> Makes one dull, vapid, smooth and tranquil scene.

His neighbour, Sir Uvedale Price, published his *Essays on the Picturesque* between 1794 and 1801; Price and Knight were generally in agreement, but the exact definition of the word 'picturesque' led to a rift. The painter whose work they most admired was not either of the Poussins or Claude but Salvator Rosa with his shaggy, wild highwaymen, twisted trees and threatening crags. The gentle English countryside does not lend itself easily to such melodrama, but we can get some idea of a Picturesque park at Hawkstone in Shropshire, a landscape created about 1790 by Sir Rowland Hill and his nephew. A rocky outcrop, riddled with caves and hollows (it may have been a Roman copper mine) provides a dramatic setting for a grotto, a rustic bridge with sketchy timbers to carry the apprehensive visitor over a deep gully, and the Cleft, a narrow, rock-hewn path between moss-covered walls of living stone – scenery to provoke shivers of awe in the visitor. Originally a bearded hermit was paid to live in one of the caves, but after fifteen years he had had enough of such a Spartan life. When living successors proved hard to find, he was replaced by a waxwork; in recent years this figure has been imaginatively replaced by a hologram-hermit in a rustic hut.

The idea of the Picturesque never really caught on in Britain; it was too extreme, too theatrical in every way, but the attacks on Brown and his followers continued. One of these followers replied to an onslaught by Uvedale Price in measured tones, the steel fist in the velvet glove:

> . . . both you and Mr Knight live among bold and picturesque scenery: this may have rendered you insensible to the beauty of those milder scenes that have charms for common observers. I will not arraign your taste; or call it vitiated, but your palate certainly requires a degree of 'irritation' rarely to be expected in garden scenery; and I trust the good sense and good taste of this country will never be led to despise the comfort of a gravel walk, the delicious fragrance of a shrubbery, the soul expanding delight of a wide extended prospect, or a view down a steep hill, because they are all subjects incapable of being painted.

Hawkstone Park, Shrewsbury. At the end of the eighteenth century gardening taste turned to landscapes that thrilled the nerves and sent shudders down the spine. This park, complete with a twentieth-century hologram hermit, is a superb survival from this period.

The good sense of the country did prevail, and Mr Humphry Repton, the author of the letter quoted above, continued to have many clients.

Repton was the genius who taught fashion-conscious park makers that they did not need to neglect or destroy their flower gardens. He admired Brown's work, but came to differ from him in preferring a house set on a terrace surrounded by a balustrade, to a house set in a sea of grass. He would place groups of shrubs around the lawn near the house, rather as he planted clumps of trees in the park, and within the balustrade he often designed a formal flower garden with symmetrical beds, an area that could be kept 'with the utmost artificial neatness' (his words). He draws a sharp distinction between landscape painting and landscape gardening (he was the first professional to call himself a landscape gardener: Brown had called himself a 'place-maker'): 'If houses were built only to be looked at or looked from, the best landscape painter would be the best landscape gardener; but to render a place in all seasons comfortable requires other considerations than those of picturesque effect.' In his famous Red Books, however, he used his skill as a painter to persuade his clients to accept his ideas. In these the reader would see the house or park as it was, and then the lifting of a flap would reveal the transformation Repton was suggesting. It was brilliant salesmanship. It also provided him with a source of practical illustrations when he came to write his books on the art of landscape gardening.

Repton was always acutely aware of the qualities of the light as it changed with the day and the season – something that is often the landscape painter's despair. He would make perspective seem longer by planting trees with light-coloured, finer foliage in front of trees with darker, heavier foliage. The driveway to the house he would usually make as short as possible, but he would also plan drives through the park with a variety of views, not unlike the compositions that Shenstone offered his visitors at The Leasowes. He appreciated that parks must also be profit-making, and was so far from opposing the introduction of cattle into his compositions that he described cows as 'peculiarly useful in showing the extent and distance of a plain surface'. As his work developed and he gained confidence, he began to diverge more and more from Brown's model. Particularly significant in this development is his work at Cobham in Kent for Lord Darnley, which began in 1790; here he included in his plans a flower garden with a fountain and some statues, a terrace garden that sounds suspiciously like a parterre and a set of ornamental steps descending to the park. In his *Fragments on the Theory and Practice of Landscape Gardening* (1816) he defended this practice as it provided 'a nice gradation from the wilder scenery of the park to the more finished and dressed appearance of the gardens'. With the terrace, the balustrade and the formal steps we are almost back to the Italian garden, which was to be a dominant influence in nineteenth-century England. The final break with Brown is summed up in Repton's own words describing Cobham: 'The house is no longer a huge pile standing naked on a vast grazing ground.'

Repton's books gave him an influence far beyond Great Britain; indeed he may be called the founding father of landscape gardening, because in his writings he articulated a theory of this art based on extensive practical experience. With Repton the English passion for flowers was harmonized with the English admiration for idyllic landscapes, or, as he put it: 'The neatness, simplicity and elegance of English gardening have acquired the approbation of the present century as the happy medium betwixt the wildness of nature and the stiffness of art; in the same manner as the English constitution is the happy medium between the liberty of savages and the restraint of despotic government.' This patriotic note has often been heard in remarks of the great eighteenth-century park makers, but it is in his distinction between the park and the garden that Repton sounds the fanfare for a new kind of taste in gardening. Here is his definition of a garden:

It is a piece of ground fenced off from cattle, and appropriated to the use and pleasure of man: it is or ought to be, cultivated and enriched by art, with such products as are not natural to this country, and, consequently, it must be artificial in its treatment, and may,

BELOW *Biddulph Grange, Stoke-on-Trent. A remarkable Victorian garden of immense ambition. From 1850 onwards James Bateman created a series of elaborate gardens to house a wide range of plants; he included a Chinese and an Egyptian garden, the exit from the latter being through a Cheshire cottage.*

ABOVE *Scotney Castle, Lamberhurst. The*
house, which incorporates earlier fragments,
was completed in 1843, and the gardens are
laid out in the Picturesque style. William
Sawrey Gilpin, nephew of the Revd William
Gilpin, defender of the Picturesque school,
advised on the siting of the house.

without impropriety, be so in its appearance; yet, there is so much of littleness in art, when compared with nature, that they cannot well be blended; it were therefore to be wished, that the exterior of a garden should be made to assimilate with park scenery, or the landscape of nature; the interior may then be laid out with all the variety, contrast, and even whim, that can produce pleasing objects to the eye.

Art is celebrated alongside nature (with no capital letter), exotic plants are to be welcomed into the garden, and there is even room for whim: we are in a new age!

No historical development happens in straight lines, and few generalizations are completely true in garden history, or perhaps in any kind of history; not everyone was making landscape parks, not everyone wanted to lose their flower gardens. The Whig view of history saw the development of the landscape park as one of the many signs of progress to greater and greater enlightenment and civilization. It is also possible to see these parks as an early sign of the Romantic revolution that was to affect all the arts of Europe at the end of the eighteenth century; like all romantic works of art, the English landscape park seeks to appeal more to the imagination than to reason. Truth for the romantics was a matter of individual perception, not of tradition or precedent; thus the paths at The Leasowes were narrow, so that a single individual could walk alone from one emotionally demanding scene to the next. And, of course, nature seemed to be the creator of all the pleasing scenes, even when it was really Lancelot Brown who had reshaped her. The curious thing is that just as English romantic poetry was reaching the height of its success, in the early years of the nineteenth century, English gardens were turning back to parterres, elaborate Italian steps, balustrades and bedding.

7

THE ENGLISH FLOWER GARDEN

EXPLORING GARDENS IN ITALY, or the Far East, or the Islamic world, the visitor may hear the exasperated exclamation, 'It's all really beautiful, but not many flowers!'; the exclaiming voice will almost certainly be English. Most Britons assume that all gardens should be like English gardens, exterior spaces decorated with flowers and containing a lawn; the lawn is just about dispensable but, for the English, if there are no flowers, there is no garden. Even the young Humphry Repton, sent by his father to study in Holland, describes in a letter looking into Dutch gardens from the canals and seeing compartments of coloured earth surrounded by dwarf box hedges – but, to his shocked surprise, no flowers! Nan Fairbrother in *Men and Gardens* writes:

> The chief love of English gardeners has always been flowers: we have seldom thought of a garden as anything but a sheltered place for growing them to perfection . . . and most of our gardening books are not books on how to make gardens at all, but on how to grow flowers. For it has seldom occurred to us that they are quite different things, as building a house is different from arranging the ornaments on the mantelpiece.

Other garden traditions place much less emphasis on flowers. Italian gardens are defined by their architectural use of light and shade, by their fountains, steps and balustraded terraces; Islamic gardens by their formal arrangement of fruit trees, by their pools and canals; Oriental gardens by their arrangement of rocks, by their subtle interweaving of indoor and outdoor space, and by their hump-back or zig-zag bridges. All of these contain flowers, but not in the profusion which the English eye expects.

How did this aberrant but intense relationship between the English and the floral world begin? Plant hunting followed the flag, like trade, and plants looted from many parts of the world were found to grow in the temperate climate of England. But even before the days of Empire the English were fascinated with a wide variety of plants. Perhaps grey skies and pearly light make the bright cheerfulness of flowers especially appealing. There is no evidence that the English have greener fingers than other races; they are just luckier to be living in a well-watered, maritime environment with few excesses of heat or cold. Gardening is therefore easier in Great Britain than in many other parts of the world; perhaps it is this that has persuaded so many Britons to take up the trowel. As early as the seventeenth century John Worlidge noticed the appetite the British had for gardening books, and, judging by the number of glossy magazines dedicated to flowers and garden-making currently available, that appetite remains unabated. In the United Kingdom there are 3,500 gardens open under the National Gardens Scheme to raise money for charity, and the National Council for the Conservation of Plants and Gardens supports 660 National Collections of particular plant genera. The briefest drive through the suburbs of a British city, let alone a visit to a village, will demonstrate the natives' love for flower gardens. Britain must be the most cultivated (in one sense, at least) country in the world.

The Romans introduced many plants to this outpost of their empire, but did they bring with them a delight in gardens full of flowers? The frescoes from the summer *triclinium* or dining room of the Villa Livia, on the outskirts of Rome, show a flourishing garden of roses and pomegranates,

ABOVE *Castle Drogo, Drewsteignton. This castle was begun in 1910, designed by Sir Edwin Lutyens. There is a valley full of rhododendrons, camellias, cornus and magnolias.*

all organized inside a low wall and a neat, trellis fence. But this is clearly an idealized, not a natural garden, since many plants, which in nature bloom at quite different periods, are seen to be flowering simultaneously. Pliny the Elder's *Natural History* contains references to plants that seem to be primarily ornamental, for example acanthus, in which his nephew took such delight, *Arbutus unedo* and cynoglossum. And in Book 19 he writes of town gardens in Rome (the translation is in Philemon Holland's delightful Elizabethan English): 'In these our days, under the name of Gardens and Hortyards, there goe many daintie places of pleasure within the very citie . . . The invention to have gardens within a citie came up first by Epicurus, the Doctor and master of al voluptuous idleness.' Places for voluptuous idleness and 'daintie places of pleasure' sound more like pleasure gardens than utilitarian vegetable gardens, but did they contain a wide variety of flowers? In the gardens of Pompeii ornamental plants were blooming in August AD 79 – lychnis, campanulas and so on. But at Fishbourne in southern England little evidence of ornamental herbaceous material has survived, so it seems unlikely that the Romans brought with them the delight in flowers that has come to typify the English.

During the Middle Ages Roman influence continued to be dominant throughout Europe. The first-century Roman farmer Lucius Junius Columella wrote a handbook on farming and gardening which continued to be used and recommended well into the seventeenth century. John Aubrey remembered John Evelyn telling him 'out of Varro, Cato and Columella, are to be extracted all good rules of husbandry'. Most of Columella's *De Re Rustica* is written in verse, but the last part of Book 11 is written in prose and is devoted to gardens – how they should be made, fertilized, enclosed and planted – but there is no mention of flowers. In matters medical the authority to whom all Europe turned was Dioscorides, a contemporary of the elder Pliny, whose

De Materia Medica was the bible on herbal cures until well into the Renaissance. He deals with only 500 plants – how to recognize them, how to gather them, how to store them and how to use them – and it was not until the sixteenth century that gardeners began to extend this limited range; Gerard in his herbal of 1596 included over a thousand species. But Dioscorides was only interested in flowers as medicines.

In medieval England, as in the whole of Europe, gardening was the concern of the religious orders and the nobility; these people alone had the leisure and surplus income to spend some of

RIGHT *Powis Castle, Welshpool, Wales. This steep, hillside garden was begun in the late seventeenth century, and shows some French influence in the giant yew buttresses and the arrangement of the terraces. The planting is imaginative and many rare plants flourish in the microclimate provided by the walls.*

it on beautifying the spaces around them. In the monastic garden, plants were largely grown for food and medicines, but who is to say that such plants were not organized to give aesthetic pleasure? The earliest reference to an English monastic garden seems to be a mention of the *gardinum sacristae* at Winchester in the ninth century; this was situated in a part of the city still called Paradise, which reminds us of the enclosed gardens of the Persian empire. Similarly, in Oxford the section of the city called Paradise is named after a garden at Greyfriars. This was most likely a monastic pleasure garden of the kind we read about existing in the late eleventh century at Romsey Abbey in Hampshire, where the nuns tended a flower garden which they used to open to the general public.

Albertus Magnus, a German nobleman who became a Dominican, writing in about 1260, gives clear instructions on how a pleasure garden is to be made, and he is quite definite that these gardens are 'of no great utility or fruitfulness but designed for pleasure . . . they are mainly designed for the delight of two senses, viz. sight and smell'. First, a lawn must be made by importing turfs and tamping them down well: 'Care must be taken that the lawn is of such a size that about it in a square may be planted every sweet-smelling herb, such as rue and sage and basil, and likewise all sorts of flowers, as the violet, columbine, lily, rose, iris and the like.' Turf benches must be provided so that visitors to the garden can sit and 'take their repose pleasurably when their senses need refreshment'. Trees should not be planted on the lawn as they might endanger the growth of the grass, and interfere with the passage of fresh breezes that blow so healthfully through the garden.

Flowers not only refreshed the senses but were also used in religious rituals: in England Pentecost was known as 'the festival of the rose' and a shower of rose petals was sometimes used to demonstrate to the illiterate the descent of the Holy Ghost. In 1405 the Bishop of St Paul's in

BELOW *West Dean Gardens, Chichester. In the early twentieth century the property was bought by William James, who employed Harold Peto to design the massive pergola. The walled gardens have been recently replanned with three huge herbaceous borders.*

ABOVE *Brook Cottage, Alkerton. This interesting garden, like Sissinghurst, was created by a couple consisting of a plantsman and an architect. This white border is one of the best; it is much more than a collection of white flowering plants shoved into the same bed.*

London wore a chaplet of red roses at the commemoration of the church's patron saint, a practice noted by foreign observers as being peculiarly English.

Gardens were not the exclusive prerogative of the Church: the earliest private English herb garden planted for medicinal use was opened in Norwich in about 1266 by Solomon, a Jewish physician. In the later medieval period royalty were also keen gardeners: Eleanor of Castile, Edward I's wife, made a great garden at King's Langley in Hertfordshire, employing gardeners from Aragon, where they might have had the benefit of sophisticated, Islamic gardening knowledge. The preferred style of pleasure garden in the thirteenth century was the 'herber', a grass plat surrounded with paths; sometimes the turf was enlivened by the insertion of wild flowers, such as Chaucer's favourite plant, the daisy. Trelliswork was much used to separate sections of a garden, and as a frame up which to grow climbing plants, usually roses. Surviving gardeners' account books refer also to lilies and peonies, and to flowering fruit trees. Vine-covered walks and arbours would provide shade and privacy. At Eltham in south-east London in 1388/9 a garden was created specifically for the King and Queen to sup in. An English illuminator, who signed his name Johannes, painted a delightful illustration for a manuscript of about 1400 showing a king and queen, sitting on turf benches, playing chess in a garden. Here the lawn is full of flowers, and in the background one can just make out what looks suspiciously like a flower border – the first record of a border in England, perhaps. Several illustrations of this period show flowers planted against the boundary wall: in an early fourteenth-century painting from the Rhineland it is even possible to identify the plants: campion, cowslip, purple flag iris, hollyhock, peony, sweet rocket, periwinkle, lychnis, lily of the valley, roses and wallflowers. However, as we saw with the Villa Livia frescoes, paintings are not always reliable sources of evidence about contemporary practice.

Chaucer loved the appearance and smell of flowers, and gardens are important in several of his works: January's walled garden in *The Merchant's Tale* is an example, but perhaps more typical (and less of an erotic playground) is the fourteenth-century pleasure garden he describes in *Troilus and Criseyde*, with its sand-strewn walks and paling fences:

> Thys yerd was large, and rayled alle the allees,
> And shadwed well with blosmy bowes grene,
> And benched newe, and sanded alle the weyes.

A contemporary of Chaucer, John the Gardener, wrote his poem *The Feate of Gardening* in English. Among the 100 plants he mentions are many of the decorative flowers we have noted elsewhere – iris, hollyhock, lychnis, lily, periwinkle and violet. Decorative these flowers certainly are, but they also had their uses: violets could be candied and eaten as sweets; irises could be used as a strong purge, particularly effective against dropsy; the dried root of peony was used to cure convulsions and even lunacy, 'If a man layeth this wort [plant] upon the lunatic as he lies, soon he upheaveth himself whole.' Even the humble periwinkle had its uses; it was recommended by Dioscorides as 'a great binder', and by Culpeper as 'good for the nightmare'.

Throughout the Middle Ages it is hard to separate English gardening from that in the rest of Western Europe, but after a civil war, the Tudor settlement and Henry VIII's severing of ties with the Roman Church we begin to hear a distinctive English voice. In Tottell's *Miscellany* of 1557 Nicholas Grimald's poem 'The Garden', the first of a long line of poems on the subject in English, celebrates the 'mixture of solace and of gain' (that is, of pleasure and profit) to be found in a garden. And what makes the garden a place of such solace? Flowers, of course:

> Beholde, with lively hew, faire flowers that shine so bright:
> With riches, like the orient gems, they paint the mould in sight.
>
> From heavy hartes all doolfull dumps the garden chaseth quite.
> Strength it restores to limbs, draws and fulfils the sight.

not great verse, maybe, but the delight in flowers and their restorative powers is clear.

Thomas Tusser's *Hundred Good Points of Husbandry* was published in 1557, and expanded into *500 Hundred Points* in 1573. This practical guide to agriculture was a perennial favourite. It was revised, amplified and republished throughout the seventeenth century; in 1710 it was reissued in monthly parts and it made yet another, final appearance in the nineteenth century. Tusser wrote in verse also, perhaps hoping to make his advice memorable even to the illiterate. His approach is strictly utilitarian and severely moral, as in this example:

> In March and in April from morning to night
> In sowing and setting good housewives delight
> To have in a garden, or other like plot,
> To trim up their houses and furnish their pot.

Did 'trim up their houses' include collecting flowers for decoration? Or perhaps he only meant doing the dusting, and laying herbs on the floor to keep away insects.

> Where chambers are swept, and wormwood is strown
> No flea for his life dare abide to be known.

He also discusses flowers for windows and pots, among which we find again hollyhocks, violets, irises, but also daffodils, amaranthus, sweet Williams and wallflowers. So perhaps even this sternly practical farming man saw the delight in growing flowers for pleasure.

Great Dixter, Northiam. A garden made famous by the influential writings of its late owner, Christopher Lloyd. He was a plantsman but also an artist of great sensitivity who used wildflowers as part of his creation.

Shakespeare's plays are full of references to all kinds of flowers, native and exotic. Sometimes he uses them as a metaphor, as in 'Lilies that fester smell far worse than weeds', sometimes for their symbolic meaning. In *The Winter's Tale*, for instance, Perdita offers Camillo and Polixenes rosemary and rue, as 'these keep/Seeming and savour all the winter long', and thus are appropriate to their age. But she objects to 'nature's bastards', the 'gillyvors', carnations or pinks, which appeared to interbreed too promiscuously for her simple but severe morality. Perdita and Polixenes also discuss the morality of humans interfering with 'great creating Nature' by grafting and breeding new varieties of flowers. This was a matter of lively debate in the later years of the sixteenth century. George Puttenham in *The Arte of English Poesie* (1598) contributed to this discussion (another discussion that has rumbled on and on, without reaching any conclusion): 'The Gardiner by his arte will . . . embellish [a flower] in vertue, shape, odour, and taste that nature of herself woulde never have done: as to make the single gillifloure, or marigold, or daisie double; and the white rose, redde, yellow or carnation. The cunning Gardiner, using nature as a coadjutor, furthers her conclusions and many times makes her effectes more absolute and strange.' Thus it is clear that by the reign of Elizabeth English gardeners were no longer content with what nature offers; they had ambitions to improve the beauty of flowers.

The seventeenth century was the great period of the florist; the word entered the English language in 1623 and meant at that period 'someone who is skilled in the knowledge of flowering plants'. One of the first great florists and botanical writers of the century was John Parkinson, whose *Paradisi in Sole* was published in 1629. This is the first book to stress the sheer aesthetic pleasure of flowers rather than their usefulness, and there is a strain of national pride when he contemplates the range of flowers that can be grown in England. His title page refers to 'a garden of all sorts of pleasant flowers which our English ayre will permitt to be noursed up'. And he emphasizes the pleasure to be derived from expanding the range of plant material in our gardens by introducing 'divers outlandish flowers that for their pride, beauty and earlinesse are to be planted in gardens of pleasure for delight'. We will hear that word 'delight' again and again in the literature of the English flower garden.

Parkinson ascribes a provenance, sometimes rather fancifully, to all the plants he discusses. For example, he says the love apple, as the humble tomato was then delightfully known, comes from 'the hot countries of Barbary and Ethiopia', but in England we grow them only 'for curiosity and for the amorous aspect or beauty of the fruit'. 'Curiosity' is a key word of the seventeenth century, both in the sense of an oddity, and also in the modern sense of a love of enquiry. Many kept cabinets of curiosities, oddities of all kinds, and these became sources of material for scientists, such as those of the Royal Society, which was granted its royal charter in 1662. The cabinet of curiosities collected by the Tradescants, after whom tradescantia is named, became the nucleus of the Ashmolean Museum at Oxford. And when Parkinson published his *Theatrum Botanicum* in 1640, he included descriptions of more than 3,000 plants, whereas Gerard in his herbal of only fifty years earlier had included only 1,000. Interest in flowers was flourishing.

John Worlidge, whose *Art of Gardening* appeared in 1677, followed closely in Parkinson's footsteps. In his preface he sings the praises of the English soil and 'its aptness to produce naturally so great variety of trees for beauty and shade, flowers for delight, and edible plants also'. Interesting to note here how the usefulness of plants as food is relegated almost to an afterthought. He aims his book not only at those who own 'fair estates and pleasant seats' but at 'the honest and plain countryman'. Worlidge feels sure of an attentive audience because 'the affections of our countrymen naturally tend towards gardening, and this explains the number of books published on the subject'. The English were, perhaps, beginning to see themselves not merely as the inhabitants of a blessed land but as specially marked out by their skill as gardeners.

The Oxford Botanic Garden was founded in 1621, and in a seventeenth-century description it is said to be 'serviceable not only to all Physicians, Apothecaryes, and those who are more immediately concerned in the practise of Physick, but to persons of all qualities, serving to help the diseased and for the delight and pleasure of those of perfect health, containing therein 300 severall sorts of plants for the honour of our nation'. 'Delight' (again) and pleasure are to be found in gardens, as is a motive for national pride. Flowers are the subject of the delightfully energetic prose of Samuel Gilbert, whose *Florist's Vade Mecum* was published in 1692. On his title page he describes his volume as 'a choice compendium of whatever worthy notice has been extant for the Propagation, Raising, Planting, Encreasing, and Preserving the rarest Flowers and Plants that our Climate and Skill (in mixing, making and meliorating apted soils to each species) will perswade to live with us'. In his 'Epistle to the Reader' he is severe with those who take a utilitarian view of flowers and only appreciate 'a Clover July Flower because 'tis good to make syrup of'. Gilbert sounds like our contemporary when he inveighs against 'the Mercenary Flower Catchers about London . . . [who are guilty of] fathering new names on old flowers to enhance their price'. And equally when he recognizes the part played by fashion in the flower garden: 'I leave out many obsolete and overdated flowers, to make room for many new ones, that yearly grow into our acquaintance.' He sees no objection to violent human intervention in the botanical world, and has a section entitled 'To Change the Colours of Several Flowers whilst in the Blossom', in which he recommends painting the petals with spirits of vitriol to turn them scarlet!

There is palpable excitement in the writing of many of these seventeenth-century florists as they describe the new plants that were becoming available in England. But while they are excited by flowers and particularly by what was novel, they seem usually to have laid out their gardens very formally as botanical collections. The beauties of a flower could be enhanced by breeding, or even, *in extremis*, by vitriol, but not yet by arranging plants in a border (a word Gilbert uses in its modern, horticultural sense) to create a harmonious colour scheme. This enthusiasm for new plants was apparent all over Europe: in Italy they even had miniature theatres in which to display their treasures. The tulip, which caused such a sensation on its first appearance in the West, was bred and distributed from Holland.

New Place, Stratford-on-Avon. The house Shakespeare bought on his retirement no longer exists, but this garden has been planted on the site. It includes a 'pleached bower' and a knot garden to suggest the Elizabethan period.

But in England how widespread was this passion for flowers? The middle classes were beginning to be great plant collectors; the Reverend Walter Stonehouse was reported to grow 866 different species in his garden at Darfield in Yorkshire in the early 1640s. Certainly the ordinary cottager could not afford the tulip when it was first introduced, but by the mid seventeenth century Parkinson was able to write of the tulip, narcissus, fritillary and hyacinth that they were 'almost in all places, with all persons'. And Worlidge in 1667 wrote that 'there was scarce a cottage in most of the southern parts of England, but hath its proportionate garden, so great a delight do men take in it'. He has a chapter called 'Vulgar Flowers', 'which every colona knoweth how to plant, sow or propagate'; note the feminine noun – it was not the man of the house who looked after the flowers but his wife. The cottager must still have been principally concerned to produce food, but perhaps some of the exotics reached his garden, to be cared for by his wife. William Hughes's manual on flower gardening, aimed at 'plain and ordinary countrymen and women', sold out in three months.

And how did these new flowers reach their homes in English gardens? Gerard tells us of a merchant from London called Nicholas Leate who collected plants in France himself, but such was his enthusiasm that 'He doth carefully send into Syria having a servant there at Aleppo and in many other countries, for which myself and likewise the whole land are much bound to him.' The Tradescants were employed by aristocrats, such as the Earl of Salisbury, to mount plant-hunting expeditions, some as far afield as Russia, which resulted in the introduction, among other things, of the first lilac. John Evelyn asked his friend Samuel Pepys, Secretary to the Admiralty, to persuade naval officers posted abroad to bring seed back with them to England. The Bishop of London, Henry Compton, was a famous florist with over a thousand exotics growing in the garden of his palace at Fulham. He had the good fortune to be also Bishop of North America, so he could employ missionaries to bring back new species for him. European missionary collectors were to produce prolific results when they began to penetrate into China in the nineteenth century.

But the ordinary individual could not afford to fund plant-hunting expeditions; he or she was dependent on gifts from the great gardens. Gardeners have always been notoriously generous in sharing their plants, knowing, perhaps, that if their own crop fails, they can restock from the gardener who has been the object of their generosity. Nevertheless there was clearly a gap in the market and the professional nurseryman stepped in to fill it. By the 1690s there were at least fifteen nurseries in and around London; the largest of these, the Brompton Park nursery, by 1705 had nearly ten million plants for sale. One of the founders of this famous nursery was George London, who had been Bishop Compton's gardener in Fulham. He took as his junior partner Henry Wise, who had trained under the royal gardener, John Rose. Of Wise Stephen Switzer wrote that he was responsible for 'forwarding the business of gardening in such a degree that it is almost impossible to describe'. And a profitable business it was; when Wise died he left more than £100,000. Partly as a result of the activities of such nurseries, the range of plant material available to the enthusiastic gardener grew rapidly; it has been calculated that in 1500 there were some 200 kinds of cultivated plant available in England; by 1839 the number had climbed to something like 18,000.

English gardening benefited hugely from the arrival of gardeners escaping persecution in Holland and France. In Norwich, where many Dutch immigrants settled, there was an annual florists' feast, which can be traced back to 1637. Around the city such quantities of sweet-smelling flowers grew that, as a visitor noted in 1728, during feast days the Norwich streets were strewed with their petals. Some of the best pinks and auriculas were produced in Spitalfields, where many Huguenot weavers had settled when they were driven out of France. The search for novelty and perfection of bloom produced intensive research and experiment, so that Parkinson in 1629 recorded 140 kinds of tulip, while twenty years later a French florist reported to John Evelyn that there were 10,000 varieties. But perhaps the mania for the tulip makes it an exception. In the eighteenth century many towns promoted flower shows with prizes; at Bristol there were two specialist shows a year, one for auriculas and one for carnations. By 1691 John Aubrey was able to write: 'In the time of Charles 2nd gardening was much improved and became common: I doe beleeve, I may modestly affirm that there is now ten times as much gardning about London as there

Edenbridge House, Edenbridge. The house is partly sixteenth century, but the garden is a modern development. The arrangement of two borders flanking an immaculately mown stretch of grass is typically English.

was in AD 1660: and we have been since that time much improved in foreign plants: especially since about 1683, there have been exotick Plants brought into England no less than seven thousand.'

Many of these exotics required special treatment, in particular protection from the cold and damp of the English winter. The great problem was what to do with the orange tree, 'that busy plant' as George Herbert called it, since it fruits and flowers simultaneously. These were much in demand as 'greens' – that is, evergreens – which could be trimmed into formal shapes and would still bear fruit. There were two possible solutions: to protect them with some kind of tent in winter, or to grow them in boxes so that they could be moved into the safety of some kind of 'green house'. In many Italian gardens the former solution was adopted, and in England John Evelyn in his *Elysium Britannicum* (*c.*1660) has a charming drawing of a four-poster bed 'furnished with a tester [covering] and Curtaines of Green' used to protect his exotics from both cold and scorching sun.

But when he visited the Chelsea Physic Garden in August 1685 he found a better solution to the problem of protecting rare plants, a solution devised by John Watts, the keeper of the garden. This is how Evelyn recorded the discovery in his diary: 'What was very ingenious [was] the subterranean heat, conveyed by a stove under the Conserveatory, which was all vaulted with brick; so as he leaves the doors and windowes open in the hardest frosts.' This was a step forward from the mere greenhouse, and such heated houses became known as 'stoves'. The effect on the range of exotic flowers that could be grown was immediately apparent. Stephen Switzer in his *Iconographia Rustica* (1718) heaps praise on the Duchess of Beaufort because she devoted so much of her time 'that many other Ladies devote to the tiresome Pleasures of the Town' to her garden; the result was seen at Badminton in Gloucestershire, where 'Thousands of those foreign Plants (by her as it were made familiar to this clime) were regimented together, and kept in a wonderful deal of Health, Order and Decency.' The duchess commissioned a Dutch artist, Everard Kick, to paint her most prized specimens, among them passion flowers, daturas, nerines, hibiscus and cacti.

And what happened to flowers during the mid eighteenth century, while the gentry were destroying their flowered parterres, uprooting their avenues and submerging their estates in acres of lawn? The answer is, of course, that not all gardeners were such abject followers of fashion. Many could not afford the exorbitant costs of reshaping the landscape; others were more interested in flowers than in grass. In the early part of the century one of the most famous collectors was Lord Petre, son of the 'villain' of Pope's *Rape of the Lock*; his garden at Thorndon Hall in Essex was conservatively French in layout, with canals, drives and a great avenue of transplanted elms. It is said his plant collection numbered 219,000 different items, including trees, shrubs and flowers. In the spring of 1740, two years before he died at the early age of twenty-nine, he planted nearly five thousand trees, including cedars of Lebanon, tulip trees and chestnuts. In his stoves he grew pineapples (then the height of fashion), bananas and limes. But his great triumph was that in 1739 he brought to flowering the first camellia introduced into England; it was kept in his greenhouse for safety.

From America through the combined efforts of two Quakers, Peter Collinson and John Bartram, came magnolias, phlox and lilies. The Dutch had established a trading monopoly in Japan, where they were confined to the tiny island of Deshima in Nagasaki harbour; nevertheless

BELOW *Knightshayes, Tiverton. The Victorian garden dates from the 1870s, but the garden we see today is largely the work of Sir John and Lady Heathcoat-Amory in the 1950s. It is designed with the greatest artistry, an example being the contrast between the low, multi-coloured garden seen opposite and the elegant, green emptiness of the garden here. The only colour, apart from green, is provided by the statue, the weeping silver pear and the water lilies.*

ABOVE *Knightshayes, Tiverton. The planting is kept deliberately low and colourful, to contrast with the garden seen on the opposite page. The latter is isolated behind a tall yew hedge, and so comes as a complete surprise.*

they managed to send plants back to Europe. From South Africa Francis Masson sent plants to Kew, which had been founded as a botanical garden in 1762 under the enthusiastic patronage of Queen Augusta, George III's mother. Later in the century Captain Cook and Joseph Banks, later director of Kew, brought back some three thousand varieties of flowering plant, new to England, from the southern seas. So, despite the mania for Brownian landscape parks, the flood of new flowering material continued.

By the mid eighteenth century the rage for novelty in flowering plants was no longer confined to the noble few, and a sure indicator of the increasing demand was their falling price. In 1777 a seed catalogue produced by Richard Weston contained 208 anemones, 575 hyacinths, at least 800 tulips and more than 1,000 ranunculi. In explaining his pricing Weston pointed out the power of fashion: 'All new-raised flowers decrease greatly in price in a few years after they are raised.' A problem for buyers was that there was no agreed method of naming plants until in the middle of the century Carl Linnaeus divided the plant kingdom into groups called genera and sub-branches called species. Another indication of the popularity of gardening as an activity in England (and the larger number of those able to read) is the number of books published on the subject: while the seventeenth century had seen about a hundred volumes on gardens and gardening, the eighteenth, by contrast, produced at least six hundred. John Abercrombie's *Every Man His Own Gardener* (1767) was reproduced in sixteen editions before 1800, and in 1787 William Curtis began to publish *The Botanical Magazine, or Flower Garden Displayed*.

By 1779 it was true of England that 'Scarce a person from the peer to the cottager thinks himself tolerably happy without being possessed of a garden.' Outside the burgeoning cities the 'improving' landlord re-housed his tenants in model villages, where each cottage would have a

ABOVE *Sutton Place, Guildford. The house dates from the early sixteenth century. In the 1980s Sir Geoffrey Jellicoe was employed to redesign the gardens; typical of his love of allegory is the lake designed in the shape of a foetus.*

garden, usually in front of the house, so that the landlord could keep an eye on how the garden was being used and on its state of maintenance. We have heard about the cottager and his garden before, but perhaps it is at this point that we can identify a cottage garden style, in which vegetables and flowers were mixed.

But the great development of the eighteenth century was the expansion in town gardening. In the confined space of a town garden, rolling lawns and lakes were not a possibility, but it was certainly possible to grow flowers, provided the air was not too polluted. And as early as 1722 Thomas Fairchild noticed how Londoners would buy plants from itinerant flower-sellers 'rather than not . . . have something of the garden before them'. The poet Cowper describes plant containers on a city windowsill:

> There the pitcher stands
> A fragment, and the spoutless teapot there;
> Sad witnesses how close-pent man regrets
> The country, with what order he contrives
> A peep at nature, when he can no more.

If it was impossible to keep even pots of flowers alive, then you had to resort to pictures of flowers like those created by the famous Mrs Delany. And as the air of the city became more polluted the richer merchants began to buy places in the suburbs. In 1700 the population of the City of London was 140,000, but by 1800 it had declined to 78,000. At the same time, however, the population of the metropolis as a whole grew from 675,000 to 900,000, with the increasing popularity of villages such as Westminster. David Garrick, the greatest actor of his day, bought a villa at Hampton – note the word 'villa', with its suggestions of Roman precedent.

Like all fashions, the rage for flowers was easily mocked. Jenny Uglow in her delightful *A Little History of British Gardening* reproduces a cartoon of an eighteenth-century lady whose cantilevered hairdo has been laid out like a formal garden with gravel walks, rectangular beds and trailing flowers. And fashion determined what plants should be grown: William Hanbury in 1770 said the hollyhock had now grown too common, but admitted that 'this custom of alternately introducing and expelling of flowers' made fashionable gardening a tricky business. This being England, class, too, played no small part in deciding what to grow: auriculas, tulips and pinks were for the poor (tulips for the poor, when in the early seventeenth century the price had led literally to bankruptcy!); the cottage gardener would grow roses and polyanthus, while the owner of a villa aspired to dahlias, geraniums and clematis. The garden was a space in which the owner was free to express himself or the gardener to express herself; it was this independence that made gardening so attractive to women, 'to whom other spheres of activity were closed', according to Keith Thomas, to whose excellent *Man and the Natural World* I am much indebted. Certainly books and articles in the newly founded magazines were aimed specifically at women, whose natural role it seemed to be to tend the flower garden, the fragile beauty of flowers echoing the fragile beauty of the daughters of Eve, perhaps.

Thomas Jefferson recommended his fellow Americans Messrs Rutledge and Shippen to visit the parks of England, but not to follow the English addiction for plant collecting; 'It is the country of all others where the noblest gardens may be made without expense. We have only to cut out the superabundant plants.' But flowers had not disappeared entirely during the rule of the magician 'Capability' Brown: they had been tucked away out of sight in walled gardens, where the ladies of the household could tend them, while the master was striding his rolling acres of lawn. Flowers would have been out of scale with the noble proportions of the Brownian landscape, and flower beds near the house would have interrupted the fine flow of the greensward. Early in the eighteenth

BELOW *Hampton Court Palace, East Molesey. This is a magnificent collection of gardens: the Great Maze dates from 1691, and the Baroque Privy Garden of William III has recently been restored. Here bedding plants and topiary are used to maximum effect.*

century Switzer had written disparagingly of 'Flowers and other trifling Decorations fit only for little Town-gardens, and not for the expansive Tracts of the Country'. But by the end of the century taste was changing, and people wanted flowers to be as visible at their country seats as they were in their town gardens.

Humphry Repton was as alert to this change of taste as he was to new plant introductions. When he designed the garden at East Cowes Castle on the Isle of Wight for his partner John Nash, he planted *Rhododendron ponticum*, now the scourge of the countryside, a shrub that had only been introduced in the middle of the century. He knew his clients would want to grow a wide range of plants, so in one of his Red Books he advises on the soil of the flower garden: American plants need 'bog earth', that is acid soil, while alpines need stone for sharp drainage. For other exotics he often designed orangeries close to the house, sometimes joined to it by a glazed corridor, where yet other tender plants could be grown. In his last book, *Fragments on the Theory and Practice of Landscape Gardening* (1816), he confesses that he has become more interested in gardens than landscapes. In particular he refers to his work for the Earl of Bridgewater at Ashridge in Hertfordshire (one of his last commissions), where he decided he wanted 'to get away from the sameness of gravel walks in serpentine lines, with broad margins of grass, and flowers, and shrubs, everywhere promiscuously mixed and repeated'. Since Ashridge had been a conventual college, he decided to design one of 'those ancient trim gardens which formerly delighted the inhabitants of this curious spot', together with a monks' garden and a rosarium.

The odd thing about the rose, which has had such a long history as the queen of flowers and emblem of royalty, is that it was not subject to the intensive interest of breeders and collectors until the early years of the nineteenth century: in 1800 fewer than 100 varieties of rose were available, but by 1826 there were nearly 1,400. With the new varieties from China, the banksian rose, the tea rose and so on, new strains of long-flowering, highly scented roses were produced, the best of which were perhaps the Bourbon roses. Rose gardens, those nurseries of disease and spindly legs, were to become a commonplace in an age that loved to mass together flowers of the same kind or colour. And, with the new plant material flowing in from an empire on which the sun never set, there was no end to the variety of flowers that could be bred in your greenhouse or stove, and then planted out into regimented beds. The early Victorian gardener could paint his garden with plants in a way that had not been possible before, and he liked to paint in bright tones. Consider just some of the colours on his palette: bright-red pelargoniums or scarlet salvias, brassy marigolds and, from South America, yellow calceolaria, purple heliotrope, blue lobelia, white petunias from Brazil, begonias, verbena and eschscholtzia. Exotics would be raised in the hothouse and planted out when the weather allowed; thus was born the 'bedding system'.

And what shape should the beds be? Listen to James Shirley Hibberd in *Rustic Adornments for Homes of Taste* (1856): 'When a lawn or terrace is to be enriched with a display of flowers, the geometric garden is most appropriate . . . There is no need of harsh outlines, indeed curves of some kind should predominate.' So geometry was back! When Shirley Hibberd wrote these words, this style of flower garden was already well established, and had already been criticized because its result was that 'Scores of unmeaning flower beds in the shape of kidneys and tadpoles and sausages and leeches now disfigure the lawn.' If this reminds you of biscuits or pastry shapes

BELOW *Broughton Castle, Banbury. This garden is rightly celebrated for its magnificent herbaceous borders; one contains colours in the range of blues, purples, mauves and red, another blue, yellow, grey and white. Here we see a simple arrangement of* Viola cornuta, Allium cernuum *and* Alchemilla mollis.

ABOVE *Hampton Court Castle, Leominster. The true herbaceous border has no woody plants in it. If shrubs are included, the border is more accurately called 'mixed'.*

created by curiously shaped metal cutters, Francis Bacon had had the same reaction to knots 200 years earlier, when he sourly commented, 'You may see as good sights many times in tarts.' There is nothing new under the gardening sun!

Another way of using flowers as exterior decoration was to group them into circular 'pincushion' beds, with the lowest at the front, the heights rising gently to a standard plant, often a rose, at the centre. The most obvious example of decorating with flowers was ribbon gardening; Shirley Hibberd defines it thus: 'It is the arrangement of plants in lines, each line being of one colour or one set of blended tints, and the plants forming the several lines of the border are so selected as to contrast against each other, and produce a harmony in the whole.' In this style of gardening the most useful flowers are those that are easily dragooned into tight shapes and elaborate patterns; it is these patterns and the bright colours of the floral display that are of interest, not the character of the individual plant. We might compare the Victorian gardener's approach to his plants with the Victorian industrialist's attitude to his workers, as caricatured in Dickens' *Hard Times*: Gradgrind was only interested in the 'hands' en masse, and then only as long as they were obedient; a single individual such as Stephen Blackpool was beneath his notice, unless he were a fomenter of rebellion.

In the tightly buttoned world of Victorian respectability nature, of course, could not be given her head. Listen to the language of Hibberd as he discusses the planting of the garden. At the front of the house he suggests evergreens – laurels, naturally, 'lauristinus' and holly – 'to give the house a substantial aspect, but all must be as trim as the Corporal's boots'. Yew or cypress might be used; they are 'somewhat gloomy, though very substantial and respectable'. And behind the house the borders should be 'symmetrically arranged as to colours'; however, this genial guide does make a concession – 'Though a formal disposition is essential, there are certain ways of breaking a rigid formality, which, to a tasteful eye, give much pleasure.' On one matter, though, he is imperious: 'Now for the geometric garden, and the beds on terraces and lawns. Here the colours are to blaze like the variegated lamps at Vauxhall, or the fireworks of the Peace celebration.' Respectable, trim sobriety at the front but a blazing show behind the house: the Victorian householder wanted to have it both ways, to celebrate his wealth but not to flaunt it in any way that might be considered vulgar.

Later in the century E.A. Bowles attacked this 'made-by-contract, opulent style of gardening . . . that relies upon Bank of England notes for manure'. John Sales quotes a gardener to the Rothschild family who had heard it said 'that rich people used to show their wealth by the size of their bedding plant list: ten thousand for a squire, twenty for a baronet, thirty for an earl and forty for a duke'. Certainly this way of using flowers was not cheap, particularly when one considers that the bedding scheme would be changed at least once during the season. Labour costs may have been low, but the raising and care of the thousands of plants in hothouses was more costly: as Hibberd warned, 'The cold pit, the forcing pit and the greenhouse must be carefully managed to keep up a succession.'

Small town gardens could imitate the pincushion bed and the ribbon planting, but they might not have the greenhouse space for exotics, which had to be bought from the flourishing nurseries; greenhouses, however, did become cheaper after the repeal of the tax on glass in 1845. They were built using cylinder glass (plate glass to us) and steel, a model that could fit the

suburban greenhouse or rise to the heights of Decimus Burton's Palm House at Kew, or, supremely, the Crystal Palace. The population of England approximately doubled every fifty years from 1750 to 1900, from 5 million in 1750 to 40 million in 1900. This meant a huge expansion in the demand for housing, and it was to the dwellers in these new, smaller town houses, each with its bit of garden, that John Claudius Loudon addressed himself.

The middle years of the nineteenth century saw gardening establish itself as a major interest of these burgeoning middle classes, and Loudon was their teacher. This extraordinary man is said to have published some sixty million words in his astonishingly energetic life; after the amputation of his right arm, he had to dictate to his wife, Jane, and this is what he was doing when he died in 1843. Loudon's interests were wide-ranging; he designed everything from glasshouses to public parks, and wrote about agriculture and architecture, garden cemeteries and gardening libraries. The bible for the apprentice gardener was his *Encyclopaedia of Gardening* (1822); this was followed in 1838 by the even more influential *The Suburban Gardener and Villa Companion*. In the latter work he divided gardens into four types according to their size and gave advice on how each might be developed. This practical, hard-headed Scotsman offered plans, suggested plants and gave hints on their cultivation, but above all he calculated the cost of a garden makeover – something our current TV pundits seem reluctant to do. Loudon had begun life as a devotee of the Picturesque, but his Continental travels had persuaded him that formal gardens also had their merits. He emphasized the garden as a work of art; it was not and could not be nature, so he gave his style the graceless name 'gardenesque'. In its celebration of the unnatural, the quirky, the odd, Loudon's 'gardenesque' gave great encouragement to the planting of, for example, monkey puzzles in suburban gardens. With Loudon's guidance the middle classes in their suburban villas discovered they could follow the example of the wealthy with their kidney-shaped beds (fewer in number, of course) cut into immaculate lawns, trimmed into respectability by Mr Budding's newly invented lawn-mower.

ABOVE *Broughton Cottage, Banbury. A true cottage garden would have contained fruit trees, a jumbled collection of favourite ornamentals and vegetables. This example seems rather to look back to Victorian ribbon planting and pincushion beds.*

Particularly in Midland and northern towns, unregulated urban development resulted in housing that was often rolled out over the countryside with no thought for health, beauty or public welfare. As Trevelyan has it: 'To millions the divorce from nature was absolute, and so too was the divorce from all dignity and beauty and significance in the wilderness of mean streets in which they were bred.' Some towns made efforts to counter this divorce by providing allotments for the factory workers; naturally these were usually planted to provide food for the family. But some allotment-holders also grew flowers. At Hunger Hill in Nottingham 10,000 plots were rented to workers in the hosiery trade for £1 a year; here they grew not only vegetables but also roses. In 1860 they held the first rose show in England, and such was their success that the great rosarian Dean Hole asked, 'Where will you see such roses as are produced upon the Hunger Hills by these amateurs?' This concentration on roses suggests a kind of local specialization, which is still apparent in some gardening clubs in the north of England: Paisley weavers specialized in breeding 'laced pinks'; in Lancashire it was auriculas, while the Pansy Society of Falkirk held its first show in 1844. More general societies were also founded, like the York Grand Floricultural and Horticultural Society, in imitation of the Horticultural Society of London, which had been founded in 1804.

Some of these societies were founded or backed by the local gentry, because gardening was felt to be a morally improving activity, and this was an age dedicated to improving the morals of others. The 'deserving poor' gardened; the 'undeserving poor' drank. Keith Thomas records that 'the love of flowers and a taste for gardening' were seriously suggested as a remedy for the high rate of illegitimacy in Cumbria. Another who testified to the salvation offered by gardening was a gentleman who wrote to *The Cottage Gardener* in 1850: he describes how he had been a victim of the demon drink, 'so much was my whole frame enervated that my arms hung almost paralysed by

BELOW *East Ruston Old Vicarage, Norwich. One of the most ambitious gardens to have been made in England in recent years. The planting is opulent, even theatrical, but also carefully structured.*

my side', but then he saw an advertisement for the magazine and now he was the proud owner of 'an allotment of four hundred yards'. A regular, female columnist of the same magazine takes up the theme: 'There is moral beauty, too, in the cultivated cottage garden. Neatness and attendance bespeak activity, diligence, and care; neglect and untidiness tell of the BEER-HOUSE' (her capitals). Maybe there are political as well as moral implications in this promotion of gardening as an improving activity. Keith Thomas goes so far as to suggest: 'The preoccupation with gardening, like that with pets, fishing and other hobbies, even helps to explain the relative lack of radical and political impulses among the British proletariat.'

The rich had no need of moral improvement, of course. In an age of such wealth they could have anything they wanted in their gardens, and some wanted everything. The Duke of Devonshire at Chatsworth in Derbyshire wanted a vast glasshouse, in which to grow the giant water-lily *Victoria regina* and exotic orchids, so for him Joseph Paxton built the largest area of glass in the world, large enough for the Queen to drive through in a coach and four. At Alton Towers in Staffordshire Charles Talbot, 15th Earl of Shrewsbury, wanted a version of Stonehenge, a Chinese temple, an Indian temple, a three-storey, Gothic, cast-iron prospect tower and a Swiss cottage with a blind harpist. The grounds were planted with a profusion of rhododendrons, heathers and exotic trees. John Claudius Loudon was appalled: 'We consider the greater part of it in excessively bad taste, or rather, perhaps, the work of a morbid imagination joined to the command of unlimited resources.'

Shrewsbury had 200 hectares/490 acres to play with; at Biddulph Grange in Staffordshire James Bateman had only 8 hectares/19 acres, but in those he sought to encompass the world. Here is David Stuart's list of what part of the garden included:

Waddesdon Manor, Aylsbury. The late nineteenth-century French-style château was built for Ferdinand de Rothschild. The south parterre has maintained its Victorian layout, but the bedding plan is different each year.

a lean-to greenhouse for tender rhododendrons and camellias, as well as glasshouses for all the fruit crops that could be cultivated in them; terraces; private gardens; a couple of parterre gardens, one for coloured sands, one devoted to all the new verbenas being bred by the nurserymen; a large patch of hardy rhododendrons surrounding a pond with an islet set in its middle; narrow winding walks and tunnels; endless rockwork, part of which was an imitation of the Great Wall of China, planted about with bamboos and some of the newly imported hostas; a pinetum . . . a bowling green; a quoit ground; a raised terrace crescent, and an Italian parterre.

That was only the beginning: there was also a wellingtonia avenue, a stumpery (a collection of oak stumps thrown together and planted with ferns), an Egyptian court with stone sphinxes, enclosed by yew hedges, from which a tunnel led into a grotto, and when the visitor emerged by a different route he came out through the door of a half-timbered Cheshire cottage. And still there was more: the area called China containing a Chinese temple, idols and joss-houses was planted with Moutan peonies, Japanese maples, hostas and soaring cardiocrinum lilies. Entry was five shillings, closed on Sunday.

Such exuberant excess could not last. In 1842 one correspondent threw up his hands in horror as he read a plant catalogue: 'What in the name of moderation, is one to do with "four thousand new seedling, shrubby calceolarias, all named varieties", beautiful as they undoubtedly are.' One problem with the fashion for bedding was its emphasis on a narrow range of plants whose habit of growth made them suitable for such exterior decoration. Verbenas and calceolarias were all the rage, but they were terribly subject to mildew and had to be dusted every two weeks or so with flowers of sulphur, a disfiguring yellow powder. Geraniums (most of them were botanically pelargoniums) were tougher; sports and selections were of huge commercial value – for example, the variety 'Tom Thumb', the first with a tricoloured leaf, was used extensively in bedding schemes. In the suburbs, the public parks and most of the great houses the fashion for bedding ruled, but in quieter backwaters of the country the mania for novelty and display had not displaced the love of old varieties or the growing of flowers for their own individual beauty. Thus when the pendulum of fashion began to swing against bedding, it was to the vicarages and cottage gardens of rural England that the prophets of the new style looked. The image of the cottage garden that emerged in Victorian England was largely the product of nostalgia for a pre-industrial age. In some literature, and much painting, the English country cottage was represented as an idyllic, sun-lit setting for laughing, smock-clad children and happy animals.

Cottage and vicarage gardens were not all fictitious. Mary Russell Mitford describes her spendthrift father's garden in a letter of 1842 to Elizabeth Barrett, soon to become Mrs Browning. The cottage was, of course, 'covered with vines and roses'; the garden contained old fruit trees now 'festooned with honeysuckle', and was planted with 'clumps of matchless hollyhocks and splendid dahlias', 'huge masses of lupines', larkspur, monkshood and oriental poppies. Roses climbed through the apple trees, a detail the great Vita Sackville-West was to imitate at Sissinghurst. The dahlias and the absence of vegetables marked this out as a gentrified cottage garden, but the jumbled opulence of the planting was to become a style much imitated. The genial Canon Ellacombe, who was born in 1822, lived and gardened for all but five of his ninety-four years at Bitton in Gloucestershire. His *In a Gloucestershire Garden* (1895) is a hymn to what he calls 'a better and more healthy style of gardening', but he regrets how much has been lost: 'The parsonage garden some years ago was a home for hundreds of good old-fashioned flowers, but I am afraid no gardens suffered more from the bedding craze, which swept them clear of all their old long-cherished beauties, and reduced them to the dull level of uniformity with their neighbours' gardens, or to miniature mockeries of Trentham and Cliveden.' He also points out that for a parson gardening is a useful way to establish contact with his flock: 'The love of flowers and gardening is so universal among the English peasantry that a country parson will often find a better introduction to a cottager through his garden than by any other means.' Snobbery had also dictated that certain plants were classified as fit only for the cottage. Mrs Earle, in her

Pot Pourri From A Surrey Garden (1897), reflects on the popular fashion for planting crown imperials, while 'In my youth they were rather sniffed at and called cottage plants.'

ABOVE *Biddulph Grange, Stoke-on-Trent. James Bateman, who created the gardens in the second half of the nineteenth century, was a great plant collector. Here we see part of his rhododendron collection, edged with bedding plants in true Victorian style.*

The standard bearer for the anti-bedding movement was the polemical Irishman William Robinson. He had worked at the Royal Botanical Society's garden in Regent's Park in London, where he had been in charge of the herbaceous collections. Robinson had taken a special interest in English wild flowers, but also had travelled widely in Europe and America. In 1870 he published *The Wild Garden*, in which he recommended the use of 'plants of other countries, as hardy as our hardiest wild flowers, in places where they will flourish without further care or cost'. A new note is at once apparent: the interests of the flowers are paramount; they should be placed where they will be happy, not tormented into patterns to fit the human will. And in his awareness of the need for economy he is the friend of every modern gardener; unsurprisingly *The Wild Garden* was reissued in 1977 and again in 1983.

But this book was only a prelude to his greatest work, perhaps the most influential book on gardening since Roman times: *The English Flower Garden*, which was published in 1883 and went through eight editions before 1900. In the foreword to the eighth edition the gloves are off; he attacks some of the most famous gardens of the day, the Royal Horticultural Society's in Kensington and Paxton's around the Crystal Palace, for what he called 'all the theatrical gardening of Versailles reproduced in Surrey'. His tone is splendidly forthright: 'I saw the flower-gardener meanly trying to rival the tile or wallpaper men, and throwing aside with contempt all the lovely things that through their height or form did not conform to this idea.' It was the narrow range of plants used in bedding schemes that particularly enraged Robinson: 'No stereotyped garden of half-a-dozen kinds of plants will satisfy anyone who knows that many beautiful aspects of vegetation are possible in a garden in spring, summer and autumn.' Unsurprisingly he found his ideal in the cottage garden: 'English cottage gardens are never bare and seldom ugly . . . they are pretty from snowdrop time till the Fuchsia bushes bloom nearly into winter.' When he asks rhetorically what is the essential charm of the cottage garden, the answer is clear: 'it is the absence of any "plan", which lets the flowers tell their story to the heart'. This is the eighteenth-century landscape rebellion against parterres and avenues writ small: geometry is again to be overthrown and nature to be reclaimed from the excesses of art.

Robinson was a tireless polemicist for his more relaxed style of gardening. In 1871 he founded a weekly journal, *The Garden*, which he edited until 1899. *Gardening Illustrated* and *Cottage Gardening* followed. When he stopped editing *The Garden* in 1899, the editor's chair was briefly occupied by his friend Gertrude Jekyll, who was a frequent contributor to the magazine. In the writings of both Jekyll and Robinson the border is a key element in the garden's design. As early as 1829 Cobbett had distinguished between borders and beds; beds contained a 'mass of one sort of flower', while in a border colours and varieties were blended, the plants being selected 'to insure a succession of blossom from the earliest months of spring until the coming of the frosts'. The earliest use of the term 'herbaceous border' dates from 1826, and the earliest examples of borders made from hardy, herbaceous plants are from the 1840s at Hatfield House in Hertfordshire and Arley Hall in Cheshire. But it was not until the later part of the nineteenth century that the herbaceous border came into its glory, marking the high point of the British obsession with flowers.

Robinson discusses borders fully in *The English Flower Garden*. His tone is characteristically hortatory and peremptory: 'Have no patience with bare ground'; 'Detestable clipped laurel, weary and so ugly!'; 'Do not pay much attention to labelling; if a plant is not worth knowing, it is not worth growing.' For him 'A simple border has been the first expression of flower gardening . . . there is no arrangement of flowers more graceful, varied or capable of giving more delight.' In that word 'delight' Robinson is, unconsciously perhaps, echoing the seventeenth-century florists. He points out how permanent planting means lower labour costs, and takes pleasure in the changes that the seasons bring. Above all, he contrasts the beauty of form seen in irises, lilies, delphiniums and evening primroses with the shapelessness of bedding plants, which 'merely give us flat colour'.

RIGHT *Glendurgan, Falmouth. Even a nineteenth-century garden famed for its remarkable collection of trees and shrubs, some of them subtropical, contains beautiful tiny wild flowers that are also found on the road banks of Devon and Cornwall.*

The arrangement of the plants must be relaxed: climbers at the back of a border are allowed 'a certain degree of abandoned grace', and plants should not always be arranged in graduated rows by height. At the end of the chapter he lists 180 genera of hardy plants suitable for a herbaceous border, everything from acanthus to zinnia. He emphasizes the merits of perennials, but allows that annuals can be tucked into the border to supply the place of plants that are over. Robinson's forthright advocacy made converts by the barrowful, particularly after 1918, when labour costs began to soar. But even earlier many gardeners were ready for a style that was more relaxed and placed more emphasis on the individual beauty of a single plant.

In some gardening histories Robinson plays the part of John the Baptist to the goddess of the border, Gertrude Jekyll. Between 1880 and 1930 this sturdy lady spoke to many gardeners in her sensible and sensitive voice, through her articles in Robinson's magazines and through her books. She was above all a craftswoman, a devotee of William Morris (who thought bedding 'an aberration of the human mind') and the Arts and Crafts movement, so her artistry was always based on practical experience and expressed with a solid understanding of what was possible. Failing eyesight compelled her to abandon painting in favour of garden design, but she always saw herself as a painter with plants: merely having a good collection of plants, she wrote, is 'only like having a box of paints from the best colourman, or, to go one step further, it is like having portions of these paints set out upon a palette'. She liked to use plants in what she called 'drifts', that is informal, often sausage-shaped groupings, where the boundaries between one group and another were blurred. Perhaps less sensitive to the form of individual plants than Robinson, she was a mistress of colour. Listen to her advice (from *Colour Schemes for the Garden*, 1936) on planning a flower border:

BELOW *The Priory, Kemerton, Tewkesbury. Peter Healing designed this border in his head while a prisoner of war. He was much influenced by the theories of Gertrude Jekyll – hence the careful grading of the colours.*

The planting of the border is designed to show a distinct scheme of colour arrangement. At the two ends there is a groundwork of grey and glaucous foliage – Stachys, Santolina, Cineraria maritime, Sea-kale and Lyme-grass, with the darker foliage, also of grey quality, of Yucca, Clematis recta and Rue. With this, at the near or western end, there are flowers of pure blue, grey-blue, white, palest yellow and palest pink; each colour partly in distinct masses, partly intergrouped. The colouring then passes through stronger yellow, to orange and red. By the time the middle space of the border is reached the colour is strong and gorgeous, but, as it is in good harmonies, it is never garish. Then the colour strength recedes in an inverse sequence through orange and deep yellow to pale yellow, white and palest pink, again with blue-grey foliage. But at this, the eastern end, instead of the pure blues we have purples and lilacs.

Jekyll had not only painted but had studied colour theory, so she understood that when the eye is saturated by strong colours it is more receptive to complementary, softer colours.

Gertrude Jekyll claimed she had learned much from cottage gardens: 'It may be two plants growing together by happy chance, or a pretty tangle of mixed creepers, or something one has always thought must have a south wall doing better on an east one.' But it takes the sharp eye of the artist to see these details among the chaos of flowers and vegetables in the real cottage garden, where favourites are crammed in wherever there is room. She was also sensible enough to appreciate that borders of a single colour are not guaranteed to work: 'A blue garden, for beauty's sake, may be hungering for a group of white lilies, or for something of palest lemon-yellow, but it is not allowed to have it, because it is called the blue garden . . . Surely the business of the blue

BELOW Ascott, Leighton Buzzard. Famous for its trees, this Victorian garden also boasts some fine borders. The plants spilling on to the path break the straight line or, to use a word dear to English gardeners, 'soften' the hard edge.

LEFT AND BELOW *Hidcote Manor Garden, Chipping Campden. The creation of the American Major Lawrence Johnston in the early twentieth century, this is one of the most influential gardens in the country; it even influenced Sissinghurst. The Red Border (left) is only one of the colour-themed gardens; there are also white, and yellow/blue gardens. The swimming pool (below) is jammed into a space dramatically too small for it.*

ABOVE *Sissinghurst Castle, Cranbrook. This is the famous and influential White Garden, originally conceived by Vita Sackville-West as a moonlight garden. The dwarf hedges around the beds are sometimes allowed to grow too high, so, to see the flowers, the visitor has to peer down, as into a grave.*

garden is to be beautiful as well as to be blue . . . any experienced colourist knows that blues will be more telling – more purely blue – by the juxtaposition of a rightly placed, complementary colour.' Her influence has been great throughout the land and no more so than in two of the great gardens of the twentieth century – Hidcote in Gloucestershire and Sissinghurst in Kent. Each has a part of the garden devoted to a single colour: the much-hymned White Garden at Sissinghurst, which is really a moonlight garden, and the Red Borders at Hidcote. Others have imitated Jekyll's carefully graded range of colours illustrated in the previous paragraph, few more successfully than Peter Healing at Kemerton in Worcestershire.

Vita Sackville-West had visited Miss Jekyll's garden at Munstead Wood in Surrey, but she had little admiration for herbaceous borders 'or for the plants that usually fill them – coarse things with no delicacy or quality about them. I think the only justification for such borders is that they should be perfectly planned, both in regard to colour and to grouping; perfectly staked, and perfectly weeded. How many people have the time or the labour?' Her practical question sounds a chill note; we are no longer in the golden afternoon of Edwardian luxury. Her gardening is bolder with colours than Jekyll's, mixing shrubs, particularly the old roses she did so much to make popular, and bulbs with herbaceous plants; it is impulsive, wonderfully personal and therefore difficult to imitate. 'The main thing,' she writes in summing up her planting design, 'is to have a foundation of large, tough, untroublesome plants with intervening spaces for the occupation of annuals, bulbs or anything that takes your fancy.' Anyone can manage that, but few can do it as well as she did.

Sissinghurst has its cottage garden also, 'but', in Vita Sackville-West's own words, 'it is a cottage garden in the academic, horticultural sense, too, for it is planted to a variety of kinds – shrubs, herbaceous plants, bulbs and corms in close association in the manner developed by Gertrude Jekyll out of traditional cottage gardening. There is, as in all the great Jekyll gardens, a pleasing touch of what I may perhaps call Marie Antoinette-ism about it. For while the method is that of the cottage gardener, the material is more sophisticated.' Miss Sackville-West thought that Lawrence Johnston's Hidcote 'resembles a cottage garden or rather a series of cottage gardens in so far as the plants grow in a jumble, flowering shrubs mingling with roses, herbaceous plants with bulbous subjects, climbers scrambling over hedges, seedlings coming up wherever they have planted themselves'.

Both of these great gardens are now in the care of the National Trust, whose gardens consultant for many years was Graham Stuart Thomas, a consummate designer with his own interpretation of the Robinson/Jekyll/cottage tradition – and a man who crossed the Channel only once, in 1951

Sissinghurst Castle, Cranbrook. Vita Sackville-West did not much like herbaceous borders – unless they were perfectly designed and perfectly staked. Many of her borders are mixtures of herbaceous material and shrubs, including old roses. The spring walk (left), planted with bulbs under tightly pleached trees, was largely the work of Vita's husband, Harold Nicolson. 'Profusion, even extravagance and exuberance, within the confines of the utmost linear severity', was her declared aim.

to spend a weekend in Paris, an experience he disliked. His voice brings us full circle in this exploration of the English addiction to flowers in their gardens. He gave a talk on the BBC in 1980 which began with words that directly echo the feelings of Samuel Gilbert, John Parkinson and many another seventeenth-century writer: 'We are very blessed in this country. We can go into our gardens and find flowers in any month of the year.' He goes on in his second paragraph to tell us what horticulture is all about – flowers.

> The transcendent beauty of flowers is something which is apt to be forgotten by young prospective gardeners, and also, I'm sorry to say, sometimes by their teachers. There would be no need to study what may be broadly called the science of horticulture were it not for the beauty of flowers, coupled of course with the beauty and use of fruit and vegetables. But it is *the beauty of flowers* [his italics] that has made us want to have beautiful gardens. We should not forget it.

Only someone steeped, as Graham Stuart Thomas was, in the English tradition of garden-making could write like this; an Italian, Muslim or Oriental garden maker would never have placed such an overwhelming emphasis on flowers.

And what of today? Certainly we English are not all making herbaceous borders à la Jekyll, and some of us prefer a formal layout. We use shrubs and bulbs in long grass; we make Japanese gravel gardens, raked into swirls. We do what we like, and there are many styles to influence us. But we still love flowers, which explains why 720 specialist British nurseries successfully offer over 70,000 different kinds of plant in the annually published *RHS Plant Finder*. The pendulum of fashion, of course, must swing again – against flowers. And we can see it happening in the gardens specially designed for the Chelsea Flower Show and in television programmes. Modish designers want us to fill our gardens with plastic, polished steel, timber, rocks, mirrors – anything but flowers. But how many people are persuaded? Few, to judge by the gardens one sees in English villages and suburbs. Gardeners are conservative people; we like gardens that resemble our grandparents' gardens, because childhood memories call us back to these models of arcadia. Simon Schama, treating a much wider theme in his stimulating *Landscape and Memory*, uses a splendidly horticultural metaphor to explain how we can never evade the influence of our personal and national past: 'The sum of our pasts, generation laid over generation, like the slow mould of the seasons, forms the compost of our future.' And the English compost heap of memory is full of flowers.

8

THE AMERICAN EXPERIMENT

ABOVE *Stonecrop Gardens, Cold Spring, New York. Originally the home of Anne and Frank Cabot, before they left to garden even further north, this is now a public garden. It lies 350 metres/1,100 feet above the Hudson Valley. This is a glimpse of the Deck Garden.*

OPPOSITE *Innisfree Garden, Millbrook, New York. This garden, or more accurately landscape, was created by Walter and Marion Beck, with the help of Lester Collis, between 1930 and 1960.*

A T THE END OF F. SCOTT FITZGERALD'S *The Great Gatsby* the narrator imagines Long Island Sound as the original Dutch settlers might have seen it:

> . . . a fresh, green breast of the new world. Its vanished trees, the trees that had made way for Gatsby's house, had once pandered in whispers to the last and greatest of all human dreams; for a transitory enchanted moment man must have held his breath in the presence of this continent, compelled into an aesthetic contemplation he neither understood nor desired, face to face for the last time in history with something commensurate with his capacity for wonder.

The stupendous scale and physical beauty of this continent still amazes the first-time visitor, particularly someone who has read only of American cities and their problems. There is so much space that the sense of possibility is overwhelming; there is room for everything and everyone, for new ideas and experiments in living differently. Such pristine freshness almost defies the past; here there seems to be only a future untrammelled by the conventions and manners of the homeland the immigrant has left. It is particularly easy to think like this if the invader/immigrant imagines the country to be empty, ignoring (or eliminating) those who were dwelling in this green paradise before he or she arrived.

In this great, green melting pot where so many of the world's cultures and traditions, prejudices and tastes meet, what new civilization emerged and with it what kind of gardens? Anything could have happened; gardens might have developed in ways history-soaked Europeans could never have imagined. The American garden style could have been revolutionary in thinking and execution; instead it remains a matter of debate whether there is such a thing as an American garden style. Perhaps while the melting pot still bubbles, and the population is still deciding what the word 'American' means, it is too much to expect an American style of garden. Where there is no national garden tradition, it is all too easy to borrow ideas from another country; this is particularly so if you have just emigrated from that country and feel that your cultural identity still depends on those foreign roots. This may account, to some extent, for the hesitant development of an American garden style.

If there is a disadvantage in the lack of a native-grown garden orthodoxy, there are also huge advantages. First, there is the freedom to rethink everything about a garden from scratch; you can do what you like, particularly when there is the cash and space to think big. Second, you can express your own artistic personality to the full without obligatory nods in the direction of orthodox good taste; this may also, though, be a treacherous temptation, since you may reveal more of yourself than you anticipated. At San Simeon in California the press baron William Randolph Hearst enjoyed to the full the freedom to do exactly what he wanted – and missed creating something beautiful by several million miles. Another advantage is that American imperialism has no garden tradition to impose on the world; McDonald's and Wal-Mart may follow the Stars and Stripes, but not the rose gardens and lawns that followed the Union Jack. The greatest advantage, however, is that American garden literature is much more diverse and more searching than in, for example, the United Kingdom. There are no assumptions about what a garden or a garden book should be, so the most fundamental questions are asked, and answered in interestingly original ways.

It used to be almost traditional in the United States, particularly on the east coast, to praise British garden writing at the expense of native products. This seems to me entirely unjust. For example, where in Britain can you find such wide-ranging, provocative and intelligent writing about gardens as that of Michael Pollan? He raises fundamental questions about what a garden is and what it should be – something which Britons know instinctively, or rather presume they know, and therefore don't need to discuss. Britons also think it more than a little pretentious to talk about the definition and purpose of a garden, since everyone knows what it is; an understanding and appreciation of gardens is bred in the bone, and so doesn't require definition, or indeed comment, let alone discussion. This kind of instinctive 'knowledge' all too quickly and easily becomes narrow-minded and bone-headed. Thus in the United Kingdom you would rarely find a book called *The Meaning of Gardens*, whereas in the US there are at least two books with this title, each of which has interesting things to say about the cultural significance of gardens.

Eleanor Perényi's *Green Thoughts* is another example, a classic of common gardening sense written in bracing, forthright prose. The Antiguan–American writer Jamaica Kincaid,has become entangled with gardening in her adopted Vermont. In *My Garden (Book)* she writes not of the peace her garden gives her but of the constant state of creative anxiety she finds herself in. She is very alert to the politics of gardening and botany. For example, she tells the story of the dahlia, a plant native to Mexico, where it was known as *cocoxochitl*; however, after it was introduced into Europe (Kincaid would probably say 'stolen'), the Swedish botanist Andreas Dahl got to work on it and thus we know the plant by his name. Gardens and botany can thus be seen as evidence of conquest and control. A reader, battling through the tangled brackets of her prose, may be fascinated or infuriated by her intelligent naivety; it is impossible not to find it stimulating. This book is typical of US garden writing in its originality – an originality that is almost obligatory, since this is not a nation that gardens because it must, because gardening is a national pastime; each individual must work out his or her motive for taking up the trowel. And nothing can be taken for granted in a nation that, as Kincaid says, 'is impatient with memory', usually preferring what is new to what is traditional. When they were writing the constitution, the fathers of the nation had to begin anew, and everything could be worked out from first principles; so it is with the best American garden writers – every idea is re-examined, tested and perhaps modified before it can be accepted.

God arrived on the American continent in various forms: the Spanish in California brought the Catholic faith to the pagan native Indians; the Pilgrim Fathers in New England brought their severe, ascetic, perhaps arrogant Christianity, and the Jamestown settlers a flexible Protestantism which could accommodate their rampant capitalist ambitions. The United States remains a country riddled with religion. Is it by chance that Americans call autumn 'the fall'? Perhaps there is a suggestion that if Adam and Eve had never eaten the blessed apple, spring would have been eternal in God's own country. The early settlers in New England certainly felt that they had been singled out by divine providence, blessed in the way God had provided them with this new land in which they could found a perfect theocracy, based on the (they meant 'their') literal interpretation of the Bible.

ABOVE *Hearst Castle, San Simeon, California. This gigantic house was built by Julia Morgan for William Randolph Hearst between 1919 and 1947. The gardens cover 48.5 hectares/120 acres, but have little character or beauty.*

And this sense that Americans are particularly blessed, indeed have some special relationship to God, persisted in the doctrine of Manifest Destiny, which justified their slaughter of the native American Indians who stood in the way of the white man's kind of better world.

What has all this to do with American gardens, you may be thinking? Religion and morality inform American thinking at the deepest level, and thus have inevitably affected the style of their gardens. Consider the burden of responsibility God has laid on the backs of his chosen people by endowing them with this paradise. They feel themselves under a divine obligation not to squander or misuse their inheritance. Moreover, would not creating a pleasure garden, for the delight of the eyes and the nose, be a gross misuse of God's gifts? After all, a Puritan should find beauty in the simple and utilitarian, thus perhaps in vegetable gardens, not in flower gardens, which serve only to delight the erring senses of fallen man and woman. Thomas Jefferson's greatest term of disparagement was to call something 'useless', and pleasure gardens are just that, unnecessary distractions from the work that needs to be done – and, worst of all, they even suggest that fallen humans can improve on God's handiwork. All these half-conscious feelings make for a kind of hesitancy in the American approach to gardens, a reluctance to commit oneself to them as works of art. And remember that the word 'garden' in the US refers only to the cultivated parts of 'the yard'. Pollan sums the matter up well when he discusses a certain reluctance in his compatriots to interfere with nature: 'At least since the time of Thoreau, Americans have seemed more interested in the idea of bending themselves to nature's will, which might explain why this country has produced so many more great naturalists than great gardeners.'

Then there is the wilderness, the God-given majesty of the great mountains, rivers and prairies, which belittle the paltry attempts of humans to create their own garden compositions. Such a landscape offers a challenge to garden makers that is not only moral but also aesthetic. To give two

BELOW *Thuja Garden, Northeast Harbour, Maine. This garden was created by Charles Savage, some of the plant material coming from Beatrix Farrand's garden at Reef Point. It consists of a series of herbaceous borders in a forest clearing; note the characteristically American sharp boundary between the cultivated and the wild.*

LEFT *Naumkeag, Stockbridge, Massachusetts. The gardens were designed for Mabel Choate by Fletcher Steele in the 1920s and '30s. The famous Blue Steps were built in 1938; their elegant curves contrast with the silver birches, while the white paint echoes their colour.*

examples: with the proceeds of her novel *The House of Mirth* Edith Wharton was finally able to create the house and garden she wanted. The garden had to be Italian in inspiration, since these were the gardens she most admired and had written about. She and her husband chose a site in the Berkshire Hills at Lennox, Massachusetts, which provided the slopes she needed, and set about laying out the garden; it has been expensively restored, and is now expensively open to the public. The layout could not be more simple: on the main terrace below the house, a flower garden on the left and a sunken *giardino segreto* on the right are joined by a walk of pleached limes. The flower garden is flat and formally patterned; behind it, dwarfing its proportions, towers the forest, dark

and dreadful. And this was so in Wharton's day, as we can see from contemporary photographs. What could she have done to avoid the sensation that the garden had been created in a clearing? Plant shrubs or even small trees in the flower garden to soften the boundary between the cultivated and the wild? Or thin the forest, removing it to a greater distance so that it no longer dwarfed the flower garden? But that would have been a kind of sacrilege, so the sharp division between forest and garden remains.

LEFT AND RIGHT *The Mount, Lennox, Massachusetts. The gardens were designed by Edith Wharton herself, following her favourite Italian models. The flower garden (left) is backed by the dark forest, with, again, little attempt to blend the one into the other. The grass steps to be seen in the picture (right) recall the 'falls' of earlier American gardens*

ABOVE AND LEFT *Biltmore, Asheville, North Carolina. This huge château (left) was built for George Vanderbilt at the end of the nineteenth century. He employed Frederick Law Olmsted to design the gardens. Wisely, Olmsted located the ornamental gardens away from the house behind a wall; he avoided competition with the beauties of the natural landscape (above) by leaving much of the space round the house empty.*

The wilderness offered a challenge even to someone as wealthy as George W. Vanderbilt, and his brilliant landscape designer, Frederick Law Olmsted, confessed, 'I am nervous, and this is because I am not quite at home when required to merge stately architecture with natural or naturalistic landscape work.' When they came to lay out the grounds of Vanderbilt's gigantic mansion, modestly named Biltmore House, in North Carolina, how could they compete with the majestic beauty of the forests, the lakes and the Great Smoky Mountains? Olmsted's solution was brilliant: wisely shrinking from any attempt to compete with the natural landscape, he created a flat bowling green beside the house, from which the views are breathtaking; the formal garden he tucked away down the hill, behind a wall, so that its smaller scale beauties could be appreciated without competition.

After Independence, the young nation was determined to establish its separate identity, and the wilderness formed an important element in what distinguished the United States from Europe; European, especially British, landscapes were characterized as beautiful while American landscapes were sublime. The difference lay in the effects produced: beauty creates mere aesthetic satisfaction, while the sublime arouses awe and rapture of an almost religious kind. Particularly among the Romantics, sublime landscapes aroused religious feelings; as early as 1739 the poet Thomas Gray, describing in a letter the landscape of the Grande Chartreuse, wrote, 'Not a precipice, not a torrent, not a cliff, but is pregnant with religion and poetry.' Burke in his essay on the sublime and the beautiful, published in 1757, defined the sublime as 'whatever is fitted in any sort to excite the ideas of pain and danger, that is to say, whatever is in any sort terrible, or operates in a manner analogous to terror'. This led some landscapers of the Picturesque School into gross extravagances, such as gibbets and other instruments of torture, as we saw in Chapter 6. But the major point about the sublime is that it is usually found, not created. And the bible-studying Americans would not have forgotten that awe in the face of God's handiwork is a way to deeper faith: 'The fear of the Lord is the beginning of wisdom.'

By the first half of the nineteenth century Americans were beginning to feel that the pristine quality of their sublime landscape was under threat. It was therefore the duty of painters to record its beauty for posterity. Thomas Cole, the distinguished landscape painter, could claim, 'We are still in Eden; the wall that shuts us out of the garden is ignorance and folly.' But J.F. Cropsey, reviewing some of Cole's pictures in 1847, took a less sanguine view: 'The axe of civilisation is busy with our old forests, and artisan ingenuity is fast sweeping away the relics of our national infancy . . .

RIGHT *Hilldene, Manchester, Vermont. The summer home of Robert Todd Lincoln was built at the end of the nineteenth century. The Formal Garden is laid out on a hill which projects into the valley, so the eye is continually drawn away from the garden.*

Yankee enterprise has little sympathy with the Picturesque.' These writers were responding to the growth of industry in, for example, the beautiful Hudson Valley, and their disquiet found an echo in government when in 1864 Congress passed a bill giving Yosemite Park to the state of California 'for public use, resort and recreation . . . inalienable for all time'. This far-sighted decision, which was the beginning of what would become the National Parks movement, is made all the more remarkable when we realize that in 1864 the nation was suffering the trauma of civil war. So Yosemite, a place that the painter Albert Bierstadt called 'the Garden of Eden' when he arrived there is 1863, was preserved and with it a portion of that God-given landscape which had promised so much to the first colonizers of America.

But the wilderness was not all good, pristine and innocent. It was a place of literal and spiritual darkness where the enemy, the native American Indians, lived. It was a place of savagery and pagan rituals, in need of conversion by enlightened missionaries. And its forests and mountains, not to mention their inhabitants, made the exploitation of the great spaces of the Midwest harder than it might have been. So the wilderness also offered a challenge to the colonists, both moral and practical. Yet deep in the American subconscious is buried the idea of the wilderness as a place of freedom and renewal, where innocence can still be preserved. At the end of Mark Twain's seminal novel, Huck Finn famously remarks, 'I got to light out for the Territory ahead of the rest, because Aunt Sally she's going to adopt me and sivilise [sic] me, and I can't stand it.' He needs to cross the frontier, that most highly charged element in American mythology, to a world that is purer, freer, less tame. It may be dangerous and uncomfortable, but the freedom to make of yourself what you will, to begin all over again, which can be found only in the emptiness of the wilderness, is intoxicating.

The wilderness has a similar ambiguity, beautiful but also dangerous, in that other great American myth, the Western film. The romantic heroes are the free-living cowboys who have no settled home but pick up work where they can, and move cattle across the empty prairie to the railhead. The enemy is the farmer who wires off his land, impeding the freedom of movement that has been a traditional right of the cowboy. That is one side of the myth, showing the wicked settler carving out of the land, which should be a common good for all, an estate of his own, wiring off his boundaries so that he can cultivate his land. The other is its opposite: the familiar scene of the circle of wagons in which a handful of gallant (often hymn-singing) settlers try to defend their womenfolk and their children from the whooping Indians who gallop in threatening circles round the camp. Here the evil, destructive, anarchic side of the wilderness is highlighted: it is the enemy of anyone who tries to tame it, to civilize it, to exploit it. It stands in the way of progress, moral and economic.

And the wilderness as the supreme place of freedom is not only some dusty myth. It offers a constant refuge to those who oppose the way American society is developing. In twentieth-century Montana they set up a free community that refused to pay any US government taxes and patrolled the boundary of their independent community with rifles to keep the Feds at bay. The right to carry a rifle, defended to the last round by the National Rifle Association, is a vestige of this wilderness spirit; people should be self-reliant enough to defend themselves, not be dependent on a society's police force. In the 1960s those who opposed the Vietnam War, if they didn't flee to Canada to avoid the draft, would often set up alternative, hippie-style communes in the hills of California, the pastures of Montana or the woods of Maine – another kind of alternative to what they saw as the corrupt rule of corporate America. To this day the alternative Fourth of July celebrations in the remarkably named West Athens, Maine, show that the anarchist spirit permitted, even fostered, by the wilderness is still alive and well in 2007.

The historian Perry Miller sees the youthful America projecting an image of itself as 'Nature's nation', an innocent, self-sufficient, outdoors people, with the strong implication that if the people followed nature's precepts they would be protected from artificiality. Ralph Waldo Emerson, to whom we will return, had a similar feeling about his country: 'Separated from the contamination which infects all other civilized lands, this country has always boasted a great comparative purity.' A pleasure garden is certainly not only artificial but also an interference with the natural beauty with which God endowed the country; what a departure it must mark from the purity of nature's

Wave Hill, Bronx, New York City. This garden lies on the edge of the noble Hudson River, and looks across to the Palisades, with their emphatic horizontal line. With great sensitivity much of the planting in the garden is kept low to harmonize with the natural setting.

ways! Carrying this baggage of half-buried assumptions about the wilderness, how is the poor American gardener to proceed without feeling self-conscious, uneasy, even a little guilty?

Yet there are beautiful gardens in the United States, and not all of them hidden away like the walled garden at Biltmore. Some of them take account of the wilderness, like the wonderful garden at Wave Hill in New York; looking across the Hudson to the Palisades with their severe horizontal line, the garden permits itself few vertical accents – in general the plantings are low and level. Or the American garden turns its back on the wilderness completely, like the supremely theatrical and brilliant garden called Lotusland in Santa Barbara, California. What we seldom find in American gardens is the gentle transition from garden to the wild that is so familiar to an English eye. But then England has no wilderness; the whole countryside is so manicured that it might well be a garden. Remember Walpole's famous saying about Kent that 'he leapt the fence and saw all nature was a garden'. That might be true in England; it could not be less true in America. America has something much purer, more significant and noble than countryside: leap the fence (there probably isn't one) in most parts of the United States and you find yourself in thick forest, prairie or desert. Even if you live in a city the inhabitants of the wilderness may come to find you out. In Chappaqua, a dormitory suburb just north of New York City, bears rummage through the waste-bins; coyotes are invading the edges of several cities, and no American book about making a garden lacks its chapter on the battle with the woodchucks.

There were gardens and orchards before the white man arrived on the continent of America; in 1540 the Spanish explorer Coronado discovered in the Santa Fe area vegetable gardens, growing squash, beans and corn, and it is probably this kind of garden that Drake reported he had destroyed in a raid on Florida in 1583. A year later sea captains in the expedition of Sir Walter Raleigh reported 'so sweet and so strong a smell as if we had been in the midst of some delicate garden abounding with all kinds of odoriferous flowers'. Certainly in Mexico there were flowers; we have already referred to the dahlia, which was prized less for its beauty, perhaps, than for its roots, which could be used for water pipes. And dahlias, like so many other plants grown in gardens at this period, were also used for medicine. The native Americans were particularly skilled in herbal remedies, to the extent that Robert Colbourne, writing in 1753, claimed:

> The Americans have been able to discover to the Europeans the most effectual remedies yet known, as the Peruvian Bark, Jalop and others; for which we are indebted to the experience of the illiterate inhabitants of the new world; whilst all the boasted learning of the Europeans has been so little productive of improvements in physic that, with respect to our own plants, we know very little more of their virtues than we have learned from Dioscorides and some other of the ancients.

But it is hard to discover much about native American gardening, because nineteenth-century America was intent on portraying the early inhabitants of the land as savages; only thus was it possible to sustain the doctrine of the white man's superiority. Writing of the expansion westward in the mid nineteenth century John Louis O'Sullivan wrote: 'It is our [the white settlers'] manifest destiny to overspread the continent allotted by Providence for the free development of our yearly multiplying millions.' Note the keywords – 'destiny', 'Providence' and 'free': they make the settlers sound like the chosen people. Painters responded enthusiastically to this idea, often representing Daniel Boone as the Moses of the white settlers, leading them fearlessly into the promised land.

The history of gardening before the revolution follows a predictable pattern. The first gardens were planted for 'meate and medicine'; they were carefully fenced to protect the food supply from domestic and wild animals. The design would probably have been rectilinear, paths bisecting raised beds, as at the Whipple House in Ipswich, Massachusetts. But, of course, medicinal plants might also be decorative – the lily and the rose, for example. The foremost gardening nation in Europe, the Dutch, created gardens in New York (then New Amsterdam), and there was a lively exchange of plants between Europe and the new colonies during the seventeenth century. In 1683 when Penn laid out his ideal town, Philadelphia, a haven of tolerance for all religions, he stipulated 'Let every house be placed . . . in ye middle of its platt . . . so there may be ground on each side, for gardens, or orchards, or fields, that it may be a green country town.' Penn was not only concerned with the beauty of his new town but also had in mind the Great Fire of London of 1666: gardens were useful firebreaks between houses. In the last two decades of the century cash crops, tobacco and, further south, cotton, began to mean that there was surplus cash, some of which could be spent on making gardens. Yet in 1705 Robert Beverley in his *History and Present State of Virginia* was not impressed by the progress that had been made towards horticultural civilization in his native colony: 'A garden is nowhere sooner made than there [in Virginia], either for fruits or flowers . . . and yet . . . they han't many gardens in that country fit to bear the name of gardens.'

By the middle of the eighteenth century, however, gardens were becoming more sophisticated: we read of a Boston garden with canals and pools, while greenhouses and orangeries were more common. For the first time we hear of the colonists no longer merely following the example of the mother country but developing a new element in their gardens: these were 'falls' – descending grass terraces, usually unbroken by any path, flower bed or planting. And in 1772 Martha Logan wrote the first book on gardening to be published in the New World, *A Treatise on Gardening*, published in Charleston.

The landscape parks of England were slow to make an impression in the colonies, and the gardens of the Governor's Palace at Williamsburg, capital of Virginia, were laid out as symmetrical, geometrical parterres, with canals and a maze. Philadelphia was the largest and richest city of the newly independent nation, and it was not long before some of that wealth was spent on creating a memorable garden. In 1785 William Hamilton began to lay out his landscape garden, Woodlands, on the banks of the Schuylkill River in Pennsylvania. Jefferson said that this garden was 'the only rival I have known in America to what may be seen in England'. Hamilton had visited England, writing, 'England as a country is an Elysium'; his emphasis was clearly intended to convey that as an imperial power, England was far from heavenly. He liked to conduct visitors around his garden by a particular route, so that his compositions could be fully appreciated. A visitor noted 'numerous copses of native trees, interspersed with artificial groves, which are of trees collected from all parts of the world'; the contrast established between the two adjectives is striking – 'native' set against 'artificial'.

The path, which guides the visitor, and the views arranged at intervals, like scenes in a play, make Woodlands sound like a *ferme ornée*, such as Hamilton might have seen or read about in England. Certainly Thomas Jefferson's Monticello in Virginia was inspired by this combination of utility and beauty. While he was Minister in Paris on behalf of the government of the new state (1785–9), Jefferson took the opportunity to visit many gardens, particularly in England. His notes show how his taste was turning away from the rectilinear, classical gardens towards something more romantic; he writes of Chiswick House, 'The gardens show still too much art.' Like the practical man he was, he would also always enquire how much things cost; at Painshill he noted, 'Grotto said to have cost £7000', but he was not always impressed with lavish spending, writing that 'The gardens at Schwetzingen show how much money may be laid out to make an ugly thing.' He was always a great promoter of native American plants; while in Paris he had given friends seeds of American trees, the white oak and tulip tree, for example. At Monticello he created a winding path on the flat summit of the hill behind his house, and along the path set out flower beds, each of which was devoted to a single species. Thus Jefferson could compare different varieties of the

Ipswich, Massachusetts. This recreation of an early American garden, behind its wooden fence, gives a good impression of what such utilitarian gardens must have been like. Plants would have been grown for culinary and medical uses, rather than for beauty.

same plant, seeing which flourished and which did not. He loved to study plants, to see which of them yielded best; for this purpose he grew thirty-eight varieties of peach, twenty kinds of cabbage and many different sorts of apple. But his granddaughter remembered how much he also loved the colours of flowers, some of which had been discovered on the Lewis and Clark expedition to the West, which he had sponsored; others were native species like the dramatic *Lobelia cardinalis*, which grew at the foot of the hill on which Monticello was built and which Jefferson included in his garden. He also, of course, grew the plant named after him, *Jeffersonia diphylla*. This protean man is no easier to define as a gardener than he is in other fields; he studied plants, but also grew them for their beauty; he designed his pleasure garden around a romantic winding walk, but also toyed with the idea of a giant cascade down a neighbouring hill and even a classical grotto.

With the birth of the new nation, it became imperative to construct an identity, particularly an identity that set America apart from England and the rest of Europe. In this the wilderness was to play a vital part. The novelists wrote of the great rivers, the mountains and the forests. Mark Twain in *Huckleberry Finn* created a character who rejected the settled life of the bourgeoisie for the freedom and anarchy of the Mississippi. James Fenimore Cooper had been brought up in the wilderness near Otswego Lake, and seems to have absorbed some of its anarchic spirit since he was thrown out of Yale; his father, however, was the founder of a settlement called Cooperstown. The son's melodramatic and fantastic Leatherstocking novels take as their subject the contest between the native Americans and the pioneers for the great spaces of the continent. After a stay in Europe his novels became more polemical in defence of his native country and more opposed to Europe. Longfellow's *Hiawatha*, and Washington Irving's 'Rip van Winkle' and 'The Tales of Sleepy Hollow', continued the myth making. The latter two short stories, set in the Catskill Mountains and the Hudson Valley, also served to give some atmosphere of romance to places which otherwise were merely beautiful. American painters, particularly, were very sensitive to the charge that their native scenery, stupendous though it was, lacked the suggestive romantic associations found in European landscapes with their plentiful ruins.

The painters were certainly doing their bit to bolster the nation's confidence and define its character. In 1819 John Shaw, who was born an Englishman, began publishing his series of aquatints entitled *Picturesque Views of American Scenery*, the introduction boasting, 'In no quarter of the globe are the majesty and loveliness of nature more strikingly conspicuous than in America.' This sublime quality in the landscape, in particular its awesome power, was the inspiration for

Monticello, Charlottesville, Virginia. Thomas Jefferson was as interested in plants as he was in everything else. His garden was the laboratory where he tested different varieties of vegetable. On the hilltop he also laid out 'a winding walk . . . with a narrow border of flowers on each side'. Here we see his vegetable garden and the pavilion.

Frederic Edwin Church's series of huge paintings of Niagara Falls (1857–67), while Albert Bierstadt found more inspiration in the Far West, where man had still not stained the pristine quality of God's creation. Few of these paintings show any human figure – the huge scale of the landscape would dwarf a person – but sometimes a native American becomes the subject, especially in the paintings of George Catlin. He made a special study of native Americans and their way of life, finding in them the primitive innocence which Rousseau had prized in the person untainted by the duplicities and compromises of society.

The master landscape painter of the early nineteenth century was Thomas Cole. In 1835 he published his *Essay on American Scenery*, which had originally been given as a lecture. He was keen to emphasize the moral value of looking intently at the landscape: 'In gazing on the pure creations of the Almighty, he [the viewer] feels a calm religious tone steal through his mind, and when he has turned to mingle with his fellow men, the chords that have been struck in that sweet communion cease not to vibrate.' And an American landscape can be more uplifting than a European; its very lack of literary, historical and mythological associations means that the mind moves at once to the contemplation of God. He even finds room for gardens in his praise of nature: 'I have alluded to wild and uncultivated scenery; but the cultivated must not be forgotten, for it is still more important to man in his social capacity . . . it encompasses our homes, and, though devoid of the stern sublimity of the wild, its quieter spirit steals tenderly into our bosoms.' So even the domestic garden can have a calming and morally uplifting effect, though on a smaller scale than the sublime wilderness.

Two better writers than Cole were to be much more influential in defining the relationship between Americans and their God-given land; R.W. Emerson's *Nature* has been called 'our [Americans'] primal book', the fountainhead 'of our greatest, our one indispensable tradition'. When Emerson published this essay in 1836, at the age of thirty-three, he subtitled the work 'as Natural History and as Human History', because he was interested in the relationship between the natural world and man. 'Nature', he wrote, 'stretches out her arms and embraces man, only let his thoughts be of equal greatness.' Like Cole (and, of course, Wordsworth), he saw nature as a source of moral improvement, but Emerson went further and found a divine spirit immanent in the landscape: 'Faith should blend with the light of the rising and of setting suns, with the flying cloud, the singing bird, and the breath of flowers.' In the forests of New England he found innocence and renewal – 'In the woods a man casts off his years . . . and is always a child'; notice again that yearning for lost innocence. Gardening he found more seductive, less morally pure, as he makes clear in a light-hearted letter to Carlyle (30 April 1847): 'The works of the garden and the orchard at this season are fascinating, and will eat up days and weeks, and a brave scholar should shun it [sic] like gambling, and take refuge in cities and hotels from these pernicious enchantments.'

Emerson's one-time friend Henry David Thoreau was a preacher of the simple life, far from what he called 'the dirty institutions' of society. He refused to pay taxes that paid for the Mexican–American war, was a lifelong opponent of slavery and wrote 'That government is best which governs not at all.' This radical, Rousseau-like belief in the innate goodness of man, which needs no regulation, except when it has been perverted by social pressures, was perhaps easier to sustain when living in the isolation of his hut on Walden Pond, on the edge of Concord, Massachusetts. Thoreau is now seen as a prophet of the ecological movement, which tries to minimize man's impact on the natural world, and as the father of civil disobedience. At Walden, however, Thoreau did make a vegetable garden, which is a fundamental interference with nature; he created his celebrated bean field and had no qualms about killing a woodchuck when it attacked his vegetables. However, he did ask himself whether he was right to destroy the weeds that were originally growing in his field: 'But what right had I to oust johnswort and the rest, and break up their original herb garden?' However, it wasn't long before he saw himself as the heroic guardian of his almost human beans, digging out pig-weed, sorrel, piper-grass and other invaders: 'Daily the beans saw me come to their rescue armed with a hoe, and thin the ranks of their enemies, filling up the trenches with weedy dead.' His gardening went no further than vegetables; he might have felt more guilt if his interference with nature were all for the sake of a mere pleasure garden.

While poets, painters, essayists and novelists were beginning to define the character of the new nation and its special relationship with the American landscape, what were the gardeners doing? Their country had been doubled in size by the Louisiana Purchase in 1803, and the range of native plants available to them had been extended by the Lewis and Clark expedition to the West. The nineteenth century was dominated by divisions between the modernizing, industrial, expanding north and the conservative, agricultural, slave-owning south – divisions that were to reach their climax in the Civil War. The southern plantation houses were, in general, surrounded by conservatively formal gardens, often Italian in inspiration, with balustrades and terraces. There were exceptions, the most celebrated perhaps being the Magnolia Gardens near Charleston in South Carolina, one of the earliest so-called wilderness gardens (a neatly capacious oxymoron). Some fine private gardens were regularly open to the public, for example Andrew Brown's Magnolia Vale at Natchez, Mississippi. On the frontier, gardens were created to provide food; only with more settled conditions were pleasure gardens a possibility. In California those made rich by the Gold Rush (1849) were creating gardens like those on the east coast, complete with lawns, groups of shrubs and bedding schemes of the brightest flowers. The only concession to the arid climate was the so-called Arizona Garden, where drought-loving plants were inserted into sand and gravel. When the great Frederick Law Olmsted visited California in 1864, he said the landscape was Cyclopean but the planting Lilliputian. And when he designed the Stanford University campus, he called for the quadrangles to be paved or made of beaten earth, but it was not long before the authorities decided a university quadrangle had to be covered in grass, however unsuitable the climate.

In the east the wealthy were growing more things in greenhouses, and becoming collectors of exotic plants. In 1838 Downing could write: 'In pretty villas in a high state of keeping, a fondness for rare plants and forcing the better fruits, Boston is half a century in advance of her sister cities. Philadelphia still holds the palm for fine exotic collections, and a general greenhouse commercial business. New York is so purely a business emporium, that in its pell-mell few find time for the indulgence of a taste for gardening.' New York even then was celebrated for its 'pell-mell'! The severe Fanny Trollope was not impressed by America or its gardens: 'From the time I entered America, I had never seen the slightest approach to what we call pleasure grounds: a few very worthless and scentless flowers were all the gardening I had seen in Ohio; no attempt at garden scenery was ever dreamed of.' It had to be pointed out to her that in England fine landscapes were created by moving earth and planting trees, while in America they had only to be revealed by judicious cutting down of the forest.

Books were published to help the novice gardener with advice for local conditions: Bernard McMahon's *The American Gardener's Calendar* (1806) and Thomas Fessenden's *New American Gardener* (1828). It was in Fessenden's magazine *The New England Farmer* that André Parmentier, a Belgian immigrant and nurseryman, wrote of the garden he had laid out in Brooklyn beside his nursery. This hugely influential garden was designed in the Picturesque style with winding paths and apparently natural plantings. Parmentier also worked at Hyde Park, the great estate on the Hudson River that later became the property of the Roosevelt family.

The first American-born landscape artist of real influence was Andrew Jackson Downing: he was the son of a nurseryman, and as a young man read widely in English gardening literature, especially the works of J.C. Loudon and Humphry Repton. Even the title of his book, *A Treatise on the Theory and Practice of Landscape Gardening Adapted to North America*, published in 1841, acknowledged the influence of Repton; in this he showed how the Picturesque, a style he considered most suited to the landscapes of America (and to the violent temperament of Americans!), could be adapted to smaller houses. In 1846 he became editor of the influential magazine *The Horticulturist*, in which he promoted his ideas on the importance of public parks and landscaped cemeteries. When Joseph Bigelow laid out Mount Auburn cemetery, 6.4 kilometres/ 4 miles west of Boston, in 1831 he had created the first large-scale, artificial public landscape in America. Downing insisted that the natural beauty of cemeteries should be enhanced by 'the tasteful and harmonious embellishment of these sites by art', harmonious meaning that the

Washington, DC. The nation's capital was laid out by Pierre Charles L'Enfant in a rigid, geometrical style. But Andrew Jackson Downing's landscaping was more romantic and relaxed. He worked here with Calvert Vaux, who went on to design New York's Central Park with Olmsted.

embellishment should be in a natural, informal style. His magazine was also the first to argue how much New York needed a public park. In 1851 he was consulted about the layout of the public space around the White House and the Capitol in Washington. But all this came to a sudden end when, the next year, he was drowned in an accident on the Hudson.

On a European tour Downing had met Calvert Vaux, an English draughtsman of great skill, and had persuaded him to emigrate to America, where the two worked together on the landscaping of Washington. Vaux was a devotee of the Picturesque landscape, though he was principally an architect; in his book *Villas and Cottages* he wrote: 'The great charm in the forms of natural landscape lies in its well-balanced irregularity.' Downing's concept of Central Park in New York had been very different from the plan eventually put forward by Olmsted and Vaux. Inspired by the Smithsonian in Washington perhaps, Downing had conceived of a park filled with many more buildings, some devoted to pleasure but most of them in some way didactic, and 'winter gardens of glass, like the great Crystal palace, where the whole people could luxuriate in groves of the palms and spice trees of the tropics', but he also called for horticultural and agricultural show grounds, museums and 'great expositions of the arts'. Olmsted and Vaux's plan was that the park should serve a social function, certainly, but in a different way: it should provide New Yorkers with 'a specimen of God's handiwork, that shall be to them, inexpensively, what a month or two in the White Mountains or the Adirondacks is, at great cost, to those in easier circumstances.' Achieving this in the narrow, rectangular strip of Manhattan Island required genius of a high order. The jury appointed to select the winning design for the park was divided along political lines – Republicans for the Picturesque style, Democrats for a more formal layout. Happily, for future New Yorkers, Olmsted and Vaux won and their brilliantly romantic park is one of the great successes of North American gardening.

In a country where newness (not mere novelty) was, and perhaps still is, seen as a virtuous sign of purity and spiritual revival, it is surprising that thus far there had been few radical, American innovations in the design of gardens. All that was shortly to change. As the railways spread their networks out from the major cities, and people chose to live away from their places of work, proudly middle-class railway suburbs developed, one of the most famous being Philadelphia's Main Line. In a book celebrating the development we hear this claim: 'Suburban life is the ideal life and the Main Line is an ideal suburb.' With this new kind of suburban development arrived the first uniquely American contribution to garden design – the common front lawn. And if you doubt that this is uniquely American, drive north from Seattle across the Canadian border; immediately you enter Canada you find fences, hedges or walls between street and garden, as well as between one garden and another, much in the English style.

So what does this giant American lawn signify? First, it is the opposite of the wilderness; nothing could be more cultivated, more artificial, more useless than the even, shaved surface. It says to the world, 'We've arrived. We no longer need to use land to grow crops, or need to fence it for our stock; we have it under control.' Just as Cardinal Ippolito d'Este could use precious water to drive his fountains at the Villa d'Este, in this extravagance demonstrating his power and wealth, so the modern American can use land in this wasteful way as a demonstration that he is no longer a frontiersman.

But there is more to it than that: these shared lawns have been called 'democratic'. It is true they are all the same, thus concealing differences of national background and of financial means; they are levellers. A common lawn shows no variety of colour and permits no unusual layout to demonstrate personal taste or individuality; all it shows is the dreariest equality. Behind the house you can do what you like, but the front lawn has become a compulsory feature of the American suburb. Recalling the time his father was treated as a pariah when he refused to mow the grass in front of his house, Michael Pollan explores the significance of this common lawn:

> One lawn should flow unimpeded into another, obscuring the boundaries between homes and contributing to the sense of community. It was here on the front lawn that 'like-mindedness' received its clearest expression. The conventional design of a suburban street is meant to forge the multitude of equal individual parcels of land into a single vista – a democratic landscape. To maintain your portion of this landscape was part of your civic duty. You voted every November, joined the PTA, and mowed the lawn every Saturday.

The lawn is so much part of the public domain that in certain towns and cities a local statute forbids the householder to let the grass grow above a certain height – in Raleigh, North Carolina, for example, the limit used to be 20 centimetres/6 inches. The public quality of these front gardens is well demonstrated at Christmas, when householders stand cut-out representations of sleighs, Father Christmases and angels on their front lawns; all these face outwards, so the family who lives in the house see only the plywood backs.

It might perhaps seem logical, in the pursuit of social cohesion, to impose this uniformity in temperate New England, but the iconic front lawn has become *de rigueur* throughout the nation, even in sunny, arid California. Consider this story told in the 2007 spring issue of *Pacific Horticulture* magazine. Jan Smithen had written a book entitled *Sun-Drenched Gardens* and so knew which plants would survive the rigours of a Californian summer. One day she was working at creating a dry front garden for her new house in Upland, not far from Los Angeles, when a passerby, who turned out to be a member of the homeowners' association, shouted to her, 'I want grass.' Even after Smithen explained to the woman that the architectural board had given her permission to plant a drought-resistant garden, she snapped back, 'Don't you know the drought is over? I don't care if you have architectural permission. I have the power to make you rip all this out.' Happily Jan Smithen, who is clearly made of stern stuff, resisted such bullying and made her dry garden. This relentless insistence on a lawn as the only suitable setting for a house, whatever the local conditions, has resulted, according to Pollan's calculations, in 13 million hectares/ 50,000 square miles of lawn in the United States, on which 30 billion dollars are spent each year.

A second idiosyncratic feature of these new suburban gardens is what is called foundation planting. This has some parallels with foundation garments; both seek to conceal or give pleasing shape to what may be unstable or unattractive. In New England villages the houses were usually built of timber on a stone foundation; in consequence the wooden superstructure could be moved from one site to another. This was usually done in winter, when the house could be jacked up on to giant sleds and towed to its new site over the frozen ground. However, the dwellers in the new American suburbs didn't want anyone to think their house might be towed away; rather they wanted to give it a settled and permanent look, by planting around its base. Not, as Ruth Bramley Dean emphasized in 1917, to conceal the foundation, but to make the house 'look as if it belonged in its surroundings'. 'A judicious amount of planting here and there', she goes on, 'will take the raw, new look away from a house and tie it down adequately to the lawn's green carpet.' She is, of course, thinking of the view from the street, since the dwellers in the house see little of the foundation planting, until it grows up to obscure the view from their windows. Michael Pollan is typically sharp about foundation planting: 'Rather than create any habitable outdoor space (which is what the same planting out along the road would accomplish), it merely adorns the house, showing it off to advantage like the setting for a gemstone.' This unselfish concern for the pleasure of the passerby is, perhaps, what helps the American community to stick together, despite the fact that it is made up of people from very different backgrounds and gardening cultures.

The lack of boundary divisions became another hallmark of the American garden. Given their attitude to the wilderness as a place of innocence, God's gift to his chosen people, who would want to isolate their land and themselves from this source of blessings? When he began to make his garden in Connecticut, Michael Pollan was reluctant to fence it off: 'Fences just didn't accord with my view of gardening. A garden should be continuous with the natural landscape, I felt, in harmony with its surroundings . . . a fence bespoke disharmony, even alienation, from nature.' Trying to understand this antipathy to fences, he found it was 'a visceral matter'. As he was American, this distaste for fences had to be rooted in religion and morality. Frank J. Scott, who published his *The Art of Beautifying Suburban Home Grounds* in 1870, wrote, 'It is unchristian to hedge from the sight of others the beauties of nature which it has been our good fortune to create or secure; and all walls, high fences, hedge screens and belts of trees and shrubbery which are used for this purpose only, are so many means by which we show how unchristian and unneighborly we are.' He talks of the 'bad feelings engendered by high outside boundary walls that so often become

Pepsico Headquarters, Purchase, New York. These gardens were begun in 1965 by Donald M. Kendall, chief executive of Pepsico. In 1980 Russell Page was called in, and it was he who designed these lily pools with their sharply sculpted grass edges.

ABOVE AND LEFT *The Sarah P. Duke Gardens, Durham, North Carolina. The original gardens were swept away by floods, but in the late 1930s the terraces (left) were designed by Ellen B. Shipman. The most recent part of the garden to be developed is the Asiatic Arboretum (above), begun in 1984.*

convenient shields to hide unclean rubbish and to foster weeds', not to mention all kinds of unclean behaviour. Robert Frost clearly felt the same 'visceral' objection to walls as Pollan when he wrote his famous poem 'Mending Wall' – 'Something there is that does not love a wall.' While his neighbour says 'Good fences make good neighbours' – a very English sentiment – Frost cannot agree, but finds it hard to explain why. Not everyone shared this loathing of barriers. Alice Morse Earle, taking a strictly aesthetic view, mourned the passing of 'every fenced-in or hedged-in garden enclosure'; all had been sacrificed to 'that dreary destroyer of a garden . . . the desire for a lawn'. Some went even further. George Washington Cable in *The American Garden* (1914) traces the two words 'garden' and 'yard' back to their common root in a German word meaning 'enclosure', and concludes that the obliteration of private boundaries has meant that 'our gardens, except among the rich, have become American by ceasing to be gardens'.

In the nineteenth century Americans used their gardens as a way of demonstrating to the world their advanced morality. Charles Dudley Warner, writing in 1870, claimed, 'The man who has planted a garden feels he had done something for the good of the world.' And Joseph Breck in his *New Book of Flowers* (1866) defended the utility of flowers, since they are 'the expression of God's love to men', but he was careful not to go too far in his enthusiasm: 'We would not advocate the cultivation of flowers to the neglect of more necessary objects.' Like Emerson, he was clearly worried that there might be something seductive in the pleasures of gardening. Henry Ward Beecher had no such qualms, but saw in the cultivation of flowers a cure for many of the nervous disorders that, he claimed, afflicted modern women: 'We are persuaded that, if parents, instead of regarding a disposition to train flowers as a useless trouble, a waste of time, a pernicious romancing, would inspire the love for it, nurture and direct it, it would save their daughters from false taste, and all love of meretricious ornament.' It might result in even further moral improvement: 'A love of flowers would beget early rising, industry, habits of close observation, and of reading. It would incline the mind to notice natural phenomena, and to reason upon them. It would occupy the mind with pure thoughts, and inspire a sweet and gentle enthusiasm; maintain simplicity of taste; and in connection with personal instruction, unfold in the heart an enlarged, unstraitened, ardent piety.' Having read this, which American parents would not immediately drive their daughters out into the flower garden?

Many of the extracts in the previous paragraphs are taken from Allen Lacy's splendid anthology *The American Gardener: A Sampler*. During his research for this volume, Lacy discovered something very striking: he could find no reference to the colour and fragrance of particular flowers before 1893. Yes, there were references to scents in general and to colours in general, but no discussion of the particular sensuous attributes of an individual flower. He asked himself: 'Was it possible that an aesthetic sense of the values of colour and scent for their own sakes appeared so suddenly and so late in American writing?' He was forced to conclude that this was so, and the explanation for it lay in 'the asceticism that was deeply ingrained in the American culture . . . The aesthetic appreciation of colour and fragrance for their own sakes, and not for obtaining some kind of moral message or theological parable, is at odds with every form of asceticism.' He attributes to Celia Thaxter's *An Island Garden* (1893) the first 'frank recognition of the claims and pleasures of the senses'. But only fifteen years later another woman, Hanna Rion, was able to write, 'The greatest gift of a garden is the restoration of the five senses', a claim which urban Americans of the twenty-first century must often wholeheartedly echo.

When man's relationship with the natural world, gardening included, comes with such a heavy, unspoken load of moral, religious and social significance, it is hardly surprising that Americans approach the whole business of gardening with great wariness. Nor that an American feels a 'visceral' antipathy to fences when he begins his interference with nature, otherwise known as making a garden. Eleanor Perényi writes of 'a nostalgia for lost innocence that is endemically American', but such innocence will never be found in the garden, with its constant warfare against the disorderly nature on which humans wish to impose themselves; it is much more likely to be found in the wilderness, where man has made only minimal incursions. Carlton B. Lees, former vice-president of the New York Botanical Garden, argues in his book *Gardens, Plants and Man*

(1970) that 'As a nation we have never considered gardens necessary', but that in the stressful twentieth century we are beginning to see their therapeutic value. Yet, according to Neltje Blanchan, 'a house may be placed in the midst of wild scenery, so surpassingly beautiful in itself, that any garden artifice attempted seems a profanation' – note that last word with its weight of religious anathema. The problem for American gardeners is not an ascetic rejection of beauty – just think of the great poets, musicians and painters the country has produced – but a deep-rooted antipathy to meddling with nature on the way to making something beautiful. Michael Pollan again: 'As might be expected, the gardens made by aesthetes are considerably more pleasing to the eye than those made by moralists. It is no accident that Americans have yet to produce many world-famous gardens or landscape architects, or to found a style of garden design that anyone else would want to copy.'

One American designer who might be considered a significant figure on the world stage is a man who redefined the garden and its use for California, Thomas Church. In a forty-five-year career that ended only in 1977 he rejected the idea of the garden as a place to be looked at from the road; gardens were for living in and should look beautiful from the house. His major book, published in 1955, is *Gardens are for People*, a title that defines his approach. 'The new kind of garden,' he writes, 'is still supposed to be looked at. But that is no longer its only function. It is designed primarily for living, as an adjunct to the functions of the house.' He was one of the first to emphasize the garden as an outdoor room, and his designs were always practical as well as beautiful, ensuring privacy in a world that was becoming more crowded and cutting down on maintenance by using plenty of paving and ground cover.

Church was a master both of the dramatically angled, straight line and of the free-flowing, sinuous curve, both of which were emphasized by generous mowing edges, curbs, low walls and paths. Most of his more than two thousand commissions were for private homes, but he also worked on the headquarters of General Motors and the San Francisco Opera Courtyard. Though his California-style gardens were known for their free forms and flowing lines, he sometimes worked in a more formal style. At Lakewold in Washington State, for example, he enhanced the classical symmetry of one part of the garden by adding formal, symmetrical beds and a pool. He wrote that all his gardens followed four design principles: unity, function, simplicity and scale. Most of Church's gardens are urban or suburban and of modest size; their beauty lies in the imaginative use of limited space, the clarity of the lines and the understanding of how modern homeowners want to use their gardens. His creations may have little relationship to the landscape, except when a view demands to be included in the composition, yet in their artistic self-confidence Church's gardens show none of the hang-ups that seem to inhibit east-coast garden makers.

Inevitably, perhaps, there had to be a counter movement to the urban neatness and contained artistry of California School gardens. In 1971 a book appeared called *Gardening with Nature*, although, as all gardeners know, much gardening is working against nature. The authors, James van Sweden and Wolfgang Oehme, ask a question that challenges many of the assumptions that lie behind any designed garden: 'Do gardens have to be so tame, so harnessed, so uptight?' In particular they find fault with trim lawns, 'prissy' flower beds and predictable annuals. They want gardens to return to something like the prairie, to be less obviously works of art; in this their reaction is very American. Listen to their revolutionary zeal: 'We have neither "foundation plants" nor "perennial borders", because we treat the entire ground plane as an integrated whole. No more piling of plants against the foundation of the house, no more useless lawns that carpet the empty space out to the curb. Instead, plants should radiate from the house in all directions, like a great tapestry or collage.' Van Sweden and Oehme call their creations the New American Garden (their capitals), although many of their ideas are derived from the work of Karl Foerster, the German nurseryman whose experiments with perennial plants, particularly grasses and ferns, opened the eyes of a generation to the possibilities of permanent plantings. 'The New American Garden,' they write, 'reflects the beauties of the American countryside, especially its meadows and prairies.' So the wheel has come full circle – from wilderness to garden and now from garden back to wilderness, although this new wilderness is organized as a work of art and thus lacks the inspiring, pristine qualities of America's original God-given heartland. At least America can now claim its own garden style since, as one critic has written, the work of van Sweden and Oehme marks 'a drastic break with our long-standing tradition of English park, estate, and cottage garden'. Independence, at last, for the American gardener!

The inhibitions that American gardeners have felt about moulding nature into a work of art does not mean there are no great American gardens. In conclusion I would like to examine how much these often deeply buried attitudes to the wilderness, nature, morality and social responsibility have affected a handful of the fine American gardens.

When Eleuthère du Pont arrived in America in 1799, he was described in his passport as 'botaniste'. He made a garden described as 'informal but regular' beside the family's gunpowder mills on the Brandywine River in Delaware, and this was to be the first of the great du Pont gardens in the area; today Winterthur and Longwood Gardens are among the most celebrated and most visited in America. The Winterthur estate of 182 hectares/450 acres had been purchased by Eleuthère between 1810 and 1818. It remained a working farm during the life of the garden maker Henry Francis du Pont, who lived there from 1926 until his death in 1969. This is a landscape park in the English tradition, and beautifully cared for. The noble trees, mostly tulip trees, white oaks and American beech, have been carefully thinned to allow light through to an underplanting of shrubs and bulbs; the collection of azaleas and magnolias is particularly fine. Many Americans like to use their gardens for sporting activities – tennis and swimming, for example. H.F. du Pont was unusual in that he turned the swimming pool into a reflecting pool, which became the centrepiece of one garden area. The croquet lawn and tennis courts were similarly eliminated to make way for a garden of scented shrubs grouped around an armillary sphere. The contours of the land are beautifully exploited to contain different garden pictures, and specialist plantings. Winterthur sits easily in the landscape, with the result that it has a relaxed atmosphere that is not typical of American gardens.

Longwood is very different. Austere Winterthur seems uninterested in showing off to the visiting public; let the trees and shrubs, the contours of the land speak for themselves, it seems to say. Longwood by contrast has a swagger to it; its aim is glamour. This was the creation of Pierre S. du Pont, who bought the property in 1906, when a fine collection of trees that had been made by the Peirce family was under threat. At his death in 1954 he left Longwood 'for the sole use of the public for purposes of exhibition, instruction, education, and enjoyment' – words that echo Downing's and Olmsted's objectives in Central Park, New York. It is more properly and appropriately called Longwood Gardens, since it consists of several display areas which are designed without much apparent thought to the relationship between one part and another. There is an artificial waterfall and numerous fountains, the tallest rising to 39 metres/130 feet; the Italian Water Garden is said to be based on the design of the water parterre at the Villa Gamberaia, but that small Italian garden has no fountains, and the pools (which replaced earlier flower beds) form part of an overall design, whereas at Longwood the layout seems arbitrary. There is a forest walk to remind the visitor of what the Pennsylvania landscape used to look like,

Longwood Gardens, Kennett Square, Pennsylvania. The du Pont family, whose fortune was originally based on gunpowder, were great garden makers. Pierre Samuel du Pont began work at Longwood in the 1930s, and continued to develop the gardens until his death in 1954. The gardens were left 'for the sole use of the public, for purposes of exhibition, instruction, education and enjoyment'.

and a managed meadow that supports a wide range of wild flowers and wildlife. Then there are Conifer Knoll, the Rose Garden, the Peony Garden and the Wisteria Garden, giving the impression that this is a botanical collection rather than a work of art.

The glory of Longwood is its series of vast conservatories, which cover 1.4 hectares/3 acres. Here it is possible to ensure a display of flowering plants throughout the year, whatever the weather outside. The main conservatory was built by du Pont between 1919 and 1921 to be used as an orangery; it has since been extended and now outstrips in opulence the most extravagant of Victorian winter gardens in Britain. Here we find immaculate lawns, waterfalls, a silver garden, an exhibition of bonsai, herbaceous borders on either side of a sinuous path, a Mediterranean garden, orchids, a palm house and a children's garden – all beautifully maintained and remarkable. But Longwood Gardens could be anywhere: only the woodland and the meadow garden bear any relationship to the surrounding countryside; the rest is a kind of horticultural Disneyland.

Both Longwood and Winterthur are spaces for the entertainment and education of the public, equipped with parking lots, restaurants, display areas and diversions for children. Dumbarton Oaks, in Washington, DC, by contrast, has still the atmosphere of a private garden. This site, too, began life as a farm, though it can have been no easy matter working these fields, as the site slopes dramatically away from the house. The garden is the result of a 25-year-long partnership between a demanding patron, Mildred Bliss, and a gifted designer, Beatrix Farrand, the only female founding member of the American Society of Landscape Architects.

When they bought the property in 1920, the Blisses had a dream of 'a country house in the city'. They were widely travelled and their taste in gardens had been heavily influenced by European examples. The development of the garden from formality near the house to comparative wilderness

ABOVE *Longwood Gardens, Kennett Square, Pennsylvania. There are 1.5 hectares/3.5 acres of conservatory garden at Longwood, displaying tree ferns, cycads, orchids, Mediterranean plants – and an immaculate lawn.*

RIGHT *Dumbarton Oaks, Washington, DC. When the property in Georgetown was bought by Mr and Mrs Robert Woods Bliss in 1920, it consisted of a derelict house and outlying farm buildings. The site is very challenging, since it consists of irregular, steep slopes, but the problems were solved by Mildred Bliss and her designer, Beatrix Farrand. The curves in these steps are typical of the taste of the period.*

QUOD SEVERIS METES

ABOVE *Dumbarton Oaks, Washington, DC. The Urn Terrace has been altered from Farrand's earlier design by the addition of English ivy. The scalloped edge to the lawn again shows the period's taste for curves.*

LEFT *Dumbarton Oaks, Washington, DC. The garden continued to be developed after the retirement and subsequent death of Beatrix Farrand (1959). This pebble garden was designed by Ruth Havey in consultation with Mrs Bliss; it replaced the earlier tennis court. The Latin inscription translates as 'What you sow, you reap.'*

on the boundary is very English. And the amphitheatre above the Lovers' Lane Pool drew its inspiration from the tiny theatre in the garden of the Academia Arcadia on the Gianicolo Hill in Rome. The care taken in designing every detail of this garden – the steps and gateways, for example – make it supremely satisfying, but never fussy or 'prissy', to use the van Sweden and Oehme word. Every vista terminates in an eye-catcher, as in the great eighteenth-century gardens of the English landscape tradition, but the garden is never predictable; there is almost always a choice of paths to take, and surprises abound. The terracing gives a feeling of control, but the terraces are not symmetrically arranged, nor treated in the same style. After Farrand's death in 1959 Mrs Bliss continued to work on the development of the garden with the designer Ruth Havey, who contributed one of the great delights and surprises of Dumbarton Oaks, the Pebble Garden.

For all its European influences, this is an American garden: in England the herbaceous borders would rarely be placed so far from the house, and here there is a swimming pool, created out of a manure pit; the changing rooms are sited where the cow sheds had stood. Trees and shrubs of the same species are grouped together, so we find Cherry Hill, Crabapple Hill and Forsythia Hill, and there is also plenty of yew, box and holly to give the garden form during the winter. This garden is a masterpiece, but it is also typical of its period, which may account for the many curving lines, not all of them beautiful, and the excessive scrollwork.

In free-wheeling, free-thinking California it should be possible to shed the burdens of social, moral and religious obligation that attach to so much of the gardening in the east. But, no! The garden at Filoli, south of San Francisco, bears a moral message in its very name. William Bowers Bourn, made vastly wealthy by the Empire gold mine, named his estate Filoli to recall his guiding moral principles: FIght for the just cause; LOve your fellow man; LIve a good life = Filoli. The gardens were begun a scant eleven years after the San Francisco earthquake of 1906 and finished

ABOVE *Filoli, San Francisco, California.*
The gardens were created in a deliberately
conservative style in the 1920s. The contrast
between the formal gardens, with their topiary
hedges and columnar Irish yews, and the
wilderness of the Santa Cruz Mountains is
very striking.

in 1921. Bourn was also the owner of the Spring Valley Water Company and laid out his estate just south of the watershed where the company's water was collected.

The main gardens are classically formal and symmetrical – the Walled Garden, the Dutch Garden and the Sunken Garden – with pools of still water, lawns scorched by the Californian sun, and beautiful stonework. And where the gardens are not walled, they are immaculately hedged with yew, the sharp lines of the hedge contrasting with the undulating, wooded hills of the wilderness that lie outside and above the garden. Artifice rules; topiary is everywhere, and the beds are planted with annuals twice a year – in the early autumn for the spring show and in late spring for the summer display, the colours massed together to eye-popping effect. So startling is this colour attack upon the senses that it is a relief to find a small garden with a central circular pool, where the only colour other than green is confined to some pots on the edge of the water. And behind this pool rises a series of small, green lawns, which seem in their simplicity to recall the falls of much earlier American gardens. The most curious feature of Filoli is that the gardens are placed to one side of the house, not in front of it. The view from the main windows is not of the gardens, which are hidden away behind walls and hedges to the left, but across the terraces to a meadow. This seems characteristically American – to create such striking gardens but then to hide them away behind walls and hedges, so that they can't be enjoyed from the house, nor enhance its architecture. Are these glamorous gardens something to be ashamed of? Are you a better person if your outlook is a meadow?

Another Californian garden is quite shamelessly theatrical and extravagant. Ganna Walska (this was her stage name; her real name was Hanna Puacz) was an unsuccessful Polish singer, but clearly a fascinating character. She married six times, often men of great wealth, so when in

RIGHT AND BELOW *Lotusland, Santa Barbara, California. This remarkable garden – including a Japanese garden (below) – was made by the singer Ganna Walska between 1941 and her death in 1980. She designed with great imagination, in particular using euphorbias and cacti to dramatic effect, for example around the front door (above).*

1941 she bought the estate that came to be called Lotusland, she had the funds to make of it what she would. At the start she knew little of gardening, though she had firm tastes. The first of several landscape architects with whom she worked, not always without friction, was Lockwood de Forest. But it was her idea to replace the traditional formal garden in front of the house with cactuses, a fact acknowledged by de Forest in a letter: 'You are wonderful! I never would have thought of using cactus at the front door, or many of the other plantings you suggested. They are very handsome and I congratulate you.' Not only did she line the drive with cactus from the New World on one side and euphorbia from the Old on the other, but she planted the cactus *Euphorbia ingens* against the front of the house, where now its weird shapes, like paint squeezed from a tube or half-melted plasticine, reach up to the gutters and run along the ground.

This planting is typical of the originality of this garden, where the exigencies of the Californian climate have been turned into advantages. She had what she liked in her garden: a floral clock, 7.6 metres/25 feet in diameter, surrounded by topiary animals, a quasi-Islamic pool and rill, stone dwarfs (brought from her house in France) to people her green theatre, paths edged in blue slag from a glass factory and a pool ringed with upturned abalone shells, fed by a fountain created from two giant clam shells. This may all sound very 'Hollywood', and it is; but there are 'quieter' parts of the garden which are equally striking. The Japanese Garden was made where an earlier owner had built a dam to provide water for his citrus crop. He had planted one or two lotus plants in the pool; Ganna Walska grew 4,000 square metres/1 acre of lotus in her Japanese Garden. The Blue Garden was created under some blue cedars; originally it was planted with plumbago, ceratostigma and delphiniums, but as the shade grew denser, these were replaced by blue fescue grass and *Senecio mandraliscae*. The last part of the estate she worked on was the Cycad Garden, where her extraordinary collection of some four hundred mature specimens (including ten out of the eleven known genera) are displayed with great artistry.

Lotusland is a garden to make the visitor gasp: at the ingenious care with which the strangely shaped plants are displayed, the sight of a bank of ponytail palm (*Beaucarnia recurvata*) standing above an immaculately watered and mown lawn, the contrasts between the arid beds of succulents or cacti and the cool dampness of the Fern Garden. It is all too much, but at the same time remarkably personal, confident and original. This garden, however, was not created by an American.

The last remarkable garden in this brief survey proclaims itself American with every justification. It is as original as Lotusland, but constructed from the elements of the Hudson Valley wilderness. Innisfree takes its name from an early poem by the great Irish poet W.B. Yeats – the

LEFT *Innisfree, Millbrook, New York. The makers of this garden have been influenced by Chinese models, particularly the garden made by Wang Wei (see page 72). Here we see the yang of the standing stone contrasting with the yin of the water. And, like any Chinese garden, Innisfree is designed as a sequence of scenes.*

ABOVE *Innisfree, Millbrook, New York. For all its oriental influence this landscape is for the most part made out of local materials – water, trees and stone. But there is great artistry in this seemingly natural scene; notice, for example, how the trees sometimes advance close to the water and sometimes retreat far from it, and how the hill conceals what is round the corner.*

only poem of his, as he said with some bitterness, that was very widely known. Yeats wrote it while living in London, but it is a nostalgic poem recording the landscape of Sligo and his longing for a simpler, rural life. Appropriately it contains a bow in the direction of Thoreau: Yeats imagines his simple life on the island in Loch Gill complete with 'nine bean rows', which were surely suggested by Thoreau's famous bean field. Innisfree garden is the work of three Americans, Walter Beck and his wife Marion, and the landscape designer Lester Collins, who continued to develop the garden after the Becks' death.

This is a garden only in the loosest sense of the word; it might be more properly called a landscape. The pamphlet available at Innisfree tries hard to root this style of garden in Chinese precedent, which seems entirely unnecessary; this is an American work of art, in a style that is its own. The centre of the composition is dark, placid, glacial Tyrrel Lake, around which an informal path leads the visitor to new discoveries. In this way Innisfree recalls Stourhead more than the gardens of China, but here there is none of the classical clutter that provided a programme for the educated, eighteenth-century visitor to the English garden. The material the designers worked with is all local – water, stone, trees and landform. Much of the moving water is driven by hidden machines – the great water jet that echoes the verticals of the surrounding pines, for example. Elsewhere a stream meanders extravagantly through a patch of grass, and is crossed by a zig-zag bridge, a detail that does recall oriental gardens. Also oriental is the use of stones, not in massive piles as in so many Chinese gardens, but either standing alone as a form of natural sculpture, or paired, one standing (the yang) and one lying (the yin).

LEFT *Innisfree, Millbrook, New York. The only part of Innisfree to be gardened in detail is this area, known as the Terrace Gardens, which dates from the 1930s. But even here the atmosphere is very relaxed, and self-sown plants are allowed to colonize cracks in the paving.*

The forest has been managed with great artistry; here it advances to the water's edge, there it retreats, or is thinned into a light woodland. And shrubs or trees are grouped for colour, the cotinus for example, or are pruned into formal shapes and planted in a quincunx. The land, too, has been sculpted to vary the composition and to create mystery; entering the garden, the visitor descends a sinuous path through trees and is allowed increasingly wide glimpses of the lake, but the whole space can never be seen since Dumpling Knoll cuts off the view. Further exploration reveals the Terraces, the only part of Innisfree where there is extensive, detailed gardening; small shrubs and perennials are planted to create a contrasting pattern of leaf colour and form. And in the interstices of the paving self-sown seedlings are allowed to flourish. Here the grass is mown short. Innisfree has everything a great garden needs – individuality, proportion, mystery, surprise, variety, harmony with itself and its surroundings – and it could be nowhere but in America.

In 1585 Ralph Lane, the governor of Raleigh's first, unsuccessful colony on Roanoke Island, wrote that he had found there 'the goodliest soil under the cope of heaven'. So why have Americans not the best gardens in the world, or at least their own garden style? We have examined above some answers to this question – a suspicion of useless beauty, a reverence for a pristine wilderness, moral and social motives predominating over aesthetic in garden-making – but is that the whole story? Eleanor Perényi, returning from a European holiday, was struck by 'the dishevelled air of our domestic landscape, the scragginess of the gardens and parks'. Is it that many Americans at some unconscious level dislike or distrust gardens? They certainly love to bury them in wood-chip mulch, which as it decays removes many of the nutrients from the soil. This country began with all the great potential Scott Fitzgerald describes at the end of his novel, a potential that had been felt much earlier; in the decisive year 1776 Tom Paine wrote, 'We have it in our power to begin the world over again.' Gardeners have received much from America, but their world has not been renewed in quite the way Paine hoped for. In the nineteenth century the explorer, politician, land speculator and disciple of Manifest Destiny William Gilpin claimed that the role of America was 'to teach old nations a new civilisation'. In gardening terms this has yet to happen.

In China, Japan and Persia, as we have seen, the first pleasure gardens were intimately connected with the spiritual life of the country, as well as with its political power structure. Yet in America, the great power of the twentieth-century world, the religion of the country seems to have inhibited the development of the pleasure garden.

RIGHT *Stonecrop, Cold Spring, New York. Like many of the finest American gardens, Stonecrop makes the best use of local conditions and materials. The lesson seems to be: don't fight the wilderness, work with it.*

BIBLIOGRAPHY

Sources for quotations not otherwise credited will be found in the following:

GENERAL

William Howard Adams: *Roberto Burle Marx: The Unnatural Art of the Garden* (Museum of Modern Art, New York, 1991)

Julia S. Berrall: *The Garden* (Penguin, 1978)

Nan Fairbrother: *Men and Gardens* (Lyons and Burford, 1997)

Mark Francis and Randolph T. Hester, Jr. (eds.): *The Meaning of Gardens* (MIT, 1995)

Jack Goody: *The Culture of Flowers* (CUP, 1993)

Anthony Huxley, Mark Griffiths and Margot Levy (eds): *The New RHS Dictionary of Gardening* (Macmillan, 1992)

Miles Hadfield: *Pioneers in Gardening* (Garden Book Club, n.d.)

John Harvey: *Mediaeval Gardens* (Batsford, 1990)

Roni Jay: *Gardens of the Spirit* (Godsfield, 1998)

Geoffrey and Susan Jellicoe: *The Landscape of Man* (3rd edition, Thames and Hudson, 1995)

Geoffrey and Susan Jellicoe, P. Goode and M. Lancaster (eds): *The Oxford Companion to Gardens* (OUP, 1991)

Giovanni di Pasquale and Fabrizio Paolucci: *Il Giardino Antico da Babilonia a Roma* (Sillabe, 2007)

Charles Quest-Ritson: *The English Garden Abroad* (Viking, 1992)

Simon Schama: *Landscape and Memory* (Fontana Press, 1995)

THE ISLAMIC TRADITION

D. Fairchild Ruggles: *Gardens, Landscape and Vision* (University of Pennsylvania, 2003)

D. Fairchild Ruggles: *Islamic Gardens and Landscapes* (University of Pennsylvania, 2008)

Penelope Hobhouse: *Gardens of Persia* (Cassell, 2003)

Ali Akbar Husain: *Scent in the Islamic Garden* (OUP, 2000)

Jonas Lehrman: *Earthly Paradise* (University of California Press, 1980)

Elizabeth B. Moynihan: *Paradise as a Garden* (Scolar Press, 1982)

Elizabeth B. Moynihan (ed.): *The Moonlight Garden* (Smithsonian, 2000)

Attilio Petruccioli: *Il Giardino Islamico* (Electa, 1995)

Titley and Wood: *Oriental Gardens* (British Library, 1992)

THE ORIENTAL TRADITION: CHINA

Ji Cheng (trans. Alison Hardy): *The Craft of Gardens* (Yale, 1988)

David H. Engel: *Creating a Chinese Garden* (Croom Helm, 1986)

Maggie Keswick: *The Chinese Garden* (Academy Editions, 1978)

Chen Lifang and Yu Sianglin: *The Garden Art of China* (Timber Press, 1986)

Andrew H. Plaks: *Archetype and Allegory in the 'Dream of the Red Chamber'* (Princeton, 1976)

Vikram Seth (trans.): *Three Chinese Poets* (Phoenix, 1997)

Osvald Siren: *Gardens of China* (Ronald Press, 1949)

R. Stewart Johnston: *Scholar Gardens of China* (CUP, 1991)

Arthur Waley (trans.): *Monkey* (Reader's Union, 1944)

Young-tsu Wong: *A Paradise Lost* (University of Hawai'i, 2001)

THE ORIENTAL TRADITION: JAPAN

Mitchell Bring: *Japanese Gardens: Design and Meaning* (McGraw Hill, 1981)

Masao Hayakawa: *The Garden Art of Japan* (trans. Richard l. Gage) (Heibonsha, 1974)

Andrew Juniper: *Wabi Sabi* (Boston, 2003)

Marc Keane: *Japanese Garden Design* (Tuttle, 1997)

Lorraine Kuck: *The World of the Japanese Garden* (Weatherhill, 1984)

Wybe Kuitert: *Themes in the History of the Japanese Garden* (University of Hawai'i, 2002)

Sachimine Masui and Beatrice Testini: *Il Giardino Giapponese* (Casa dei Libri, 2007)

Ivan Morris: *The World of the Shining Prince* (OUP, 1964)

Lady Murasaki, (trans. Arthur Waley): *The Tale of Genji* (Allen and Unwin, 1965)

Lady Murasaki (trans. Richard Bowring): *Diary* (Penguin, 2005)

Gunter Nitschke: *Japanese Gardens* (Taschen, 2007)

Sakuteiki: Visions of the Japanese Garden (trans. Takei and Keane) (Tuttle, 2001)

David Slawson: *Secret Teachings in the Art of Japanese Gardens* (Kodansha, 1987)

THE ITALIAN TRADITION

Helena Attlee: *Italian Gardens* (Frances Lincoln, 2006)
David R. Coffin: *The Villa in the Life of Renaissance Rome* (Princeton, 1979)
David R. Coffin: *Pirro Ligorio* (Pennsylvania University, 2004)
Pierre de la Ruffinière du Prey: *The Villas of Pliny* (University of Chicago, 1994)
Linda Farrar: *Ancient Roman Gardens* (Sutton, 1998)
Georgina Masson: *Italian Gardens* (Thames and Hudson, 1966)
Alessandro Tagliolini: *Storia del Giardino Italiano* (Usher, 1991)

THE ENGLISH LANDSCAPE PARK

Richard Bisgrove: *The English Garden* (Viking, 1990)
John Dixon Hunt: *William Kent* (Zwemmer, 1987)
John Dixon Hunt: *Garden and Grove* (Dent, 1986)
Fleming and Gore: *The English Garden* (Michael Joseph, 1979)
Edward Hyams: *The English Garden* (Thames and Hudson, 1964)
Edward Hyams: *Capability Brown and Humphry Repton* (Dent, 1971)
Susan Lasdun: *The English Park* (Andre Deutsch, 1991)
Charles Quest-Ritson: *The English Garden* (Penguin, 2003)
Christopher Thacker: *The Genius of Gardening* (Weidenfeld and Nicolson, 1994)
Horace Walpole: *The History of the Modern Taste in Gardening* (1770)

THE ENGLISH FLOWER GARDEN

Reginald Blomfield and F. Inigo Thomas: *The Formal Garden in England* (Waterstone, 1995)
Jane Brown: *Gardens of a Golden Afternoon* (Allen Lane, 1982)
Canon Ellacombe: *In a Gloucestershire Garden* (Century, 1982)
Shirley Hibberd: *Rustic Adornments for Homes of Taste* (Century, 1987)
William Robinson: *The Wild Garden* (Century, 1983)
Anne Scott-James: *Sissinghurst* (Michael Joseph, 1975)
David Stuart: *The Garden Triumphant* (Viking, 1988)
Keith Thomas: *Man and the Natural World* (Allen Lane, 1983)
Jenny Uglow: *A Little History of British Gardening* (Pimlico, 2005)

THE AMERICAN EXPERIMENT

Balmori, McGuire and McPeck: *Beatrix Farrand's American Landscapes* (Sagapress, 1985)
The Book of Nature (Hudson River Museum, 1998)
Thomas Church: *Gardens are for People* (McGraw Hill, 1983)
Thomas Cole: *A Landscape Book* (New York, 1868)
Sharon Crawford: *Lotusland* (Companion Press, 1996)
Garrett Eckbo: *Home Landscape* (McGraw Hill, 1978)
Charles Elliott: *The Transplanted Gardener* (Viking, 1996)
Ralph Waldo Emerson: *Nature* (1836)
Mac Griswold and Eleanor Weller: *The Golden Age of American Gardens* (Abrams, 1991)
Robert Hughes: *American Visions* (Alfred A. Knopf, 1997)
Jamaica Kincaid: *My Garden (Book)* (Vintage, 2000)
Allen Lacey (ed.): *The American Gardener* (Farrar Strauss, 1988)
Diane Kostial McGuire (ed.): *American Garden Design* (Macmillan, 1994)
Eleanor Perényi: *Green Thoughts* (Pimlico, 1994)
Michael Pollan: *Second Nature* (Delta, 1991)
Witold Rybczynski: *A Clearing in the Distance* (Simon and Schuster, 1999)
Henry D. Thoreau: *Walden, or Life in the Woods* (1854)
Frederick Jackson Turner: *America's Great Frontiers and Sections* (University of Nebraska Press, 1969)
Katherine S. White: *Onward and Upward in the Garden* (Noonday Press, 1979)
Walter Muir Whitehill: *Dumbarton Oaks* (Belknap Press, 1967)
Andrew Wilton: *American Sublime* (Tate, 2002)
James van Sweden: *Bold Romantic Gardens* (Spacemaker, 1998)
James van Sweden: *Gardening with Nature* (Random House, 1997)

INDEX

Page numbers in *italic* refer to captions

A

Abd al-Rahman I 36, 37, 38
Abd al-Rahman III 38
Abercrombie, John 201
Abhaneri, Rajasthan *48*
Addison, Joseph 16, 167-8
Agra 50, *50*, 51
Agra Fort, Agra, India *53*, 54–5
Aislabie, John 174
Akbar 49, 50–1, 52, *53*, 55
Alberti, Leon Battista 38, 125, 128
Albertus Magnus 192
Alcazar, Cordoba 35, *35*, 36, 128
Alcazar, Seville *27*, *28*, *34*, 42
Alhambra, Granda 27, *32*, 39–43, *39*, *40*, *42*
allotments 207
Alton Towers, Staffordshire 208
Amber Fort, Rajasthan *49*, *51*
American gardens 218–49
Amida/Amitabha 95, 98
Andalucian gardens 34–44
Anguri Bagh, Agra *53*, 54–5
Arab gardens 34–46, 57, 124
Archer, Thomas *163*
Arley Hall, Cheshire 211
Ascott, Bedfordshire *213*
Ashikaga Yoshimasa 101, 102
Ashikaga Yoshimitsu 100–1
Ashridge, Hertfordshire 204
Assur-Banipal 12
Assur-Nasir-Pal 12
Assur-Uballit 11
Assyria 11–12
Athens 14
Atticus, Valerius 121
Attiret, Jean-Denis 86–7, 183
Aubrey, John 190, 198–9
Audley End, Essex *172*

Aurangzeb 54, 55

B

Babur 19–20, 34, 47, 48, 49
Babylon 11, 13
Bacon, Francis 205
Badminton, Gloucestershire 199–200
Bagh-e Naranjastan, Shiraz *31*
Bahadur Shah II 50
Balsamand Palace, Jodhpur *56*
bamboo 66
Banks, Joseph 201
Barry, Sir Charles 158
Bartram, John 200
Bateman, James *186*, 208, *210*
Batsford Park, Gloucestershire 112–13
Beck, Walter and Marion 247
bedding schemes 205, 209, 211
Beecher, Henry Ward 237
Beihai Park, Beijing *59*
Beijing Botanical Garden *60*
Benedict, St 124
Beverley, Robert 228
Biddulph Grange, Staffordshire *8*, *186*, 208–9, *210*
Bierstadt, Albert 226, 231
Bigelow, Joseph 232
Biltmore House, North Carolina *224*, 225
Blanchan, Neltje 238
Blenheim Palace, Oxfordshire 181, *181*, 182, 183
Bliss, Mildred 240, 243
Boccaccio 27, 124
Bodhidharma 104
bonsai *59*, 76, 94
Borghese, Miki 155
'borrowed' landscape 75, *81*, 100
bosco 139–40, 146, 149
botanical gardens 14, *16*, 37, 71, 152, 183

Boughton, Northamptonshire 166
Bourn, William Bowers 243, 244
Bowles, E.A. 205
Bramante, Donato 128–9, 134
Branitz 7, 8
Breck, Joseph 237
Bridgeman, Charles 171, 172, 173, 180, 181
broderie parterres 8, 140, *142*, 144, 163
Brompton Park Nursery 163, 198
Brook Cottage, Oxfordshire *193*
Broughton Castle, Oxfordshire *204*
Broughton Cottage, Oxfordshire *206*
Brown, Lancelot 'Capability' 122, 152, 165, *165*, 172, *172*, 173, 180–2, 183, 184, 185
Buddhism 63, 93, 94, 95, 98, 102, 104
  Esoteric Buddhism 92, 96, 98
  Zen Buddhism 91, 98, 102, 103, 104
  see also monastic gardens
Bulkawara Palace, Samarra 32
Burke, Edmund 225
Burle Marx, Roberto 24, *24*
Busbecq, Ogier Ghiselin de 47
Buscot Park, Oxfordshire *163*
Byodo-in, Uji 98

C

Cable, George Washington 237
Cabot, Anne and Frank *219*
Caesar, Julius 122
Caetani, Ada Wilbraham 153
California School gardens 238
Canadian Embassy, Tokyo 116
Cang Lang T'ing, Suzhou *62*, 63, *63*, 76, 78
carp stones 99
Cassino 124

Castello di Celsa, Siena *142*
Castello Ruspoli, Vignanello 140, *140*, *141*, 149
Castle Ashby, Northamptonshire 180
Castle Drogo, Devon *190*
catena d'acqua 159
Catherine the Great 183
Catlin, George 231
Caversham Park, Berkshire 181
Central Park, New York 19, 233
Chambers, Sir William 87, 183–4
char bagh 32, 36, 50, 55
Chardin, Sir John 31
Charles II of England 163, 166
Chasho Senrin 107
Chatsworth, Derbyshire 208
Chaucer, Geoffrey 17, 194
Chehel Sotun, Isfahan *15*
Chelsea Physic Garden, London 199
cherry blossom 19, 97, 103, *113*, 114
ch'i/ki 63–4, 77, 116
Chigi, Cardinal Flavio 144
Ch'in Shih Huang 70
Chinese Garden, Sydney *89*
Chinese gardens 17, 21–2, 24, 58–89, 183–4
chinikhanas 54, 55
Chiswick House, London 183, 229
chrysanthemums 65, 71, 114
Chuin Tung *89*
Church, Frederic Edwin 231
Church, Thomas 238
Cirencester Park, Gloucestershire 172
City Palace, Udaipur *19*
Cixi, Empress Dowager 85, 86, *87*
Claremont, Surrey 171, 172–3, *173*
Claude Lorrain 17, 168
Cobham Hall, Kent 185–6

Colbourne, Robert 228
Colchester, Maynard 164
Cole, Thomas 225, 231
Collins, Lester 247
Collinson, Peter 200
Columella, Lucius Junius 125, 190
Compton, Henry, Bishop of
 London 198
Confucianism 63
Constable, John 183
Constantinople (Istanbul) 46–7
Cooper, James Fenimore 230
Cortile del Belvedere, Vatican City
 128, 129
cottage gardens 201–2, 208,
 209–10, 211, 213, 215
Croome Park, Worcestershire 181
Cropsey, J.F. 225–6
Culbertson Garden, Pasadena 159
Curtis, William 201
Cyrus the Great 12, 30, 31
Cyrus the Younger 30

D

Daguanyuan Gongyuan, Beijing
 83, 83
Dahl, Andreas 220
Daisen-in, Kyoto 104, 105
Daitoku-ji, Kyoto 102, 103
Dar el Mokri, Fez 44
Darius the Great 31, 89
De Forest, Lockwood 246
Dean, Ruth Bramley 235
Delos, Greece 14
Diodati, Ottavio 144
Diodorus Siculus 13
Dioscorides 190–1, 194
Dorion, Thessaly 14
Downing, Andrew Jackson
 232–3
Dr Sun Yat Sen Garden,
 Vancouver 88
dragon symbol 65, 65
dry gardens 98, 99, 101–5,
 103, 104
Du Pont, Eleuthère 239
Du Pont, Henry Francis 239
Du Pont, Pierre S. 239
Dumbarton Oaks, Washington,
 D.C. 240, 240, 243, 243
Dutch gardens 164, 168, 189, 228

E

Earle, Alice Morse 237
East Cowes Castle, Isle of Wight
 204

East Ruston Old Vicarage,
 Norfolk 207
Edenbridge House, Kent 199
Egyptian gardens 13, 21
El Badi Palace, Marrakech 33
Eleanor of Castile 193
Elgin, Lord 85
Ellacombe, Canon 209
Eltham, Greater London 193
Emerson, Ralph Waldo 226, 231
English flower gardens 188–217
English landscape parks 162–87
Este, Cardinal Ippolito d' 133,
 135, 234
Evelyn, John 165, 166, 190,
 198, 199

F

Fairbrother, Nan 189
Fairchild, Thomas 202
Fan Chung-yen 78
Farrand, Beatrix 240
fermes ornées 178–80, 229
fertility metaphor 12–13, 17
Fessenden, Thomas 232
Filoli, California 243–4, 244
Finlay, Ian Hamilton 179
Fishbourne, West Sussex 119,
 190
Flitcroft, Henry 176
flower symbolism 65–6
Foerster, Karl 238
Fontainebleau 167
Fontana, Carlo 144
Forbidden City, Beijing 64, 66
foundation planting 235, 238
Fouquet, Nicholas 20
French gardens 8, 20–1
Frois, Luis 111
Frost, Robert 237
Fujiwara Michinaga 98

G

Gambara, Cardinal 129, 139
Garden at the Dawn of History,
 Kyoto 114–15
garden buildings
 Chinese gardens 23, 72, 78–9,
  82
 English gardens 163, 170, 171,
  172, 176
 Islamic gardens 31–2, 31,
  38, 46
 Japanese gardens 91, 101, 111
Garrick, David 203
Generalife, Granada 43, 44, 135

geomancy 97–8
Gerard, John 196, 198
German gardens 8
Ghinucci, Tommaso 131, 134
Giambologna 131
Giardini della Landriana, Tor San
 Lorenzo 154–5, 155, 156
Giardino Giusti, Verona 135,
 136, 139
giardino segreto 127, 146
Gibberd, Sir Frederick 174
Gilbert, Samuel 197, 217
Gilpin, Revd William 184, 248
Ginkaku-ji, Kyoto 106, 107
giocchi d'acqua 148–9
Giverny 113
glasshouses 205–6, 208–9
Glendurgan, Cornwall 211
Goethe, Johann Wolfgang von
 135
Gomizuno-o 109
Gonzales de Clavijo, Ruy 47
Gothic style 171–2, 174
Governor's Palace, Virginia 228
Gray, Thomas 225
Great Dixter, East Sussex 194
Greek gardens 13–14
green theatres 149, 150, 158–9
Grimald, Nicholas 194
Grimethorpe, Lord 152, 153
Griswold, Ralph E. 158
grottos 123, 165, 169, 176

H

ha-has 171, 171, 180
Hadrian, Emperor 11, 123
Hall Barn, Buckinghamshire 174
Hamilton, William 228–9
Hampton Court Castle,
 Herefordshire 167, 205
Hampton Court Palace, Surrey
 163, 203
Hanbury, Daniel 152
Hanbury, Sir Thomas 152
Hanbury, William 203
Hanging Gardens of Babylon 13
Hatfield House, Hertfordshire
 211
Hatshepsut, Queen 13
Havey, Ruth 243
Hawkstone Park, Shropshire
 184, 185
Hayat Baksh, Delhi 55
Healing, Peter 212
Hearne, Lafcadio 113
Hearst, William Randolph 219

Hearst Castle, California 219,
 220
Heathcoat-Amery, Sir John and
 Lady 200
Heian period 95–8, 101
herbaceous borders 211, 213, 215
Herbert, George 199
Herculaneum 120
Hibberd, (James) Shirley, 204,
 205
Hibya Park, Tokyo 113–14
Hidcote Manor Garden,
 Gloucestershire 214, 215
Hill, Sir Roland 184
Hilldene, Vermont 225
Hoare, Henry 17, 176
Hofu 102
Hole, Dean 207
holy springs 13–14
Horace 123, 169, 170
House of Ancora Nera, Pompeii
 120
House of Loreius Tibertinus,
 Pompeii 119, 121
House of the Vettii, Pompeii
 119, 120
Howard, Lelia and and Hubert
 153
Hsieh Ling-yun 71
Huerto del Rey, Toledo 37
Hughes, William 198
Hui Zong 72
Humayun 49, 50
Humble Administrator's Garden,
 Suzhou 79, 80, 81, 82
Hung Shen 72
hunting parks 70, 72, 73, 149

I

Ibn al-Baitar 37
Ibn Bassal 37
Ibn Luyun 37–8
Ibn Wafid 37
Il Sacro Bosco, Bomarzo 8, 139,
 139
India 47–55
Inkpen Old Rectory, Berkshire
 163
Innisfree, New York 219, 246–8,
 246, 247, 248
Inverewe Garden, Wester Ross
 189
Irving, Washington 230
Ishme-Dagan 11, 12
Islamic gardens 12, 15, 16,
 26–57

Isola Bella, Lago Maggiore *151*
Istanbul 46–7
Italian gardens 21, 118–61
I'timad-ud-Daulah, Agra *50*, 52

J
J. Paul Getty Museum, California
  159
Jahangir 51, 52, 55
Japanese Garden, Seattle *91, 94*
Japanese gardens 16, 24, 90–117
Japanese Gardens, Curragh *7,
  115*
Jefferson, Thomas 183, 203, 221,
  229–30
Jehan, Shah 52, 53, 54, 55
Jekyll, Gertrude *206*, 211,
  212–13, 215
Jellicoe, Sir Geoffrey *202*
Ji Cheng 61, 81–2
Jian Gong 71
Jisho-ji, Kyoto 101–2
Jodo/Pure Land style 98–9
John the Gardener 194
Johnson, Samuel 169, 179
Johnstone, Lawrence *214*
Jonangu Shrine, Kyoto *116*

K
Kairaku-en, Mito 112, *112*
Kanazawa 112
Kashmir 14, 55–6, 57
Katsura Imperial Villa, Kyoto
  108–9, 111
Katsura Tadaharu 102
Kent, William 170–1, 172,
  173–4, 180
Kentai Yoshiro 106, 107
Keswick, Maggie 70, 72
Kew Gardens 87, 201, 206
Khusrau (Chosroes) 33
Kincaid, Jamaica 220
King's Langley, Hertfordshire 193
Kingston Lacy, Dorset *171*
Kinkaku-ji, Kyoto 101
Knight, Sir Richard Payne 184
Knightshayes, Devon *4, 200,
  201*
Kobori Enshu 107, 108, 109
Koishikawa Koraku-en, Tokyo *96*,
  111–12, *111*
Kolymbetra, Sicily 45
Konchi-in, Kyoto 107–8, 111
Koran 27, 29, 31, 33, 40
Kublai Khan 72–3
Kyoto Garden, London *114*

L
La Biviere, Sicily 155, 157
La Fontaine, Jean de 20
La Mortola, Ventimiglia 152, *152*
La Zisa, Sicily 45–6, 57
Lacy, Allen 237
Lakewold, Washington State 238
land enclosures, eighteenth-
  century 166–7
Lane, Ralph 248
Lao (Laos) 15–16
Lao Tzu 64, 66
lawns, common 234
Lawson, Edward G. 158
Le Balze, Fiesole *156*
Le Clerc, Luc 135
Le Nôtre, André 20, 163
Le Vau, Louis 20
The Leasowes, West Midlands
  179, 185, 187
Leate, Nicholas 198
Lees, Carlton B. 237–8
L'Enfant, Pierre Charles *233*
Li Bai 66, 67, 71
Ligorio, Pirro 133, 134
Linnaeus, Carl 201
Little Sparta, South Lanarkshire
  179
Liu Garden, Suzhou *67, 68*,
  78–9, *79*
Livia, Empress 122, 123
Lloyd, Christopher *194*
Logan, Martha 228
London, George 163, 198
Longleat, Wiltshire 163, 180
Longwood Gardens,
  Pennsylvania 239–40, *239*,
  240
Lotusland, California 227, *245*,
  246
Loudon, John Claudius 206,
  208, 232
Louis XIV of France 20–1
Lu Shan parks 71
Luang Prabang, Lao 15
Lucullus 120–1
Lysander 30

M
Maccarone, Curzio 134–5
MacEarchern, Neil 153
Machi Bawan, Agra 54
McMahon, Bernard 232
Madinat al-Zahra, Cordoba *29*,
  38–9, 56
Maecenas 121

Magnolia Gardens, South
  Carolina 232
Magnolia Vale, Mississippi 232
Mahtab Bagh, Agra 53–4
Mansion of Prince Gong,
  Beijing *61*
Marchetti, Lauro 154
Marsh, G.T. 113
Masson, Francis 201
Masson, Georgina 140
Masuno, Shunmyo 115–16
mazes 148
Medici, Cosimo de' 125
Medici, Giovanni de' Cosimo dei
  125
Medici, Lorenzo de' 125
medicinal plants 37, 124, 193,
  228, *229*
medieval royal gardens 14–15
Mencius 70
Mesopotamia 11
Mifei 116
Milton Abbas, Dorset 181
Minamoto no Toru 96
miniaturization *67, 76, 82*
miradors 38
Mitford, Mary Russell 209
Mollet, André and Gabriel 163
monastic gardens
  Buddhist 71, 98–100, 101,
    102–5, 107–8, 115
  European 124, 192
Monet, Claude 113
Mongols 33, 72–3
Montagu, Lady Mary Wortley 46
Monticello, Virginia 229–30, *230*
moon gates *81*
moonlight gardens 53–4, 55
Morocco 45
Mount Auburn cemetery,
  Massachusetts 232
The Mount, Massachusetts
  222–3, *223*
mountains 67, 75
Mughal gardens 14, 19–20, 27,
  47–57
Mumtaz Mahal 52–3, 55
Mundy, Peter 51
Munstead Wood, Surrey 215
Munyat al-Rusafa, Andalucia
  36, 37
Murasaki, Lady 96, 97
Murin-an, Kyoto 114
Muskau, Germany 8
Muso Soseki 98, 99, 102, 116
Mussolini, Benito 153

N
Nanzen-ji, Kyoto *108*
Nash, John 204
National Gardens Scheme 189
National Parks movement,
  USA 226
Naumkeag, Massachusetts *222*
Nebuchadnezzar II 13
Needham, Joseph 88
New American Garden 238
New Place, Stratford-on-Avon
  197
Nezu Institute of Fine Arts,
  Tokyo *93*
Nicolson, Harold *216*
Nineveh 12
Ninfa, Latina *24*, 153–4, *154*
Nishat Bagh 56
Nogachi, Isamu 113
Nur Jahan 48, *50*, 52
nymphaea 120, *126, 137*

O
Oehme, Wolfgang 238, 239
Okakura Kakuzo 69
Olmsted, Frederick Law 19, *224*,
  225, 232
Oriental tradition *see* Chinese
  gardens; Japanese gardens
Orsini, Ottavia 140
Orsini, Vicino *8*, 139–40, *139*
Orti Farnesiani, Rome *21*
Ottoman kiosks 46
Oxford Botanic Garden 196

P
Padua *16*
Paganini, Niccolò *150*
Page, Russell 154, 155, *235*
Painshill Park, Surrey 183, 229
Painswick House,
  Gloucestershire *182*
Palazzo Farnese, Caprarola *4, 130*
Palazzo Piccolomini, Pienza *135*
Palermo 124
Pan En 74
paradise gardens 29–30, 56–7
  see also Islamic gardens
Parkinson, John 196, 198, 217
Parmentier, André 232
parterres *8, 137*, 140, *141, 142*,
  144, 163
Pasargadae *12*, 31
Patio de los Naranjos, Cordoba
  35, *36, 37*
Paxton, Joseph 208